She has Done a Beautiful Thing For Me

An Asian artist's presentation of the first Easter morning, showing Jesus appearing to the "holy women." From a Syriac Gospel Lectionary manuscript of the thirteenth century. The Syriac script means: "And behold Jesus met them and said, 'Hail.' And they came up and took hold of his feet and worshiped." (Matthew 28:9)

She has Done
a Beautiful Thing
For Me

PORTRAITS OF CHRISTIAN WOMEN IN ASIA

ANNE C. KWANTES

FOREWORD BY
ANDREW F. WALLS

OMF LITERATURE INC.
Manila, Philippines

All Scripture quotations, unless otherwise indicated, are taken from the *Holy Bible: New International Version*®. NIV®. Copyright © 1973, 1978, 1984 by the International Bible Society. Used by permission of Zondervan. All rights reserved.

The following materials have been used by permission:

Frontispiece

The Resurrection Appearance of Christ to the Holy Women (Matthew 28:9). From a Syriac Gospel Lectionary manuscript of the thirteenth century. British Library. Add. 7170 f.160r. Reproduced by permission of the Trustees of the British Library.

The anointing of Jesus depicted by Kim Ki-Chang on page 16. From *The Life of Jesus: Collection of Sacred Paintings by Kim Ki-Chang.* Seoul, Korea: Israel Cultural Center–Korea n.d.[1984]. Reprinted by permission of Kuk Yang.

Photo of Pandita Ramabai and her students on page 131. Reprinted by permission of Mukti Mission.

Amoy Mission seal on page 184. Reprinted by permission of the Western Theological Seminary Collection at the Joint Archives of Holland.

Photo of Pastor Lim Jin-gi and his family on page 188. From *God's Bridge or The Story of Jin-gi* by Tena Holkeboer, 2nd edition. Reprinted by permission of Wm. B. Eerdmans Publishing Company.

Photo of Ibu Sutirah on page 208. From *De Gereformeerde Zending in Midden-Java, 1931–1975* by Dr. Chris G.F. De Jong. Reprinted by permission of Uitgeverij Boekencentrum, Zoetermeer, The Netherlands.

Photo of Dr. Geertruida J. Dreckmeier on page 221. Reprinted by permission of PKN Foto-archive, Kerkinactie, The Netherlands.

She Has Done a Beautiful Thing for Me

Cover and page design by Jonathan De Vera
Typesetting by Marianne Ventura

Published (2005) in the Philippines by
OMF Literature Inc.
776 Boni Avenue
Mandaluyong City, Metro Manila
www.OMFLit.com

ISBN 971-511-894-1

Printed in the Philippines

Remembering all women in Asia,
past and present,
who have made it their aim
to do a beautiful thing for him.

Contents

Foreword

"She has done a beautiful thing," said Jesus about the woman who had just poured out her love and gratitude at His feet in one extravagant act of devotion. Some among those present thought the action quite out of place. There were better ways, they argued, to employ such a valuable asset. More fundamentally, the woman should not have been there at all.

In the beautiful book now before us, Dr. Kwantes has brought a rich offering compounded from the best products of the Asian continent, and packed with the distinctive aromas of its diverse lands. It is manifestly the product of dedicated labor and persevering search: It is equally clearly a work of love. Any who think that historical research does not hold a high place in the Kingdom of God may judge such labor wasted, and others may be surprised to see a work of serious research that is devoted to the activities of women in Christian history. To such, the book itself will give sufficient answer.

It is universally believed among Christians that God brings about salvation not only *in* history, but by means of history. We can understand little about the Incarnation of God in Christ unless we recognize that it was not an isolated event but the climax of a process that took many centuries to complete and that incorporated the whole history of Israel. Further, the process has been continuing, in the Church and in the world, for two subsequent millennia, and will do so until the New Jerusalem comes down from heaven at the last day. As the writer to the Hebrews reminds us in his eleventh chapter, the various generations of those who respond to God in faith are parts of a single continuing story that stretches across the ages. When we explore any part of that story, we are searching out the works of God.

The writer to the Hebrews also reminds us in his catalog of the ancient heroes of faith that the story is about women as well as men, about Sarah and Rahab and the Shunamite woman as much as about Abraham, Joshua or Elijah. Later historians have not always reflected this insight, and the place of women in Christian history has been obscured or neglected. What is more, Christian history has suffered a long Western captivity, where the historical lens has been directed to events in the West, while events that took place in Asia and Africa have lain unnoticed. Dr. Kwantes, with scholarship, sympathy and insight, shows us how, across the largest of the continents, God's salvation has been displayed in earlier times and in our own, employing the agency of the female half of humanity. She has done a beautiful thing, and we are all in her debt.

Professor Andrew F. Walls
Centre for the Study of Christianity in the Non-Western World
University of Edinburgh, Scotland

Acknowledgment

Biography is a thread but history is a web in which time is broad as well as long.[1]

How true and accurate this is.

The lives portrayed in this book are like threads, woven by the Master. However, when we see the whole, as when we see an armful of balloons together, or a bouquet of flowers, we get a new appreciation of the color, design and intricacy of each one.

Each individual is special, each life an offering of love, and that is how the chapters fit together. This bouquet of lives in Asia forms part of that web which makes up history. It shows God at work in Asia over the centuries, as well as in the life of each person in her own environment.

It would be impossible to piece together the experiences of these people without the help of others who knew or know them, and I wish to acknowledge here the help of all those who added facts and gave valuable insights.

Professor Minato Akiko, Mrs. Lucy Apostol and Dr. Melba Maggay told their own stories, they took the time to reminisce for the purpose of this book, and then to make suggestions and corrections. I especially acknowledge Dr. Maggay's literary input. Although Minato Akiko and I had not met before, Lucy Apostol and I have known each other for twenty-five years as colleagues and friends, and Melba Maggay and I have been acquainted for several years. The greater part of these three chapters is based on our conversations. I did not closely document the words the three women spoke in our discussions, as so many notes would be too distracting and the source is clear.

Relatives of some of the subjects had stories to tell. While Tong Tan Tjien Nio's daughter-in-law Freda's book gave the essentials, several sons talked or wrote about their mother. Freda was helpful in answering questions and read the chapter manuscript for accuracy. Quotes from the book have few notes, it is clear where they originated.

Though ninety-three years old, Tena Holkeboer's younger sister Chris Holkeboer Homkes was alert and remembered her sister well. She died a few months after our visit. Two of Tena's nieces, Cecilia Holkeboer Mereness and Jean Homkes Rockett have vivid memories of their aunt, and set aside time to talk about her. A granddaughter and granddaughter-in-law of Lillias Underwood wrote, searched for photos and were helpful via the telephone; I like to express special thanks to Grace Underwood Harkness. Margaret Ballagh's great-grandson James Ballagh Moore and his wife, and Isabella Thoburn's great-grandnephew Crawford R. Thoburn readily supplied information and sent family photos.

Ed Van Baak, the little boy who was told that he'd become a missionary some day, never forgot Tena Holkeboer's words, and now looks back on a lifetime of mission involvement. And the now aged anonymous friend of Truus Dreckmeier spent days thinking of what she would tell, and then, when we met, poured out her story with emotion.

Some people have gone out of their way to help with information and logistics and I wish to acknowledge the time spent by my sister, Cathy Van Kampen and her husband Jaap in the Netherlands as they showed me around, my brother Anton Laninga in Canada for his improvements of faded photographs, and Ishak Suhonggo Wonohadidjojo in Indonesia for accompanying me to Magelang. Natsuko and Katsuomi Shimasaki in Manila first introduced me to Professor Minato, and I am grateful.

Over the past several years I found numerous resources at Regent College in Vancouver, BC, Canada; at the archives at Hope College in Holland, MI, USA; at the library of Calvin College, Grand Rapids, MI, USA; and at the Asian Theological Seminary library in Manila, the Philippines — I have appreciated the kind services of library personnel in each place. Mr. Feije Duim of the Kerkinactie in the Netherlands kindly sent two recent papers on Truus Dreckmeier. I have valued Dr. Walls's interest in and encouragement for this project as well as his writing the Foreword. Joanna Nicolas, editor at OMF Literature, has been a practical and capable editor.

My dear husband, Dick Kwantes, has cheered me on as I worked on this and listened patiently when I talked about the people and stories of this book. There are others who have helped and who are unnamed here. To all of you, I thank you sincerely!

I have tried to be historically accurate but, of course, any errors are mine.

Anne C. Kwantes
February 2005

Early believers in Persia lived among people of the Zoroastrian faith. This religion was founded by Zarathustra (Zoroaster, in Greek), around 500 BC. Zoroastrianism is among the earliest teachings that say there is only one god. Zarathustra saw all of life as a struggle between good and evil and believed that at the end of time, evil will be destroyed and good will prevail. In this religious system, fire is a symbol of the one god and his sayings are part of the holy book.

The religion became very popular throughout Persia (today's Iran and Iraq) and was the state religion in this area for about a thousand years. Because of the prominence of this religion Christians in Persia were suspect. After all, Christians had a different holy book and worshiped a God the Zoroastrians did not know. Politically, Zoroastrian leaders had power, and advised their rulers not to tolerate Christianity, for it was associated with the Roman Empire. Jesus, though a Jew, was part of that hated empire. The two empires, the Persian and the Roman, fought each other bitterly for centuries. Persians feared that Persian Christians might join Roman Christians in time of war and oppose their own government.

This was the beginning of the suppression of Christianity in Persia, and during the early centuries after Christ there were severe persecutions of Christians. Especially around AD 400 thousands and thousands of Persian Christians were martyred for their faith. Among these were an unknown number of Christian women of whom only a few have been identified.

This book was written so that we may remember some of the thousands of the women in Asia, from Jesus' time until now, who have been devout Christians. They have served God because, their sins being forgiven, they have wished to share their thankfulness for God's love and to do what Jesus asked, namely, to let God's light shine in all the world. Many Christian women in Asia today continue to devote their lives to this great goal.

Introduction

The story is familiar, both Matthew and Mark tell it.[1] It happened shortly before Jesus' death, when the Jewish leaders were trying to find some way to arrest Jesus without angering the many people who had come to Jerusalem to celebrate the Passover.

Jesus had gone to Bethany, where he was invited for dinner by Simon the Leper, who may have been someone who was healed from leprosy by Jesus. The Jewish religious leaders wanted to kill Jesus, and soon one of his own followers would betray him for money, but here in Bethany he was shown hospitality.

While Jesus and his disciples were enjoying dinner, a woman entered the room. Neither Matthew nor Mark identifies her, but we can assume that she was driven by a sense of thankfulness. She may have heard that Jesus had freed a little girl of her demon possession when the girl's mother, a Greek woman who lived near Tyre, begged Jesus to heal her child (Matthew 15:21–28). She may have been touched by the story of Jesus' conversation with the woman in Samaria (John 4:7). She may have heard that Jesus forgave sinners, and believed. Or, again, she may have been in the crowd when Jesus was teaching and said, "Come unto me, all you who are weary and burdened, and I will give you rest" (Matthew 11:28).

The Bible omits many details of what happened. She was probably bashful in the presence of these men, reclining at the table as was their custom; but, intent on what she was about to do, she held tightly in her two hands her costly alabaster jar as she resolutely stepped toward Jesus.

The anointing of Jesus, as depicted by the Korean artist Kim Ki-Chang. Jesus and the people around Him are depicted in traditional Korean clothing and the house is in Korean style. From *The Life of Jesus: Collection of Sacred Paintings by Kim Ki-Chang.* Seoul, Korea: Israel Cultural Center-Korea, n.d. [1984]. *Photo courtesy Kuk Yang.*

It was a fine jar of translucent material, and held spikenard, a precious ointment. The jar was sealed, to prevent the ointment from evaporating, and the spikenard could only be poured out after breaking the neck of the vessel.

As the woman approached Jesus, her face must have glowed with thanksgiving and love. And then she broke the neck of the jar and poured the fragrant ointment on Jesus' head. Immediately the pleasing aroma of the spikenard filled the room.

The men around Jesus did not think much of the woman's sacrifice. They immediately began to criticize, complaining that the woman had wasted the valuable, fragrant perfume. Why, it was worth more than a year's salary! If it had been sold, the money could have been given the poor! And they cold-heartedly scolded the woman.

Simon, the host, must have been ashamed to see the woman come into the men's midst. It was not acceptable for a woman to break in on a men's dinner party. He must have known her, and felt ill at ease about what was happening. But Jesus, the dinner guest, neither complained nor was embarrassed; he praised the woman. "Leave her alone," he said to the accusing dinner guests, "Why are you bothering her? She has done a beautiful thing for me."[2]

Quoting the Old Testament, Jesus then reminded the men that the poor and needy would always be around, whereas he would not. He said that the woman's anointing him with spikenard was a preparation for his burial, and he declared that what the woman had done will always be remembered when the gospel is preached.

Several clergymen have used this story speaking at commissioning services for female missionaries. They have emphasized the anointing woman's complete dedication to serving the Lord, and have stressed the words Jesus spoke to His companions, "She has done what she could." Yes, when women and men have dedicated themselves to God's service they have done what they could. In a positive way, the title of this book emphasizes the outright praise of our Savior when he said, "She has done a beautiful thing for me." We can expect that a smile accompanied the spoken words.

Since New Testament times women have been active in Christian society if not always conspicuous. Frequently, women were dynamic partners with men. When Paul completed his letter to the Romans he gave it to Phoebe, a woman, to deliver. This letter contains personal greetings to numerous people and includes the names of several women.[3]

A number of women of the Roman Empire are remembered for their faith and, sometimes, their martyrdom. Women took part in European mission programs during the 700s, the time of Boniface (the English missionary who became famous for cutting down a sacred tree in Germany while an awed crowd looked on). During the Protestant

women valiantly defied the ban on the Bible and
ook when soldiers came searching. There was Erdmuth,
hardworking wife of the German pioneer missionary
endorf, and there were many more courageous Christian
wo... e western world, but their names and deeds seem to have
been washed away with time.

The same is true in Asia. Only a few Christian writings survived
the centuries and women are mentioned rarely. But although we
may not know personal names, some documents bear testament
that Asian Christian women have lived dedicated lives of service
throughout the centuries.

About two hundred years after New Testament times the first
known Syrian missionary after the time of the apostles, Bardaisan, wrote
about "Christian sisters" in the areas now known as Afghanistan and
northern Iran.[4] Both of these regions had many Christians in the early
centuries after Christ. About the same time there were men and women
who wished to lead holy Christian lives and called themselves "Sons
and Daughters of the Covenant."[5]

Women in Asia formed a critical component of the early Christian
community in Central Asia as leaders, ministers and martyrs. There
were ordained deaconesses, and orders of virgins and widows. Some
widows were entrusted with the work of teaching and of pastoral care.
The names of several women who were religious leaders and workers
among the poor have been preserved.[6]

The lives of Christian women and martyrdoms were hailed as
exemplary by men of the age, even though women at that time were
generally viewed as having little value. How paradoxical, that
women, who had a low social position, were held up as great
in the Kingdom of God, showing that they too were
God's precious children. The Almighty God delights in the
testimony of "lowly" women.[7]

> *The lives of Christian women and martyrdoms were hailed as exemplary by men of the age, even though women at that time were generally viewed as having little value.*

History tells of a number of Christian women in West Asia, in the area of today's Iran and Iraq, who were martyred. Candida was one of these, a prisoner-of-war who, as one of a group of resettled Christians, was taken into the harem of the Persian king[8] around the year AD 300. She became a favorite of the king; other women in the harem became jealous and sent the king a message that Candida served a god other than the one of the Persian Zoroastrians. Candida persevered in following her Christian faith and would not be persuaded even by the king to convert to Persian ways. She was then martyred.

Another woman whose story is remembered was a Persian young woman called Martha,[9] whose father had been a Christian prisoner-of-war, and whose mother was a Persian Christian. Martha decided to remain a virgin, a choice popular among early Christians who believed that the spiritual was more pure than the physical, and that celibacy was an encouragement to live a holy life.

Ancient documents tell that it was probably in AD 341 when Martha was arrested on Easter Sunday, the day after her father was murdered for his faith. A Zoroastrian priest told the king about Martha, and the king ordered Martha to renounce her Christian faith. If she refused, she would be forced to marry. Marriage would, of course, end her vow of celibacy. If she would agree to neither she should be put to death.

Martha stood firm in her Christian testimony, and remained unmoved by either the Persian king's promise of honors and gifts or his threats of torture and death; she would not revoke her vow of celibacy. After much debate she finally declared, "I have decided, like my father, to become the object of abuse for the sake of my father's God, and I will die like him because of my faith in God."

Exasperated, the attending Zoroastrian priest snarled he knew Christians were hard of heart and guilty of death. Yet, he tried again to persuade her, when he told Martha that she was young and pretty and ought to marry. Martha replied that she was already betrothed, that her fiancé was in heaven, that he would come in glory, and take all those betrothed to him to a place "not made by hands, but built in

Jerusalem." When the king heard this he sentenced Martha to die on the very spot outside the city where her father was killed the day before.

Martha was brought outside the city that Easter Sunday. Before she was executed she knelt to thank God for letting her endure and to ask for faithfulness for other persecuted Christians. Many people watched while Martha was martyred.

For a few hundred years there were prominent Christian women in Arabia including Christian queens, one of whom established a Christian convent. Among the names on a list of Christian martyrs there are several names of women, and many more, whose names are not recorded, were killed for their faith.[10]

Soon after they became Christians West Asians began to travel east to do evangelism, joining merchants on their trade routes. For more than a thousand years Christians walked along the several ancient Silk Road routes to bring God's message to people along the way. Many of these people had been educated in the schools of Mesopotamia and Persia. They brought Christian literature and medical knowledge, and built churches and monasteries along the way. In time several tribes of Central Asia were converted from local religions, mainly shamanism, to Christianity. There are tombstones in some Christian cemeteries in Central Asia that bear the names of outstanding Christians, including women.[11] Here and there Christian women are noted in histories as leaders of tribes, as religious leaders, and even as wives of Nestorian priests. Sorkaktani, the subject of a later chapter, was a Christian princess who became the mother of four Mongol rulers when the Mongol empire was most extensive and powerful. There were other Christian women who held high positions in this society.

Christian women are noted in histories as leaders of tribes, as religious leaders, and even as wives of Nestorian priests.

The wife of Japan's military leader, Hideyoshi, had

a sister and a friend who were Christians. This was during the first flush of Christianity in Japan, in the late 1500s, when Portuguese Jesuit missionaries were welcomed. But when political intrigue developed Christianity was no longer tolerated, and thousands of humble peasants died for their Christian faith. There were Christian women even in the palace. Lady Hosokawa, a prominent Japanese noblewoman, was baptized Gracia, and she was killed for her faith.

While names of only a handful of women are remembered, there were of course many more Asian Christian women who faithfully served their Savior. For centuries Christians were persecuted in many parts of Asia, and we wait still for historians to tell us more stories about them, particularly about women. There is a dearth of information about Christianity during these centuries when it nearly disappeared from Asia.

With Europeans exploring east and then Asians traveling west a new chapter opens in the book of church and mission history of Asia. This era of exploration coincided with the Protestant Reformation, which ushered in a revival in the Church in Europe. Immediately after the Protestant Reformation of 1517 we hear of overseas mission efforts and, though overseas missions took time to develop, from the beginning European men took their wives with them on their mission travels.

CHAPTER TWO

"Indeed, I have often said to Bishop Roots that, in view of the trouble women missionaries make, if I were a Bishop, I would not have one of them in my diocese; unless of course, I wanted to have some work done."

~ The words of an Episcopal female missionary in China, who trained Bible women for twenty years, to her mission director in the USA, in 1918.

Women in Mission

One of the first European missionary wives we hear about is Dorothy Carey. When her husband William came home and told her that he felt God calling him to go to India, she was expecting their fourth child. Not knowing anything about living conditions in India, or how they would earn a livelihood, she at first refused to go. When she did accompany her husband to India, in 1793, it was with great reluctance. She battled loneliness, guilt, illness and hardship, and, after years of being mentally disturbed, Dorothy Carey died in India.

Pietism in Germany, the Methodist Revival in Great Britain and the Great Awakening in the American colonies, all in the 1700s, brought far-reaching changes in ways of thought of many Christians who were serious about their personal faith and their sense of Christian responsibility to carry the gospel to non-believers. The emphasis on a personal conversion and piety left an indelible impression and had permanent consequences. Around 1800 a new mission awareness in Europe and in North America led to the founding of numerous mission societies, and both women and men were involved in these.

Revival and awakening had brought out the idea that, as creatures before God, women and men are equal. Both need repentance, forgiveness and renewal of spirit. Though a woman's social role might be primarily in the home, new ideas led to the development of literacy among girls as well as boys, in order that girls would also be able to read the Bible.

Gradually women began to have more opportunities outside the home. They began to take their place in church activities, and then in society. Yet, it was courageous of the American woman Mary Webb and her fourteen Baptist and Congregational companions to establish in 1800 the Boston Female Society for Missionary Purposes. It was their goal to glorify God and to collect money for the work of benevolence wherever that might be; annual membership dues were set at two dollars.[1]

Because two dollars was quite a sum for many housewives another American woman, Mrs. Mehitable Simpkins, began a "cent society." She collected one penny each week from friends, giving the copper coins to her husband, who was treasurer of the Massachusetts Missionary Society, sending where the money was needed.[2]

After 1812, when the first American missionaries left for overseas service, several women's mission groups were begun in America. Women were captivated by the courage of Christian missionary women in far-away places; they met in each others' homes to give their small coins and to pray specifically for the work of these missionaries. Sometimes a visitor would speak at these meetings, and tell them about special people or projects, and the women would return home marveling at what was happening in the world. At home, they would tell their families about missions. Many children learned about mission work and needs at their mother's knee, and grew up believing that God had issued a personal call to them to join the missionary workforce.

Women's opportunities in missions were limited. It was long thought improper for a woman to go overseas alone, so at first only married women were sent to the mission field together with their husbands. Most Protestant mission boards believed that missionaries ought to go as couples or families, and were even hesitant to send single men. William Carey, the well-known pioneer missionary to India, considered it the duty of a male missionary to be married and, following this thought, "some of the most vigorous recruiting for service was performed by single male missionaries in need of wives."[3] Numerous marriages were transacted after whirlwind courtships, often when the missionary candidate had completed his studies and urgently needed someone who was willing to marry a missionary and ready to travel. More than half of the early missionary couples had been married less than a year when they set out for their mission career.

One of the most astonishing stories of such brief courtship concerns two male missionaries who were ready to leave for Hawaii in 1819. Both men had been engaged to be married, but when the time came to marry the mothers of both of their young women decided not to allow their daughters to leave for such an unknown place. One of the two men was then introduced to a girl and married her within eighteen days. The other met a young woman on the day of his missionary commissioning service, discovered that she was willing to be the wife of a missionary, and married her in less than a week.[4]

Emily Prankard Gilmour came to China in 1874 to marry James Gilmour after a brief courtship by mail. She made several missionary journeys into the desert with her husband, until prevented by illness. She was deeply mourned by her husband when she died after twelve years, leaving James Gilmour "both father and mother" to their three young "laddies."

It was years before a widowed female missionary was permitted to remain at her deceased husband's overseas post, and before single women were sent overseas. Even then, at first, unmarried women always traveled and lived with a family. Once on the mission field, single women could work in the community, but married women were expected to stay at home to take care of their families. Both were limited to working with local women and children.

All women were considered assistant missionaries, even single ones. The first single woman to be sent by any mission board was Mrs. Charlotte H. White, who was sent to Burma in 1815 by the American Baptist Board of Foreign Missions. She had offered to do evangelism accompanying a couple who had been appointed to Burma. Twelve years later the American Board of Commissioners for Foreign Missions, the first American mission society, began sending single female missionaries when it commissioned Cynthia Farrar to go to India. After fifty years of Protestant missions about one hundred single women had been sent overseas, while there were many more married female missionaries. All of the work of these women was supervised by men.

Everything changed when women of several denominations began to organize their own mission boards. In 1861 American women formed the Women's Union Missionary Society. This pioneering work spurred others into action, so that by the turn of the century there were forty-eight women's boards in Canada and the USA.

Missionaries of various backgrounds and countries and living earlier or later in the 1800s had different experiences but they shared many challenges and barriers in addition to their call. This century has been called the "Great Protestant Century of Missions" and women took part in a major portion of the tasks. Like their male counterparts, female missionary workers formed an interesting assortment of individuals, for there were many ways to think about and to deal with the unknown.

What motivated Western women to enter the missionary life which, two hundred years ago, was so unknown and even now intimidates many? Basic to all other consideration is the issue of call. Whether the call came from hearing Bible and missionary stories in childhood, reading about evangelistic work, or personal contact with missionaries, biblical teaching is clear on the prompting of the Holy Spirit in the heart. If, in the early days of Protestant missions, a woman felt a call, there was no opportunity for mission service unless she was married. It is easy to understand that, aware no doubt of the male missionary's need for a wife, young women who wished to enter missions flocked around young male missionary candidates. It is almost comical to read of courtships which lasted but a few weeks, but not so comical to note the unhappiness in some missionary families when, after the wedding, husband and wife discovered that they really were not compatible. Both husband and wife loved God and were devoted to Christian service, but they were not always devoted to each other. Under such circumstances life looked grim for the woman who was far from the support of her family and country. The husband had his mission assignment, but the woman's task was in the home. Maintaining the home was much more wearisome than in the homeland, relatives were missed, and many adjustments had to be made. While this made some women pine for their former lives, new situations pushed others into creative ways of expressing their own Christian love for those around them.

Fortunately, most missionary couples learned to love and appreciate each other as time went by, and became, perhaps unwittingly, models of partners in a Christian marriage. Alexander Duff (1806–1878) was among those missionaries who were so intent on their theological studies and missionary future that they did not even think about marriage. He told an older friend that the idea of marriage had not even crossed his mind until after he was ready to go abroad as a missionary. The friend suggested to him that Duff quietly look around and added, tongue-in-cheek, "if you make the acquaintance of one of the daughters of Zion, traversing, like yourself, the wilderness of this world, her face set thitherward, get into friendly converse with her." He added, "If God puts it into her heart to be willing to forsake father and mother and cast in her lot with you, regard it as a token from the God of providence that you should use the proper means to secure her Christian society."[5] Duff caught the drift of this advice and married Anne Scott Drysdale, taking care of one more item on his list of preparations for missionary service. They left for India that year. He and his bride endured two shipwrecks, in which they lost all their belongings, before they arrived in Calcutta in 1830. Being young and spirited, they were able to deal with the experience. They served in India for more than thirty years, and Alexander Duff became a renowned missionary educator. After thirty-six years of being a missionary wife and raising her family, mostly in India, Anne died. Her husband never remarried.

A few brave young women agreed to marry men they knew little or not at all. They traveled to the mission field without knowing their future husbands, and immediately married the men to whom they had committed themselves.

When Emily Prankard, living at home with her mother in England in 1874, received a marriage proposal from someone she did not know in Beijing, she must have been stunned. Emily's sister and her husband were missionaries in

A few brave young women . . . traveled to the mission field without knowing their future husbands, and immediately married the men to whom they had committed themselves.

China, and Emily probably had no idea that her photograph, on the wall in her sister's home, had been admired by James Gilmour, a single missionary in Siberia and Mongolia. However, she promptly agreed to marry James, and before the year was finished she had traveled to China and married him.

Emily happily shared her husband's life of pioneering in desolate areas. Living without conveniences in tents in the vast desert among people whose language she had to learn and whose food she found difficult to digest was not easy. Emily was not strong and, after their first child was born, she had to remain in Beijing while James went on long missionary journeys.

After eleven years of marriage and giving birth to three children, Emily became ill with a "serious complication of her lungs" and died, leaving her husband with three young boys. James mourned the death of his dear wife and felt his family's needs keenly. He entrusted the baby to the care of Emily's sister in Beijing, but this little boy lived only for two years. James was unable to take the other two boys with him in his extensive travels, but eventually he decided that he had to send them to Scotland, where relatives would care for them and they could get an education.

James Gilmour prepared to say farewell to his boys and wrote the following words one evening, "I am most anxious to be with the children much these last days. Oh, it is hard to think of them going off over the world in that motherless fashion!"[6] And he wrote a friend, "The laddies are with me now, and I am both father and mother to them. Tonight I darned three stockings for them when they went to bed."[7]

Emily Gilmour's husband James is remembered for his dogged perseverance in spite of little result, but he is also known for the moving letters he wrote his boys far away in Scotland. The letter which he wrote to his children after their little brother died in Beijing is shown here. Its clear, easy-to-read script, and its melancholy yet encouraging tone make it easy to imagine the loving and lonely father, bent over the paper and pouring out his love and concern. This letter is an example of how Emily Prankard Gilmour lived on in the hearts of her family.

PEKING   DEC. 16. 1887

MY DEAR SONS

JIMMIE AND WILLIE

I AM WELL AND THANKFUL FOR IT. I HAVE A VERY SAD DUTY TO PERFORM. IT IS TO TELL YOU THAT YOUR LITTLE BROTHER ALEXANDER DIED THIS MORNING AT TEN O'CLOCK. THE DEAR LITTLE LAD HAD BEEN ILL A WEEK OR MORE. AT FIRST HE WAS NOT THOUGHT TO BE VERY ILL. LATER IT WAS SEEN THAT HIS HEAD WAS AFFECTED. THAT WAS MORE SERIOUS. I HAD JUST GONE TO TIEN-TSIN AND WAS SENT FOR. I LEFT TIEN-TSIN ON MONDAY MORNING AT TWO O'CLOCK A.M. AND REACHED PEKING TUESDAY EVENING AT DARK. ALICK DID NOT KNOW ME. HE LINGERED ON TILL THIS MORNING, FRIDAY, AT 10 O'CLOCK. HE DID NOT SUFFER MUCH MOST OF THE TIME, AND EVEN WHEN HE SEEMED TO SUFFER

I DON'T THINK HE WAS VERY CON- SCIOUS. THE FUNERAL IS TO BE ON MONDAY. HIS LITTLE COFFIN IS TO BE PLACED NEXT TO MAMAS.

POOR DEAR WEE ALICK HE NEVER WAS VERY WELL SINCE MAMA DIED. HIS BACK BONE— HIS SPINE— BEGAN TO CURVE SOME MONTHS AGO.

NOW MY DEAR SONS, HIS BROTHERS, DON'T BE TOO SORRY ABOUT HIM. HE HAS GONE TO MAMA, AND TO GRAND MAMA AND TO JESUS, IN THAT CITY OF BEAUTY WHERE NO ONE IS EVER SICK AND WERE ALL IS BEAUTIFUL. THERE ARE LOTS OF LITTLE GIRLS AND BOYS PLAYING ALL ABOUT, AND NO BAD BOYS OR BAD PEOPLE TO ANNOY HIM OR TEACH HIM EVIL. AND WOULD NOT MAMA RECEIVE HIM INTO HER LOVING ARMS JUST AS SHE

USED TO HOLD YOU AND HIM
WE WHEN SHE WAS HERE. DEAR
DEAR OLD PRETTY MAMA, DEAR
DEAR WEE ALICK. I THINK I SEE
HER HUGGING HIM, AND HIM
NESTLING ON HER BOSOM JUST
WHEN HE ARRIVED

                    THEY ARE FOR
EVER WITH THE LORD. JESUS
LIKES TO SEE THEM. THEY.
LIKE TO SEE JESUS. THE ANGELS
AS THEY PASS STOP TO LOOK
AT THEM AND SAY "YOUR SON?"
THE ANGELS SAY "HAS HE ANY
BROTHERS AND SISTERS?" MAMA
SAYS "TWO BROTHERS AT SCHOOL
IN HAMILTON SCOTLAND"
THE ANGELS SAY "PAPA?" MAMA SAYS
"PAPA IS A MISSIONARY IN CHINA"
THE ANGELS SAY "THE BROTHERS
AND PAPA WILL ALL COME SOME
DAY IF THEY BELONG TO JESUS"

MAMA SAYS "WONT THAT BE NICE"
NOW BOYS BE SURE YOU BELONG TO
JESUS AND YOU ARE ALL RIGHT.
TELL JESUS YOU ARE GLAD HE IS
TAKING SUCH CARE OF MAMA
AND ALICK. ASK HIM TO TAKE
CARE OF YOU, AND TO TAKE
CARE OF ME, AND SOME DAY
WE'LL ALL BE THERE TOGETHER.
MEAN TIME LET US BE VERY CARE-
FUL TO DO AND SAY JUST
WHAT JESUS LIKES.
                    I DONT KNOW WHO
WILL GO FIRST. PERHAPS GRAND-
PA. WONT THEY ALL BE GLAD TO
SEE HIM AND WON'T THEY ALL
GIVE HIM A GOOD WELCOME. I KNOW
GRAND-PA WANTS JESUS TO SAVE
HIM AND I KNOW JESUS WANTS
TO SAVE HIM. MEAN TIME
GOOD BYE MY SONS. ASK JESUS
TO KEEP YOU. DONT SORROW
OYER ALICK. HE IS WITH JESUS
        YOUR LOVING PAPA.

Besides the emotion of the basic call there were numerous other reasons which drove young women into missionary service. It might be the death of a loved one, a family situation, a wish to escape drudgery, or even the wish for adventure. As education became more available to women, however, there were as yet few opportunities in Europe and North America to put special studies to use.

Once they were on the mission field most married women found that there were many ways in which they could serve, for they were more free than their husbands to respond to the needs they saw around them. They neither received a salary nor wrote regular work reports, and since mission leaders had no or few professional expectations of them, they could each choose their own role in missions, though nearly always within the limits of their home and family.

It was clear that it was more economical to employ women than men. This was plainly worded in an article in an American missionary magazine of 1868 in which the author claimed that a woman was "even less trouble and expense than a man. I believe the ladies are the cheapest missionaries the Board sends out."[8] Though there was no financial remuneration, women were appreciated for the stability they created in the home, for the help they gave their husbands, and also for their flexibility, their interest in the work, their language learning, and their ability to engage in the local women's lives.

A confidential report about two Episcopal missionary couples in the 1830s states, "Both men are dull, but worthy. They will make good settlers. Their wives I expect will prove to be by far the best teachers in the colony."[9] Decades later an Episcopal missionary deaconess with more than twenty years experience in teaching Chinese women to be church workers, wrote to the American mission board office, "Indeed I have often said to Bishop Roots that, in view of the trouble women missionaries make, if I were a Bishop, I would not have one of them in my diocese; unless of course, I wanted to have some work done."[10]

For many couples it was, and perhaps still is, typical for the wife to become more fluent during early language study than the husband. She was the one who had to do the talking at the market, and with whoever came to the house, while the husband struggled with more formal language training as he studied biblical language for future preaching. Such differences in fluency easily led to jealousies and hard feelings, but would fade as the husband began to speak more with nationals. Eventually many husbands far outdid their wives in language competence.

Why was it that men gave so little credibility to women's education and ability? Today some women still feel discriminated against, but two hundred and even one hundred years ago it was common for men to criticize, belittle and even oppose women's participation in missions. They declared it improper for women to speak publicly and many sincerely believed that to be true. On the other hand, those most critical were usually the men who battled with their own struggles in language learning, adapting to another culture, or work-related problems.[11] Women understood this; still, it was downright frustrating for a female physician in Pyongyang, Korea, who saw the need for a medical doctor, but was discouraged from practicing simply because a male physician resented having a woman share in his work.[12]

It was often difficult for women when they were treated condescendingly and, when positions of leadership were denied them, tensions often flared. One wonders if it was mere modesty when a bishop, writing about his second wife, did not even mention her being a physician when his glowing description of her takes up nearly a page of writing, and refers to her, below a full-page photograph, simply as "Mrs."[13] This custom has not entirely disappeared today.

> *It was often difficult for women when they were treated condescendingly and, when positions of leadership were denied them, tensions often flared.*

Many couples, and also single women and men, co-operated beautifully as they sought to bring the gospel across the ocean. They readily filled the roles of sisters and brothers, aunts and uncles, and other relatives and friends during their years on the mission field.

Adele M. Fielde, the first single Baptist woman to Thailand, was a teacher who traveled to Hong Kong to marry her fiancé, but when she arrived there she learned that he had died. The mission board then allowed her to stay, but offered a salary half that of a male missionary. The offer was raised slightly only because of her loud complaints. This woman worked in mission in Thailand, and then in China, for a total of thirty-three years, and, though she

Missionary Auck C. Laninga, the author's mother, with two Javanese students of a sewing class in Magelang, Indonesia, 1932. Women missionaries looked for the opportunity to meet with Javanese women and girls, and often organized sewing classes. During these times they talked about many other things as well, such as literacy, hygiene and the Christian way of life. *Photo courtesy Laninga family.*

was a controversial person and had numerous spats with both colleagues and mission leaders, she was praised, ten years after her death, with the words: "She had done 'a man's work.'"[14]

Women were a significant element of the Student Volunteer Movement, which was an association of energetic and mission-minded Americans, college students or college graduates. Within a year of a conference in 1886 over two thousand one hundred volunteers — five hundred of whom were women — were ready to commit themselves to mission. The Student Volunteer Movement blossomed for more than thirty years, and many hundreds of its female members became overseas missionaries to Asia.[15]

As the years rolled by, more and more single Protestant women joined the missionary work force, and by 1900 they outnumbered the men in many mission stations. Some of the women became the second or even the third wife of male missionaries who had been widowed. Occasionally a missionary wife outlived her husband, and carried on the work, or married another missionary and joined him. A few women outlived more than one husband, but usually it was the male missionary who married two or three times. A mission scholar tells about the grave of one "American patriarch," buried in China, whose tomb is surrounded by the graves of seven wives."[16]

Efforts to obtain women missionaries failed time and again, and when there was a shortage of personnel the future of the work looked hopeless. During forty years of missionary work in China (1819–1859) fifty-one wives died, representing one-fourth of all Presbyterian missionaries. At that time people expected that missionaries were able to live and work in China for some seven years before they would perish.[17] Women's participation was crucial in all kinds of work among women. When women missionaries died heartaches were paired with the need for replacements in their specialized work.

Discouragement flowed from his pen when David Hibbard, principal of a mission school in the Philippines, wrote the Presbyterian board in 1905 recruiting a teacher for girls, "Personally, I should prefer that she should be businesslike and not very good-looking, as we have several unmarried men in the mission, and we cannot afford to lose our teacher when she gets out here,"[18] he wrote.

Child mortality was high and the death of children brought great sorrow. Malaria, smallpox and various fevers were some of the enemies of Caucasian women and children. The American pioneer missionaries who left America in 1812 included three women. Traveling was dangerous, long, and toilsome. One of the women had a miscarriage before reaching her destination, while another of the couples buried a child only days after their arrival on the mission field.

In 1844 two missionary families arrived in Xiamen (Amoy), China, to begin a pioneer work. Fever and death soon visited these families and, after one and a half years, one of the two men returned home to England with his two children and two children of the other family, leaving behind the graves of both wives and their other children.[19]

Other hardships need to be faced when children were sent to the homeland because of health or education, or when they were left behind when parents returned to their work at the end of a furlough. In some cases the mother stayed with the children for a year or two while the father returned to his mission work overseas. Sometimes these farewells turned out to be final, as in the case of Sarah Boardman Judson and her son George.

Sarah Boardman and her husband George were among pioneer missionaries in Myanmar (formerly Burma). When their firstborn, a two-year old daughter, died in 1829 the parents were crushed. Because there was no one else to do it, Sarah wrote, "my dear husband performed the funeral service"[20] Fifteen months later their second child died, and Sarah wrote, "Our hearts have been pierced anew by the loss of our dear babe."[21] Their third child, George, lived but then, after a six-year marriage, Sarah's husband died at age thirty.

Three years later Sarah married a colleague and old acquaintance, another missionary in Myanmar, Adoniram Judson. Adoniram had been a widower for about eight years. Sarah's young son George now had a father again. But George was sickly, which made Sarah and Adoniram decide that he should be sent to America. Sarah knew that the change would be hard for delicate little George, but when she said goodbye to him she did not know that he was to die in America. Her diary reads,

After deliberation, accompanied with tears, and agony and prayers, I came to the conviction that it was my duty to send away my only child, my darling George, and yesterday he bade me a long farewell.... Oh I shall never forget his looks, as he stood by the door, and gazed at me for the last time. His eyes were filling with tears, and his little face red with suppressed emotion. But he subdued his feelings, and it was not till he had turned away, and was going down the steps that he burst into a flood of tears. I hurried to my room; and on my knees, with my whole heart gave him up to God; and my bursting heart was comforted from above.... My reason and judgment tell me that the good of my child requires that he should be sent to America; and this of itself would support me in some little degree; but when I view it as a *sacrifice*, made for the sake of Jesus, it becomes a delightful privilege.[22]

When reminiscing, my missionary mother spoke more than once about a woman in pre-World War II Indonesia who always looked sad after she and her husband sent their two sons to Europe for high school studies. And I myself recall the exquisite pain of leaving our seventeen-year-old daughter behind, even though she was ready to enter college. Such parting happened three times more, as our three sons, one after another, returned to North America while we continued our mission assignment in Asia. But even though it was painful to let the children go, there was always that comfort of which Sarah Boardman Judson wrote.

There were times when family separation resulted in resentment and a break in the parent-child relationship. Ida S. Scudder (1870–1959) was born to missionary parents in India. She chose to follow in her father's footsteps and enrolled in medical studies in the USA. She repeatedly told her friends that she would never follow the family's medical tradition in India, she looked forward to life in the USA. She resented having lived in India as a child, while her physician father and busy mother fitted right into what was becoming a Scudder tradition.

Ida felt the painful emotions when, as a teenager, she was left in the USA to study for years. Years later her mother once said, "Indian people can't understand how I could come to India and leave six children behind in America. They would not do it. *And I don't think I could again.*"[23]

Eight years after her parents returned to India, when Ida was a young woman and nearing the end of her medical studies, a telegram came from India, saying that her mother was ill and needed her. Ida went, expecting to help her mother and then to return to the USA as soon as possible.

One evening while Ida was in her parents' home in India she answered the door three times when desperate men whose wives were in childbirth came to ask for help. All three of these Hindu men asked Ida to attend to their wives. Ida explained that her father was the physician qualified to treat the women, and though she was willing to come along to help, she was not the doctor. Each of the three men sadly said that this would be impossible, a male physician was not permitted to treat women in childbirth. Reluctantly each man left. Ida was deeply affected when she discovered later that all three of the women had died, and reflected on the fact that she could have helped the women if she were a physician in India.

In the end Ida's resentment of being separated from her family and of her parents' commitment to medical missions in India gave way to her own sense of Christian responsibility. That was her call. She returned to the USA, completed her medical education, and then returned to India. For the rest of her life she worked to develop medical services and training, and her lifework climaxed when a complete medical center, the Christian Medical College and Hospital, was opened in Vellore, South India. Though she struggled a great deal for the founding of this center, Ida became known especially for her rural work and for making medical help available to the villagers of the countryside. When she was elderly, after fifty years of a rewarding but difficult career, this remarkable woman's comment was simply, "God has been very good to me."[24] Eventually forty-two Scudders of four generations became part of mission work in India.

It was natural for the early female missionaries to work among women and children, they had no choice. It was against the custom in most Asian countries for a male physician to treat a woman, and even female medical personnel had to gradually gain the confidence of the people they hoped to serve. Before they had opportunity to tell Bible stories they had to build relationships, and attend to immediate physical needs of the people around them. They made friends when they spent time distributing food and clothing, and bandaged wounds, but constantly faced barriers and delays.

Married women often found it difficult to be part of the work because of family size, for missionary families were generally large. Today it is hard to imagine how it was possible for some of these women to achieve as much as they did when they bore so many children.

Rachel Milne and her husband Robert, the second missionary of the London Missionary Society, married in 1812. They left London and sailed for China the next month. When she died, seven years later, she had delivered five children, including a set of twins, and only three of them were still living.

Five couples in a group of fifteen newly-wed missionaries in Hawaii in the 1830s had four children each in less than ten years. Adoniram Judson, one of the first group of American missionaries to Asia, married three times, and fathered a total of twelve children, of whom eight died young or before birth. Letitia Vinton, missionary wife in China, bore eight children in twelve years; four of them died. She herself died from childbirth complications in 1903.[25] My own parents were missionaries in Indonesia during the 1930s. They left home as honeymooners and returned for furlough, six years later, with three children, two of them ill.

Single women, though at first always sent together with a family and rarely given an independent mission assignment, came into their own when mission programs became broader based and women were specifically recruited as medical and social workers and educators. Women's work, together with or alongside that of men, received much support from women in the homeland, and flourished with that encouragement.

As times began to change, perceptions of women's social roles underwent adjustments. Towards the year 1900 numerous missionaries, both women and men, were convinced that conversion to Christianity resulted in society's raising the status of women. They taught Asian women about western-style Christian living, the Christian home, and social values. Such attitudes eventually helped lead to the concept of "the white man's burden," the idea that white people were superior to people of color, and were responsible for sharing their blessings. Christianity and western values became integrated in the ventures of numerous missionaries. Today some people still appear to struggle with the shedding of these attitudes, though it seems to me that some Asians who are engaged in cross-cultural missions have shown signs of similar perspectives.

It would be interesting to learn more about the unexpected in women's work. Who would expect that two of four "godly women," sent to Tahiti in the early 1800s as brides for men of the London Missionary Society, would become a real problem, and one of them was said to have eventually drunk herself to death?[26]

Whoever thought that the British Gladys Aylward, considered an unsuitable mission candidate by the China Inland Mission, would travel to China by herself in 1932 with her cooking pots tied to her suitcase? Or that she would be the woman chosen to convince Chinese mothers to stop the painful and debilitating footbinding of their daughters? Or that she would become a Chinese citizen, and during World War II, lead some one hundred Chinese children from a dangerous place to safety?

Then there were missionary wives who had no sense of calling. One such example is the fiancée of Robert W. Carter who applied to the Presbyterian board in the early 1900s to go to the Philippines. When asked her reason for applying, she replied, "It is my purpose to go as the wife of a medical missionary — not as a missionary."[27] Another young woman, a physician, answered a question about her personal views of biblical teachings and of the Presbyterian Church rather frankly. She wrote, "I know nothing of the Confessions of Faith of the Presbyterian Church . . . I have no regular habit of Bible study."[28] This woman received a missionary appointment, together with her husband, but no assignment. She was, perhaps, an exception.

Most female missionaries went to their overseas assignments with a dedicated heart. Eleanor Chesnut, a doctor, carried medical supplies with her when she went to China in 1893. In China she had a hospital built with bricks paid for out of her salary. She refused to be repaid for them, for she insisted that that would "spoil all her fun."[29] This was the courageous doctor who — by herself — amputated the leg of a Chinese laborer. The skin at the place of amputation did not immediately heal properly, and when the man did recover he told others that Doctor Chesnut had taken some skin from her own leg and transplanted it to his.

The first unmarried female missionary to Iran traveled together with a missionary couple, in the mid 1800s. Fidelia Fiske found it very difficult to enrol girls in her classes because parents had no interest in their daughters being educated. Eventually she started her first class, and Fidelia taught literacy and Bible lessons to Nestorian women and girls for some fifteen years. Run-down, she returned to America and died at the age of forty-seven. After her death a letter came from an Iranian girl with the question, "Is there another Miss Fiske in your country?"[30]

For many centuries after the time of the Genghis Khan we hear nothing about Asian Christian women but then, where there was response to the gospel, they reappeared on the scene. It seems that few Asian women have kept journals or wrote about their lives, but missionaries did. At first letters and reports, perhaps as part of the men's reports, but also separately, told about conversions. The gospel was new to Asian women. Missionaries mentioned that women responded to the Christian call, but this correspondence rarely mentioned who the women were. Usually no names were attached.

Next came stories of women who had responded to the gospel and had become leaders. No training was needed, of course, to tell family members and neighbors about one's new-found faith, but if women were to work among women they needed at least Bible lessons. Many Christian women in Asia became so-called Bible-women, who had received some Bible training and usually continued to have lessons from the missionary as they traveled into the villages and towns to teach the Christian faith. They had the same language and culture as the people they visited, and were therefore perfectly suited for working among the local women. Some women studied further and became leaders and teachers, and several women's names were recorded. Everywhere in Asia where Christian work was done there were three inseparables: church, school and hospital.

Ibu Sutirah of Indonesia was one of the first women to enrol in a theological course in a men's school, and became an evangelist specifically for work among hospital patients. Later she became the principal of a school in middle Java for future female evangelists.

From the beginning, medical missionaries taught women and girls how to give basic nursing care to patients. Sometimes it was difficult to attract girls to this work. Wealthy parents thought it below their daughters' dignity to wash patients, change bed linens, and to do what seemed menial work, while peasant girls usually had no education and needed even the most basic instruction. The first three nurses in the Philippines went into training merely because the mothers were appreciative of what the male missionary physician had done for them, they coerced their daughters to enroll in the training which the doctor offered.

As soon as there were Christian converts it became imperative that they be taught more about the faith, and, if they were going to read the Bible, they would have to learn to read. Classes were set up for anyone wishing to learn, and those who did well and had teaching gifts were soon invited to become teachers. Schools were not only for literacy, they also included Bible lessons. Further education was offered after the simple literacy classes and many mission schools later excelled and became famous. Asian women had opportunities to study in these schools and to become professionals. Gradually the statistics of early reports were fleshed out as names and life stories of women were told.

Mission literature includes names of numerous Asian teachers who were outstanding Christians and did splendid work. Some of them became principals and other educational leaders. For instance, Christina Wang, a Chinese Christian, became a teacher in southern China. She left for Manila when communists took over in China. She was principal of Hope Christian High School, in Manila, until she died in 1966.

One of the reasons why missionaries hoped to educate Christian girls was so that young pastors would be able to find Christian girls to marry. Newly educated pastors were usually young, and it was vital that they should start a Christian home. The Asian way of choosing a wife for a young man was very effective in this, and many pastors became practiced in choosing Christian wives for their parishioners.

Once it was acceptable for women to take positions of leadership Asian women were seen as leaders in their field of expertise. A young Christian Filipina graduated from a missionary training school and was invited to be an associate pastor in 1938. When she married a pastor the next year, she and her husband became co-pastors in the church. When her husband died nineteen years later, it seemed only natural for her to continue as *pastora* [female pastor]. But soon this full-time task was too heavy, for she was raising seven children.

In her position as executive director of the Translators' Association of the Philippines Helen Madrid has the opportunity to encourage future Bible translators in Asia. *Photo courtesy Helen Madrid*

Further years of education, of church work and of teaching at the Bible College resulted in the ordination of Rev. Angelina B. Buensuceso, the first ordained female *pastora*, of the Convention of Philippine Baptist Churches, Inc.[31]

One of many examples of an Asian woman giving Christian leadership today is seen in the Philippines. Helen Madrid,[32] a Filipina born in 1943, grew up in rural northern Philippines. Seeds for her future were sown when she was young and met a foreign couple, both Wycliffe Bible Translators. One day her mother sent her to the village

> *Once it was acceptable for women to take positions of leadership Asian women were seen as leaders in their field of expertise.*

on an errand, to the house of the translators. The lady of the house spoke to Helen about the Lord Jesus. Later a pastor taught Bible lessons in the home of Helen's parents. Helen was touched by the story of Lazarus and the rich man (Luke 16:19–31), and wondered how she might be a good Christian. She observed the Wycliffe couple teach literacy to local people and was impressed by their work of translating the Bible into the local language.

While completing high school Helen studied part-time at the nearby seminary. During this time she saw the poverty of local pastors, several of whom had to augment their income with extra work. This gave Helen the idea of setting up a business of dress design, and to give part of her income to a pastor's family. For this she needed to study business, and she enrolled in a university in Manila. She was able to cover her educational expenses by being a seamstress, as she had learned to sew.

During her last semester at university she was challenged to apply for a scholarship for a summer course in linguistics. Remembering the Wycliffe couple of her youth, Helen prayed for guidance and said to God, "This is the test. If I apply and pass I will do what you want me to do." She received the grant, took the course, then decided to forget about the dress design shop and to become a Bible translator instead. This decision was confirmed by God.

For eight years Helen worked as a Bible translator and then studied in the USA. In 1985 she received an MA in Linguistics from the University of Texas at Arlington and returned to the Philippines, ready to do further translations. But again there was a change, for Helen was asked to work in office administration. This was a difficult decision for Helen, for it meant giving up the field work she loved. But she followed the Master's leading and, for seventeen years, held various positions in the Translators' Association of the Philippines (TAP).

It was an unexpected joy when church leaders in Ifugao Province asked Helen to be a consultant in their Bible translating project, for this would put her back in the primary work of translation. Again she trained new translators, gave advice on translation problems, checked completed work for publication, and felt fulfilled in her work.

Since 2002 Helen has been the Executive Director of the Translators' Association of the Philippines, and a member of Wycliffe International, Inc. It is demanding work, but Helen is encouraged when she receives messages such as, "As a leader you have a vision and we want to be part of that vision." It is Helen's vision that, by the year 2025, TAP will send about two hundred and fifty Filipino Bible translators into other areas of Asia where people do not yet have Christian Scriptures in their own language. This is the prayer and happy hope she shares.

Today Christian women can be found in many different Christian endeavors as listeners, motivators, planners, followers, executors, officers, women who pray. Together, Christian women in Asia continue to be witnesses of the gospel.

The stories of the women in this book are written so that they and their achievements will not be forgotten, for their example speaks today. Whether they lived long ago or are with us today, they have done the best they could in lives of Christian service.

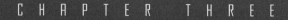
There seems to be no painting or drawing of Sorkaktani, mother of Kublai Khan. There is, however, a well-published picture of the wife of Kublai Khan, and Sorkaktani would probably have dressed much the same. The picture shows Sorkaktani's daughter-in-law wearing a tall, red headpiece, matching her outfit. She does not smile, her mouth is small. Her eyebrows are straight lines, marked in with blackening, for this was the fashion among Mongol women of that day.

Normally, in the early 1200s, Mongols wore animal furs, to keep warm in the cold north. The fur's hair was on the inside while the skin faced the outside. It is said that the early Mongols paid no attention to hygiene. Theirs was an animistic society and its people believed that water was a symbol of the spirits, that it should not be dirtied. So they washed neither their bodies nor their clothes, not even their dishes.[1]

When winter ended the people eagerly looked for the first animals of spring, because food supplies were all but finished by then. As soon as small animals such as foxes were seen they were hunted, and when spring came and deer and fish might be caught the Mongols prized the new source of nourishment.

Mongol existence was hard, often cruel, and life was cheap. Women may have been second class citizens among the Mongols, but their contributions to tribal life were important. One of these, of course, was that of bringing up children, and of teaching them the basics of the nomadic life. In addition to that Sorkaktani, her sisters and other Christian women passed on to their children the Christian faith as they knew it.

Mother of Four Rulers

Sorkaktani[2] (died 1252)

Because Mongol history was first written in Persian, Arabic and Chinese, before translation into European languages, numerous spellings of names have resulted. For example, the name of the founder of the Mongol Empire, though usually spelled as Genghis Khan, is sometimes written as Chingis Khan, Jenghiz Khan, or something similar. Sorkaktani's son Kublai is often referred to as Khubilai Khan, or even Qubilai. Sorkaktani's name is spelled in at least eight ways.

It must have been frightening for Sorkaktani to be given away as a prize in a war settlement. True, life in northern Asia in the 1200s was often cruel and tribal warfare common. Still, when she and her older sister were led away by the conqueror, the Khan of the Mongols, she must have been distressed as she pondered her future.

Who was Sorkaktani, and what was significant about her?

It is doubtful that Sorkaktani left behind a life of luxury when she was brought to the tents of the Mongols and married the khan's youngest son; her life among the Mongols was one of struggles and hard work. Her heritage, however, was royal; her father was the brother of a king, as well as a powerful local chieftain. She and her sisters used the title *beki*, a title which was used only for people in high levels of society, and probably meant "princess." They belonged to the Kerait tribe, a largely Christian tribe among mostly Buddhist nomads who moved as seasons changed and local food supplies were exhausted.

The Kerait tribe was one of the numerous nomadic tribes wandering in areas north and west of China, always in search of grasslands and water for their animals. Five kinds of animals were especially important to these nomads.[3] They prized their horses, because they were a fast means of travel. They raised sheep, goats, and yaks for food as well as for fuel, and for making clothing and tents. They used camels for transport, especially in desert travel. To the north, east and west of the vast steppes where they roamed were mountain ranges, and to the south was the enormous Gobi Desert.

During the summer they had to take advantage of lush grass and hunt and fish because when autumn came food became scarce. The people of the steppes had to harden themselves against the bitter cold of winter. During the severe winter weather they were forced to kill many of their animals for food, and invariably they became hungry when there was little left to eat. During those months they hunched around the fire in their *gers*, round felt tents (also called *yurts*). There was no firewood on the plains, and the dung used for fires filled the tents with smoke, of which only a part could escape through the vent at the top of the *ger*. It was a time of planning new battles, of telling stories, of waiting for the cold to abate. Then, when spring came with the promise of new greens, the *gers* were folded and placed on wagons, the animals were rounded up and the whole tribe moved to a new place. This is how people in this part of the world lived for centuries.

Clans and tribes made friends with neighboring tribes or fought each other, depending on their current need to have allies or to claim certain grasslands for their own animals. Jealousies between clans often led to warfare, and it was common to steal women and animals. Even the chief's family did not escape this. It was because of the victorious Mongol khan's demand that Sorkaktani and her sister were forced to leave their mother's tent for good while they were still young girls.

The Old Silk Road, a trade route winding through the Gobi Desert and along the plains of Asia, already existed before the time of Jesus. When the Christian Church was still very young, missionaries from Syria and western Persia traveled eastward along the same roads as the merchants did, and some of the merchants themselves were missionaries. As they traveled during the day and spent the nights around campfires or in towns these Christian merchants and missionaries spread the gospel in Central Asia, even in East Asia. Christian churches were built; some large cities of Central Asia, such as Merv and Samarkand, became centers for evangelism, and from there missionaries fanned out further and further.

Around AD 1100 a number of people of the large nomadic tribes north and west of China began to be converted to the Nestorian Christian faith.[4] The Kerait tribe, south and east of Lake Baikal, was the earliest to see conversions, and a century or so later the whole tribe had become Christian.[5]

The Keraits were prominent among the nomads, and when the powerful Christian Kerait chieftain Toghrul helped their Chinese neighbors win a victory, the Chinese honored him, in return, with the title of *Wang*. He came to be called Toghrul Wang Khan (*Wang* for king, and *Khan* for leader) by his people.

Toghrul Wang Khan was asked by Temujin (c1162–1227), a young man of the neighboring Mongols, to make a friendship pact, and became like a father to Temujin. Later they became blood brothers and together they fought numerous battles. But friendship pacts could and were broken. After Temujin emerged as a strong ruler among the Mongols he heard that Toghrul had become disloyal; it took him little time to attack and conquer the Keraits and to kill Toghrul.[6] As part of the peace agreement the Mongol leader demanded that two young nieces of Toghrul be given to him; he took the elder sister for his wife (but later gave her away as a reward to one of his brave generals), while he gave the younger sister, Sorkaktani, as wife to his youngest son Tolui. A third sister later became the wife of Temujin's eldest son.[7] These three sisters were all of the Christian Kerait tribe.

Even if she were afraid, Sorkaktani probably held her head high when she was brought to the Mongols' camp. She was familiar with the ways of the Mongols whose lives she shared from this time. She was a young girl, but, even though she was used as a pawn in restoring peace, she was brought up in the ways of royalty; moreover, she was intelligent and ambitious.

But who were the Mongols, and who was their leader?

Temujin was the eldest son in a minor family of Mongol tribal rulers. When he was a young boy his father, the chief, was poisoned by a neighboring enemy tribe. Most of those warriors who had been loyal to his father saw little future in remaining with the widow and children of their leader, and joined other clans. This left the family destitute, for they had no wealth, and Temujin, as new head of the clan, was young and inexperienced. His mother, though, was an able woman and did her utmost to provide for her children and to teach them to survive.

It seems that Temujin was strong and agile and could hold his own. He learned to hunt, fish and fight as he grew up, and gradually was able to attract some of his father's former followers back to the clan. These men joined Temujin under his white banner with the nine yak tails. In times of battle the banner of each tribe became a symbol of which they were proud and it united the men as they rode in the desert and searched for their unit.

Temujin and his men traveled east to wage battle and returned victorious. They went west and again Timujin came back the conqueror.

Timujin did not govern the areas he won, for he did not care about ruling those he vanquished. All he wanted was victory in war, power, and plenty of grassland and water for the well-being of his people. He simply fought to defeat the tribes around him and to become great. For instance, when he heard that Toghrul Wang Khan had betrayed his loyalty he immediately plunged toward the Keraits, seeking revenge.

Temujin was clever, and proved himself as he won battle after battle. Ruthless and cruel, he was able to gain power and, eventually, to unify many regional tribes into one entity under his white banner of the nine yak tails. When he achieved this he called together a *kuriltai* (council of tribal chiefs) in 1206 and was able to have himself proclaimed head of them all. At the suggestion of a shaman (priest) he was given the title *Genghis Kha Khan* (the Greatest of Rulers, the Emperor of All Men).[8] He now claimed to be the ruler of "all tribes who live in felt tents," and all of those people, as a group, now became known as Mongols. Even those tribes he had conquered were now called Mongols.[9] From then on he was known as Genghis Khan; he was thirty-nine years old, and would live for another twenty-one years.

Although Genghis Khan ordered a writing system to be developed for his people, no Mongol history was written during his lifetime. The authors of *The Secret History*, written by Mongols after Genghis Khan's death, as well as those Persian, Arab and Chinese who described the history of this time, were impressed by Sorkaktani. They described her as "extremely talented and able and she was elevated over all the other women of the world,"[10] and "a queen who trained her sons so well that all princes were amazed by her administrative skills."[11] Even a Roman Catholic missionary, who was sent by the pope to visit the Mongol camp, commented that she was highly honored. Such praise of a woman, written by men, was very unusual during the Middle Ages.

We do not know how old Sorkaktani was when she married Tolui, Genghis Khan's fourth son, but she must have been very young, because she lived some fifty years after she was brought to the Mongol tents. There is no literature about their relationship as husband and wife. We do know that Tolui was often away, accompanying Genghis Khan on

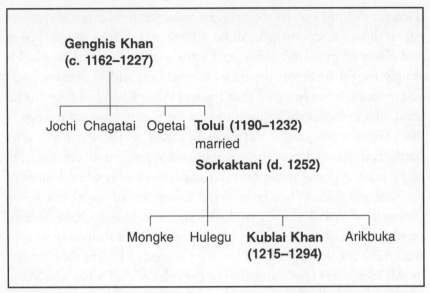

Sorkaktani, daughter-in-law of Genghis Khan, had significant Christian influence on her four sons. The family tree shows Genghis Khan who brought Sorkaktani to his people and gave her to his son Tolui as wife. Sorkaktani became the mother of four sons, all of whom became important important leaders, but Kublai Khan became the most famous. He was the fifth Great Khan of the Mongols, and also founded a Mongol dynasty, the Yuan Dynasty (1279–1368), in China.

his military campaigns. We also know that there were other wives, but that Sorkaktani was the main wife. To the Mongols this meant that her children would be the heirs of Genghis Khan, though children of other wives and concubines would also be recognized as his offspring. In fact, the several wives and concubines and their children often were the reason for the splintering of society, and for the numerous branches and clans within a tribe.

It was quite common for nearby tribes to take Kerait wives for their chief's family, because the Kerait were powerful, and an alliance with them was usually an advantage. Kerait women enjoyed a good reputation. Stealing women was quite common among royals, even when women were already married. Even Genghis Khan's mother had been forcibly taken, her life taking a sudden turn when, after her wedding and on her way to her new husband's home, she was abducted by Genghis Khan's father's people. In spite of her previous wedding, she was married to Genghis Khan's father.

Though a princess, Sorkaktani would have a life of many responsibilities. Individual women's lives had little value, yet women often had much authority. After all, women were an important symbol of the workforce. They cared for the clan. They were trained to fight. They prepared for the frequent moves of the clan and then moved the *gers* from grassland to grassland. They took care of animals, saw to it that the clan had enough food, and they were in charge when the men were away. Many were expert horsewomen. Some even went to war with the men. They had the privilege of divorce, and some of them exercised great influence as priestesses. At the same time, their social status was so low that the author of *The Secret History*, writes about the "fair-cheeked girls, and the fine-shanked geldings" as desirable war booty in one breath. Throughout *The Secret History* horses are described in detail, much more so than those desirable "fair-cheeked girls."[12] In fact, the horse was crucial in the Mongols' rise to power, and it is fascinating to read how horses enabled warriors to strike out in lightning raids and to escape quickly when necessary; how riders could cover eighty miles a day on long-distance expeditions, and how horses could travel through what seemed impassable deserts and across insurmountable mountain ranges.

Life was cheap during Mongol rule. Thousands of people were killed in battle, as Mongols destroyed cities and murdered all of their victims except those they considered useful. All this was done to ensure that they would have large areas of grasslands, and impose taxes on the conquered people. Yet, in spite of the savage and cruel ways of the Mongol warriors their chief, Genghis Khan — merciless ruler of an immense empire — was said to have been deathly afraid of his mother and of his wife.[13]

As the wife of Genghis Khan's youngest son Tolui, Sorkaktani was in the background for many years. During this time she and Tolui had four sons, and she devoted

> *Though a princess, Sorkaktani would have a life of many responsibilities. Individual women's lives had little value, yet women often had much authority.*

herself to educating them. Being a Christian, she had a unique opportunity to teach them the Christian faith. She was a dynamic woman and was determined that her sons would one day be leaders.

Sorkaktani saw to it that her boys were properly trained to use bow and arrow, and that they learned the other skills essential for life on the steppes. She had ambitions for her sons, and taught them to know the needs of their subjects. She made sure that each of her boys learned the language of another area, so that they would be more familiar with people outside of the Mongol homeland as the empire grew.

Sorkaktani was unable to read, but she understood the importance of the written page. Her father-in-law, Genghis Khan, was also illiterate, yet thought it important for his people to learn reading and writing. Before the Mongols had a system of writing, their neighbors to the south were already largely literate. These were the Uighurs, a partially Christian tribe. Once Genghis Khan interviewed an Uighur prisoner who was a scholar, and learned about their system of writing. He was so impressed that he ordered people to learn this system, and he made the Uighur script the official script of the Mongol empire.[14] Sorkaktani hired an Uighur tutor to teach her sons to read and write.[15] But more than that, she taught her boys values. Two of her sons are said to have become Christians. All of them acquired values which were foreign to the ruthless, destructive Mongol way of life.

It is said that, until she died, Sorkaktani lived a Christian life. This example certainly was the best witness she could give her family. She also taught her sons to be tolerant of others' religious beliefs. This was not easy in the Mongol setting where there was so little acceptance, but she herself was a model for her sons by consistently allowing others to follow their own faith. She showed in her life that, though she was a Christian, she tolerated other religions. It is well possible that this was also for political reasons, because Sorkaktani was a shrewd administrator, and knew that much more can be accomplished with smooth relationships than with stormy ones. Sorkaktani not only tolerated but even supported Buddhists and Muslims as well as Christians. She taught her boys that it was useless to exploit peasants, as the Mongols usually did. After conquering an area they usually destroyed the agricultural lands because to them, grasslands were the most necessary. But Sorkaktani made her sons understand that, if they were to benefit from the food which farmers could provide, they must protect them rather than make life more difficult for the farmers.

While Sorkaktani was bringing up her sons her father-in-law, Genghis Khan, was reaching the peak of his sovereignty. He was masterful in planning his battles and sending his generals on military campaigns. He conquered his enemies by violent warfare and brutal devastation, and was merciless towards his victims.

The Mongols won battles in distant places where they conquered other people, afterwards the soldiers pillaged and then returned home with goods that Mongols had never seen. Genghis Khan and his men learned to appreciate the beautiful silks, the delicious foods, and exotic items from other places. Gradually, as they learned about other people's ways, their own way of life began to change subtly. Nomadic life made way for a more settled lifestyle. While they roamed the country as tribal clans the Mongols had no central city, but that began to change when Genghis Khan chose to make Karakorum, the former Kerait center, his headquarters. His son would later make the town a more permanent base, and employ advisors of different faiths, including Christians, to help him rule the vast lands and people of various backgrounds.[16] And years later Sorkaktani's son Kublai Khan would move the Mongol capital to Khanbaliq (also spelled as Khanbalik), today's Beijing.

Genghis Khan established a code of laws by which he ruled. These written laws were absolute and of fundamental importance to all his subjects. Christian influence can be detected in some of these rules, and is said to have been due to his Nestorian Christian advisers.[17] The first law read, "All men are to believe in one God, Creator of Heaven and Earth."[18] The second rule showed Genghis Khan's religious tolerance, "Leaders

> *Genghis Khan established a code of laws by which he ruled . . . Christian influence can be detected in some of these rules.*

of a religion, preachers, monks, persons who are dedicated to religious practices, the criers of mosques, physicians and undertakers are to be freed from public taxes and charges."[19] There was no lenience in cases of disobedience. Throughout his life Genghis Khan spread warfare, death and destruction around him as his empire became more widespread.

When he was old one of his advisors said to him, "Thou has conquered a great empire in the saddle. Thou canst not govern it so."[20] This advisor clearly understood that the way of the nomads could not continue when people acquired lands and goods; a central system of government would have to be devised for the growing empire.

In his sixties and ailing, Genghis Khan understood that actions needed to be done so that Mongol rule might continue. When his eldest son Jochi died, Genghis Khan decided to bypass his second son, Chagatai, and appointed Ogetai, his third son, to succeed him.

Genghis Khan considered his task as yet incomplete. When he was on his deathbed he said to his sons, "With Heaven's aid I have conquered for you a huge empire. But my life was too short to achieve the conquest of the world. That is left for you."[21] Then he urged them to agree with one another and to be united, so the empire would not break apart.[22] His sons did, for some time, continue to defend the empire's borders, but could not keep it unified as their father had done. In a short time the race for succession was causing tensions, and Sorkaktani was on the alert for the sake of her sons.

According to Mongol custom, the youngest son of a man's main wife inherited the rule over the home estate, rather than other areas, and he was called the *otchigin* ("Hearth Prince"). It appeared that this would be the lot of Tolui, Genghis Khan's youngest son and Sorkaktani's husband. And that did happen. Tolui ruled the home region and died during the reign of Ogetai, his older brother. History barely mentions it, but it is worth noting that, after Tolui's death, Ogetai regularly asked Sorkaktani for advice.[23]

Upon Ogetai's death regents ruled for a few years and then his son Kuyuk succeeded, but Kuyuk was sickly and died after two years. After Kuyuk's death his mother, who was also a Christian and a competent politician, was plotting to place her own nephew on the throne, and it was then that Sorkaktani saw her opportunity. It was Mongol custom to convene a *kuriltai* (council of tribal chiefs), whenever a new leader had to be elected. Sorkaktani convinced these council members that the next Great Khan should be a direct descendant of Genghis Khan, rather than the nephew of a daughter-in-law, and then shrewdly persuaded the council members to elect her eldest son, Mongke, to be the next Great Khan.

Sorkaktani's brilliant planning, political skill, and dedication to the future of her sons resulted in all of her sons becoming leaders. It is impossible to know how much she influenced her sons with her own Christian faith, but it is clear that she exposed them to the same Christian principles which guided the numerous advisors at the Khan's court, where Christians were respected. The wife and daughter of Mongke, Sorkaktani's eldest son, were said to be Christians, and Mongke hired a Christian tutor for his son. During Mongke's time as Great Khan there was much freedom for Christians, and worship services were held openly. Mongke even accompanied his wife to the tent of worship, a European visiting missionary wrote.[24]

Mongke commissioned his brother Hulagu (Sorkaktani and Tolui's second son) to capture the Islamic states in the western lands. Hulagu's troops struck west, destroyed much of West Asia, and then founded the Il Khan dynasty in Persia.

Hulagu's wife, Queen Dokuz was a Christian Kerait princess, and well known for her devotion. When she traveled with her husband their caravan always included a portable chapel, set on a cart. Hulagu's army assaulted Baghdad in 1258 and destroyed the city. Many Christians were saved because of the personal pleadings of Queen Dokuz. Some historians claim that Hulagu was a

It is impossible to know how much she influenced her sons with her own Christian faith, but it is clear that she exposed them to the same Christian principles which guided the numerous advisors at the Khan's court.

Christian, others that he was a spirit worshiper. Though he favored Christians and proclaimed freedom of worship in his domain, and forbade Muslims to interfere with Christian practices, he himself nevertheless adopted certain Buddhist customs.[25] When Mongke heard what had happened in the west and how Dokuz had interceded for the Christians he told Hulagu that he would do well to consult the Queen in all his affairs.[26]

Sorkaktani and Tolui's second son, Kublai, seems to have been his mother's favorite. She took extra care in his education and seems to have given him much advice. She saw to it that Kublai learned to read and write the Mongolian language.[27] When she saw that he was becoming involved in China she insisted that he learn to speak Chinese and understand Confucian thought. Sorkaktani knew that Confucianism was basic to the Chinese way of life, and that an understanding of the Chinese language and lifestyle would be essential in governing China well. Though she prepared him to be a great ruler, Sorkaktani was not to see her son Kublai when, as Great Khan and Emperor of China, he was the most powerful man of his time.[28] She died before this happened. It is obvious that it was because of his mother's influence that Kublai Khan supported the small group of Nestorian Christians in China, once he was in power there. A year after her son Mongke became Great Khan, Sorkaktani became sick and died. At her funeral Mongke honored her with the title of "Empress." Then she was buried near her husband Tolui.[29]

Sorkaktani and Tolui's youngest son's ambitions for the throne never materialized. Following Mongol tradition this youngest son, the *otchigin*, "Hearth Prince," was posted in the home territory and ruled there.[30] And so Sorkaktani's sons all became distinguished leaders in the short-lived Mongol Empire (1206–1368) which, at its height, was larger than any empire before or after, and reached from Korea to Western Russia in the north, and from Burma to Iraq in the south.[31]

Sorkaktani was respected for her beauty, her boldness, her modesty, and her Christian faith. The Mongol Empire, in which Sorkaktani played an important role, was bloody. The words death and destruction describe it well. But for Christians it was a period when their faith was tolerated, even protected by the khans, and a time of freedom of worship. The Mongol Empire did not last long; for several reasons, including alcoholism and mismanagement, it came to an abrupt end in less than a century and a half. Even before its demise Christian freedoms vanished as Mongols turned to Islam. An era was closed.

Sorkaktani died when Mongol sovereignty was nearing its peak. She never could have realized that, in spite of slaughter, plunder and war, the Mongols ushered in a period of peace between nations, a period during which Asians and Europeans traveled along the ancient trade routes, exchanged ideas, and laid the foundation for a new age. That new age would enable European missionaries to come to Asia and introduce the Christian faith, for the second time in some areas of Asia.

We may ask what Sorkaktani's understanding of the Christian faith really was, and whether or how much she compromised her faith. After asking these questions it may be reasonable to remember that this illiterate woman kept her faith throughout life during a time when even the Queen's head could roll very quickly if she offended her husband, the Khan. In the maze of people, events, places and time of the great Mongolian Empire Sorkaktani will always be remembered as one of the Christian princesses who dared to live their faith.

We may believe that, when Sorkaktani's life on earth ended our Savior said of her, "She has done a beautiful thing for me."

Western women became missionaries or missionary wives for various reasons. In the 1800s schools for girls became more common in Europe and North America, but initially there were few work opportunities for female graduates. Some women married missionary candidates for love, others in hope of future adventures, still others because they believed that they had something to contribute.

European missions to Asia began during the early 1700s, yet Dorothy Carey, who traveled to India nearly a century later, is remembered as the hapless wife of the pioneer missionary, William Carey. She, William and their children spent some anxious years in India around 1800, when the British East India Company, which basically ruled India, wanted nothing to do with Christian missionaries on the continent, and did their best to drive them out should they try to come.

It was 1812 when the first American group of missionaries to Asia embarked for India. Some of these young people would eventually sail on to Burma (Myanmar) or to the Isle of France (Mauritius), some 2,400 kilometers east of Africa.

The nineteenth century has been called the "Great Century of Protestant Missions," and many women left home and family in Europe or North America for mission service, either as single missionaries or as missionary wives. These women left their stamp on the work of education and medicine, but perhaps even more significant was their impact as Christian individuals who did their utmost so that others might hear about Jesus.

A Teenaged Pioneer Missionary

Harriet Atwood Newell (1793–1812)

Two hundred years ago it was very "modern" for American girls to go to an academy. The government of Massachusetts had decided that all children had to go to school, but usually that did not include girls, who learned to read and sew at home. Many Christian parents wanted their children to know how to read so that they would be able to read the Bible. By the end of the 1700s it became more common for American girls to attend school, at least to learn to read and write.[1]

In 1803 church members opened the Bradford Academy, one of the earliest recognized private schools which also accepted girls. Girls studied the usual reading and writing and handcrafts, but there was more, for here they studied other courses, such as geography. The town of Bradford was on the Merrimack River; trading ships went from this town to American ports, but also across the ocean to West India and Great Britain and parents in Bradford wanted their children to learn about geography and navigation.[2] Clearly, they looked beyond their own community. Harriet Atwood was twelve years old when her parents enrolled her at the Bradford Academy, about a kilometer from their home. As her father was a businessman, it was no surprise that Harriet was sent to school, where she enjoyed her studies, and loved to read books.

During Harriet's first year at Bradford Academy there was a spiritual revival at the school, and she was one of the students who was

Harriet Newell, nineteen-year old American pioneer missionary.

impressed by it. "Must I be born again?" she asked. All her life she had learned about salvation and the Bible, but now the question became personal. She took the matter very seriously, and in time Harriet experienced a spiritual renewal. In her church, young people usually made a public confirmation of their faith during a worship service, but Harriet did not do that. Because there were arguments and bitterness in the congregation Harriet did not feel comfortable, and kept quiet.

Having failed to follow up on the promises she had made to follow her Lord Harriet fell away from her commitment for some time. Then, when she was fourteen, her father died. There were nine children in the family, and Harriet must have thought about life and death as she worked hard to help her mother at home. Perhaps that was the reason why her heart was touched by a sermon she heard, and she remembered the promise she made to God that she would live a Christian life. She repented of her sins, believed that she was forgiven, and resolutely determined to follow Jesus.

Harriet loved to write in her diary and to correspond with friends. She used the flowing language of her day to describe her innermost feelings. "What am I, what am I, that I should be blessed with the gospel's joyful sound, while so many are perishing in heathen darkness for lack of the knowledge of Christ?"[3] A few months later she publicly confirmed her faith during a worship service. She wrote a friend, "I have now publicly confessed my faith in God. I have taken the vows of the covenant upon me, and solemnly surrendered myself to him eternally. Entreat God to have mercy upon me, and keep me from falling." She told her friends about her father's death, how he had died calmly, trusting

God. And that, though she cried when she visited his tomb to pray, she was certain she'd see him again in heaven.[4]

Harriet took her faith seriously, and when she had turned sixteen she wrote, "I have now come to the close of another year. How various have been the scenes which I have been called to pass through this year. But what have I done for God? What for the interests of religion? And what for my own soul?"[5]

In the same year that Harriet Atwood enrolled in Bradford Academy, a young man, Samuel Newell, eight years older than Harriet, was studying at William College at Harvard, not far away. Samuel was a devout Christian; he and some friends used to get together outdoors to talk about world affairs, and to pray for people in other places, as well as about their own future. Once, when they were out in a field, there was an unexpected storm, and they took shelter beside a haystack in the field. They made an important commitment that day in 1806, when they decided to become missionaries. This meeting came to be known as the Haystack Prayer Meeting, and was the beginning of the founding of the first American overseas missions.

When Samuel Newell and his friends were ready to enrol in seminary they did not go to Harvard, which was gaining a reputation for liberalism, but entered Andover Theological Seminary, a new Congregational school, based on more conservative principles. Samuel Newell and some of his friends spoke with some school and church leaders about their hope to become missionaries, and in 1810 they sent a paper to the Congregational church leaders of the area. In this paper they stated that they were committed to missions, and they asked advice as to whether they should go east or west, join an existing missionary society [the London Missionary Society in England] or just forget the whole idea. The

> *They made an important commitment that day in 1806, when they decided to become missionaries. This meeting came to be known as the Haystack Prayer Meeting, and was the beginning of the founding of the first American overseas missions.*

church leaders appointed a committee and this was the beginning of the first American missionary society, called the American Board of Commissioners for Foreign Missions (ABCFM or American Board for short).

Harriet corresponded with her friends and enjoyed their company. One of her friends was Ann Hasseltine, who was five years older, and who had been one of Harriet's classmates at Bradford Academy. Ann was an energetic young woman; after her graduation she began to teach, and was soon known for her Christian personal work among students.[6] One day when Ann was visiting Harriet she gave her the shocking news that Adoniram Judson, one of Samuel Newell's friends of the Haystack group, had proposed marriage to her, and that she had accepted, though she hardly knew Adoniram. This marriage proposal meant more than marrying, it also indicated an agreement to go overseas, "to endure the sufferings of a Christian amongst heathen nations, to spend her days in India's sultry clime."[7] It seemed natural to choose India as a place to do mission work. There had already been correspondence with the London Missionary Society, and perhaps the young and inexperienced American missionary candidates could join William Carey, who by then had been in India for nearly twenty years.

Clearly, Ann's relationship with Adoniram was not a romantic one at first, but a woman's sense of call from God to become a missionary spouse. It set Harriet to thinking, and that evening she wrote in her diary,

> How did the news affect my heart! Is she willing to do all this for God; and shall I refuse to lend my little aid, in a land where divine revelation has shed its brightest rays? I have felt more for the salvation of the heathen, this day, than I recollect to have felt through my whole past life.[8]

For Harriet it was the beginning of a quest to discover God's will for her life.

Three days after this visit Harriet met Samuel Newell. Her diary for 23 October 1810 reads simply that someone "... introduced Mr. Newell to our family. He appears to be an engaged Christian. Expects to spend his life in preaching a Savior to the benighted pagans."[9] Samuel was back the next week, and Harriet wrote,

> He gave me some account of the dealings of God with his soul. If such a man, who has devoted himself to the service of the gospel, has determined to labor in the most difficult part of the vineyard, and is willing to renounce his earthly happiness for the interest of religion; if *he* doubts his possessing the love of God: What shall *I* say of *myself*?[10]

Harriet must have been in contact with Ann Hasseltine over the next several winter months, and thought about her own future, wondering if she might also be asked to consider becoming a missionary. And then it happened, in the spring of 1811, when she received a letter from Samuel Newell. That evening she confided in her diary,

> This was not a long wished for letter, — no, it was a long-dreaded one, which I was conscious would involve me in doubt, anxiety, and distress. Nor were the contents such as I might answer at a *distant* period; they required an *immediate* answer. And now what shall I say? How shall I decide this important, this interesting question? Shall I consent to leave for ever the parent of my youth, the friends of my life; the dear scenes of my childhood, and my native country; and go to a land of strangers, "not knowing the things that shall befall me there?" O for direction from heaven! "O for that wisdom which is profitable to direct!" I will go to God, and with an unbiassed [sic] and unprejudiced mind, seek his guidance. I will cast this heavy burden on him, humbly trusting that he will sustain me, and direct me in the path of duty.[11]

It is clear that Harriet's first reaction is related not to the thought of marrying Samuel, but to the prospect of becoming a missionary in a faraway place. Her concern was such that she wrote in her diary that she had not slept for three nights because she was so upset. One evening she was so tired that she fell asleep after dinner and for a while forgot about India and all the related questions. But later in the evening, in her bedroom, it all came back and she related that her heart almost burst as she asked God for guidance.

Harriet was away from home when she received Samuel's letter, and she could hardly wait to go home and talk with her mother. She had an idea — what if her mother would refuse to let her go? "Perhaps my dear mother will immediately say, *Harriet shall never go.* Well, if this should be the case, my duty would be plain. I cannot act contrary to the advice and express commands of a pious mother."[12] But she was not given the easy answer she probably hoped for secretly, for her mother told Harriet that she had to make the decision herself.

It was hard to come to a resolution, but Samuel was waiting for a reply. Harriet wrote him that were she to follow her own wishes, she would "decidedly answer in the negative." She then mentioned that she was so young, only seventeen, and she trembled at the idea. Her mother would neither encourage nor advise her, and so she concluded her letter with the request, "Will Mr. Newell remember Harriet at the Mercy Seat? Will he implore for her the guidance of that covenant Redeemer, whom she has professed to love?"[13]

Apparently Samuel spent two weeks in Bradford that month of April, so Harriet and he probably met repeatedly. The next month Harriet wrote a friend that Samuel had visited several times then, too. In June she told a friend that Samuel and she spent an evening discussing the proposed mission, its dangers and difficulties, and that the conversation had left her depressed and in doubt. In her words,

> Sometimes I can reflect upon this subject with composure, and even long to be on missionary ground, where superstition and idolatry usurp the sway; I think I can bid my dear friends a last farewell, with calmness, and follow, with delight, the leadings of Providence. But at other times I fear that this is not the situation God has designed for me.... My greatest fear is, that I shall lose all courage and perseverance, should I go, and not only be unhappy myself, but make those wretched who are with me.[14]

Faced with so weighty a decision, perhaps she sensed the danger of being wrongly motivated by the "strong attachment" of which she had written in her diary. Was she falling in love with the man who was courting her? After all, she was a teenager of seventeen, and it must have been romantic to be given so much attention by a gentleman.

Samuel left in June for Philadelphia, to take a basic medical course as part of his missionary preparation. Harriet wrote in her diary that she would not see him for nine months and added that she could "hardly feel reconciled to his departure, but the will of the Lord be done." However, she was certain that it would be useful for Samuel to take some medical training. "Why then, should I object?" Obviously she was in love by now.

Soon after Samuel left, Harriet wrote him, "I think upon the whole that I am decided." Yet there was another issue. What if she would be a burden instead of a help for Samuel? What if she could not help him in time of trouble, or lighten his burden? If that were the case, she wrote, *"I ought not to go."* She definitely wished to be useful if she'd accompany Samuel as his wife. Around that time she shared a joy with Samuel when she told him that a friend "has greatly lessened every discouragement, and given me a 'passion for missions,' which I never felt before." Yet, until she left for India Harriet repeatedly doubted if it was really God's will for her to go.[15]

It is no wonder that the decision was so very difficult for Harriet. Travel was difficult and life in distant countries had many unknowns. There was no experienced American missionary wife to whom she could go for advice. It would be so much simpler for a young woman, and certainly for the teenager that Harriet was, to look for a different future.

Harriet lived during a time often called the "Second Great Awakening," a time when Americans became convinced that missions was a task of the Church,[16] and it was a time when women were encouraged to help needy women and children. Among women the emphasis was on "women's work for women." It was all so new to Harriet. Missions far away from home and friends seemed a dark prospect.

> *Harriet lived during a time often called the "Second Great Awakening," a time when Americans became convinced that missions was a task of the Church. . . .*

Samuel had only recently come into her life. She was very young. Marriage and missionary duty were so closely intertwined, and there seemed to be so many reasons for choosing to stay at home. But the urge to do her Christian duty and to help bring the gospel to the people of India was stronger for Harriet than her personal wishes.

Plans and preparations were made, and it was time to go. It was February 1812, and cold wintry weather in Massachusetts. Five men, Samuel Newell, Adoniram Judson, Gordon Hall, Luther Rice and Samuel Nott, were ordained into the ministry, and the three women who would accompany them were commissioned with the men to serve as missionaries to India. Ann and Adoniram Judson were already married, while Roxana Peck and her fiancé Samuel Nott, and Harriet Atwood and Samuel Newell were about to be married. Roxana Peck was not able to attend this commissioning service because of bad weather. An overflow crowd filled the large church of Salem, Massachusetts, and, though people were excited about these young mission pioneers, it was "as silent as the chamber of death when the pastor spoke to the young missionaries."[17]

What was remarkable about this commissioning service was that in the pastor's sermon he also addressed the women. This was probably the first time that missionary wives were ever given a specific missionary task other than helping their husbands. The pastor told them,

> It will be your business, my dear children, to teach these women, to whom your husbands can have but little, or no access. Go then, and do all in your power . . .
> Teach them to realize that they are not an inferior race of creatures . . .
> Teach them that they have immortal souls . . .
> Teach them to accept of [sic] Christ as their Savior, and to enjoy the privileges of the children of God.[18]

Harriet appeared composed at the service, peaceful in her decision to marry Samuel Newell and to devote her life to mission. One

Ordination and commissioning of the first American missionaries to Asia, on 5 February 1812, at Haverhill, Massachusetts. Five young men are kneeling to be blessed by leaders of the American Board of Commissioners for Foreign Missions, but where are the three women who were part of this group of American pioneer missionaries? They were called "assistant missionaries," and as such, had no official standing. Still, the pastor addressed Harriet, as representative of the women, and gave her advice for her future work in mission.

cannot help but wonder about her thoughts as she prepared for what she expected to be her final family farewells.

Three days later, on 9 February 1812, Harriet and Samuel were married, and ten days later they left by ship for India, together with Ann and Adoniram Judson. Roxana and Samuel Nott, Luther Rice and Gordon Hall left a few days later on another ship. Roxana was twenty-seven, Ann twenty-three, and Harriet eighteen; three young women, each with a new husband and a new mission.

Harriet and Ann were happy to spend the nearly four months aboard the same ship. Because they had known each other for years they could laugh and talk together, but they could also cry, and commiserate with each other when they were seasick or lonely. And though winds and storm slowed them down the young couples had a

FAC SIMILE, FROM MRS NEWELL'S JOURNAL AT SEA, AUGUST 11TH, 1812.

My wicked heart is inclined to think it hard, that I should be doomed to suffer such fatigue and hardship! But hush, my wavering passions! It is for Jesus who sacrificed the pleasures of his Father's kingdom to redeem a fallen world, that thus I wander from place to place, & feel no where at home,

Harriet Newell's personal journal reflection, written aboard an India-bound ship, 11 August 1812.

"My wicked heart is inclined to think it hard, that I should be doomed to suffer such fatigue and hardship. But hush, my warring passions! It is for Jesus who sacrificed the pleasures of his Father's kingdom to redeem a fallen world, that thus I wander from place to place, and feel nowhere at home."

variety of experiences, and Harriet and Samuel had time to develop a closer relationship during the many weeks at sea. They ate turtle soup; they met ships on their return to America; they walked the deck for exercise; they enjoyed the warm climate as they traveled south, and then around the tip of Africa. The four missionaries met daily for devotions, Bible studies and spiritual discussions. Samuel was sick for a week, and Harriet wrote her mother that she was pleased that she felt useful when she helped him. When they arrived in India, Harriet was pregnant. William Carey, Hannah and Joshua Marshman, and Mary and William Ward, Baptist missionaries who were already in India, warmly welcomed the new arrivals and took them in.

And then — disappointment. The British East India Company, which practically governed India at that time, was violently opposed to Christian missions for fear it would hurt their trade. It was 1812. Great Britain and America's relationship was very tense, war had just broken out. "We are ordered by government to leave the British territories, and return to America immediately. Captain H. will be ready to sail in three weeks.... Thus is our way hedged up — all our prospects are blasted," Harriet wrote her mother. The Newells and the Judsons were dismayed. This crushing news seemed illogical, it did not fit with what they believed God had called them to do. After long prayer sessions at the missionary community and several interviews at the government office they were told that, rather than return to America, they would be allowed to travel to the Isle of France, which Great Britain had recently captured from the French.

The Isle of France (Mauritius today) was a small tropical island in the Southwest Indian Ocean. It lay east of Madagascar, some 2,400 kilometers east of Africa, and its new British governor welcomed Christian missionaries. Perhaps the American missionaries could begin their hoped for evangelism there. A ship was set to leave Calcutta in early August, but had available space for only two passengers. Harriet was five months pregnant now, so it was decided that Harriet and Samuel should go, and that Ann and Adoniram would follow at the next opportunity. It would be another long voyage, one of 5,800 kilometers, and it was expected to take about six weeks; still, the Newells expected to arrive at the Isle of France well in time for their baby's birth.

Again, there were problems. Conditions on board were appalling. Harriet came down with severe dysentery. There was such a fierce storm that after more than a month they were still in the Bay of Bengal, east of India. The ship sprang a leak, and they had to go ashore for repairs. That delay took more than a week, but it was a chance for Harriet to recuperate.

Still three weeks before they reached the Isle of France Harriet went into early labor and delivered a baby girl. It must have been agonizing for both Harriet and Samuel when Harriet gave birth, the only woman aboard the ship, without conveniences and few comforts. We may assume that Samuel's medical course had not included midwifery! Harriet and Samuel named their child Harriet Atwood, after the baby's mother.

There was a strong wind and it rained hard, and facilities on the ship could not adequately protect Harriet and the baby. They both caught colds, and little Harriet sickened. Harriet and Samuel feared for her health so, rather than wait for a more traditional opportunity, Samuel baptized little Harriet aboard ship when she was four days old. The next day she died. It must have been a chilling experience for the new parents to commit the little body to a "watery grave" in the sea. Harriet never recovered. Soon after the baby died she herself became ill and recognized the familiar symptoms of consumption (tuberculosis), the disease which had brought about her father's death some four years earlier.

Eventually, when they arrived at their destination, the crossing from Calcutta to the Isle of France had taken three months rather than six weeks. It was early November 1812. Samuel rented a small house and gently took care of Harriet; they both knew that she would not live. Harriet anxiously looked forward to the Judsons' arrival, and hoped that they would come while she was still living. She desperately wished that together they could celebrate the Lord's Supper before she died.

When they knew that the end was near, Harriet and Samuel had communion together, and while she could still speak, Harriet gave Samuel farewell messages for her family and friends. She asked him to tell them that she had never regretted becoming a missionary. And that, though she had not even begun work among the women of India, she felt a bit like David who loved God and wanted to build a temple, but was not allowed by God to do so.

Harriet died twenty days after their arrival on the Isle of France. She had turned nineteen on the way from Calcutta. Samuel was the only mourner when her remains were buried under an evergreen tree in a cemetery on the Isle of France.

When they knew that the end was near, Harriet and Samuel had communion together.

When the Judsons arrived, not long afterwards, Ann was stunned to hear about her friend's death. She wrote in her diary, "Harriet is dead. Harriet, my dear friend, my earliest associate in the Mission, is no more . . . she is gone, and I am left behind, still to endure the trials of a missionary life."[19] Little did Ann know that she and Adoniram would wander for some eighteen months before arriving at their own place of mission work in Myanmar (Burma), nor could she guess that she herself would die at age thirty-seven and be buried in Asia.

After Harriet's death Samuel Newell wrote long letters to Harriet's mother to tell her exactly what had happened.

> Oh Harriet, Harriet, my heart bleeds afresh at the sound of thy name; and yet I love to repeat it, and to dwell upon the sound. How often did I wish, my dear mother, for your presence, during Harriet's illness — in the closing scene, — and especially the night after her death, which I spent with no person in my house but my negro man, while the remains of our dear Harriet lay enclosed in the gloomy coffin before me.[20]

Once, in a letter to his mother-in-law, Samuel enclosed a twig and a bud from the tree under which Harriet's remains lay buried.

Samuel Newell asked Dr. Leonard Woods, professor at Andover Seminary and charter member of the ABCFM, to preach at a memorial service held in the USA for Harriet. In his sermon Dr. Woods claimed that, because a woman finds her greatest joy in home and family, the missionary wife offers a greater sacrifice than her husband when she leaves for missionary service.[21] This must have sounded strange to many ears, yet it seemed so appropriate in Harriet's case.

While he was on the Isle of France Samuel Newell received news that his colleagues had received permission to establish mission work in Mumbai (Bombay), India. The governor there was a devout Christian, and he negotiated for permission for Christian missionaries to evangelize in his territory. Samuel Newell then returned to India and joined his colleagues in the work he had so long looked forward to doing.

A missionary wife in Mumbai felt sorry for Samuel, and suggested he write to a friend of hers living in Salem, Massachusetts. Samuel did so and, though he did not know her at all, he relied on the missionary wife's suggestion and proposed marriage to the lady in Salem. She replied positively, traveled to Mumbai, and she and Samuel Newell were married. This marriage was also short-lived, for Samuel Newell died three years later of cholera. He was thirty-six years old when he died.

Harriet was one of three young women who were part of the first group of American missionaries to cross the ocean, and she was the first American female missionary to die overseas. But that is only one reason why people wrote about and remembered her. Harriet's many letters and entries from her diary show readers a Christian teenager who was committed to serving God, and who, out of a sense of Christian duty, left her home and country for an unknown future. Each step of the way she depended on God's grace. This was why she became a model for others.

We may believe that, when Harriet Atwood Newell's life on earth ended our Savior said of her, "She has done a beautiful thing for me."

CHAPTER FIVE

The earliest Christian missionaries to Japan were Jesuit priests. Francis Xavier, one of the founders of the Society of Jesus, was the well-known pioneer Roman Catholic missionary who landed in southern Japan in 1549. As the Portuguese knew no Japanese it was difficult to communicate, yet Xavier reported that, while visiting a feudal lord, his Japanese fellow traveler,

> . . . showed a beautiful picture he had brought from India, of the blessed Mary and the child Jesus sitting on her lap. When the prince looked upon it, he was overwhelmed with emotion, and falling on his knees, he very devoutly worshipped it, and commanded all present to do the same.[1]

In the beginning the Jesuits enjoyed success, and after thirty-two years they claimed to have one hundred and fifty thousand converts.[2] But this soon changed, and severe persecution of Christians followed as the Japanese government tried to root out the new faith in their country.

It was a new era when Christianity re-entered Japan; this time Protestants were in the foreground. Now most missionaries were married and brought their wives.

When Margaret Ballagh came to Japan in 1861 there were already a few missionary women. It was still the nineteenth century, and wives were not yet officially counted as "missionaries," yet their important contribution to mission was mostly recognized and appreciated.

Ten years after Protestant pioneer missionaries began their evangelistic efforts in Japan the first unmarried female missionary joined the work and, after a time of language study, began to teach in a new school. There were few educational opportunities for women then and, because of the rapid modernization of Japan which was taking place at this time, many Japanese parents opted for mission schools for their daughters. By the time Protestant missionaries had been in Japan for thirty years there were one hundred and seven single women out of a total of two hundred and fifty-one female missionaries, far outnumbering the one hundred and forty-eight male missionaries.[3] Most of these female missionaries were involved in the basic education of a new generation of Japanese women.

From the beginning both female and male missionaries faced numerous difficulties, yet they persisted, motivated by their faith, dedication and determination. They overcame prejudices and took on tough challenges, undeterred their readiness to do a beautiful thing for the Master.

Margaret T. K. Ballagh was one of the women who led the way.

Letters Home from Japan

Margaret T. K. Ballagh (1840–1909)

"Now Aunt, I must tell you of the little palefaced baby who has come to cheer our loneliness . . . on the twenty-sixth of last month [26 June 1862] Dr. Hepburn [the attending physician] brought her to me and asked me what should be her name? I answered immediately, 'Carrie Virginia, for my sister and native state'; but her papa afterwards called her Elizabeth, so we shall have her christened some day, 'Carrie Elizabeth.'"[4]

This is a rare glimpse into Margaret Ballagh's real feelings, for she was a cheerful and brave woman, and seldom admitted feeling downhearted. She was optimistic, but loneliness was part of her life at this time, as she was still a newcomer to Japan, where she and her husband had come a year earlier. She was not yet fluent in the language, and they lived in a two hundred year-old Buddhist temple which was difficult to redecorate as a cozy home. Yet Margaret felt happy as she held her baby, and felt much loved by her husband, James H. Ballagh.

James H. Ballagh was raised by a prayerful mother. From the time she married, James's mother had asked God that, if she should have children, God would send some of them to the mission field in her stead. This prayer must have influenced the way she raised her ten children; some indeed did become cross-cultural missionaries, James was one. From the time he was a young boy he wanted to serve God in his life.

James H. Ballagh, of New York, had been appointed as missionary to Japan for the Reformed Church in America, but was at twenty-eight still single. Most people believed that the stability and support which came with having a spouse and a home was an important factor in being an effective missionary, and no doubt James was encouraged to look for a wife.

James Ballagh Moore, great-grandson of Margaret and James, chuckles as he relates how Margaret came to marry James.[5]

> Of course he had to visit churches to ask for prayer and financial support, before he could leave for Japan. One church he visited was the Presbyterian Church in Timber Ridge, near Lexington, Virginia. Here he stayed at the home of Elder and Mrs. Kinnear, a couple who had only one child, a daughter. Margaret Kinnear was a bright young woman of twenty. She had read letters written by Ann Judson and other missionary wives, and had a longing to become a missionary herself.
>
> When James was ready to return to New York it rained hard. Bridges were washed out, travel was impossible for two weeks, and James was invited to stay with the Kinnear family until it became possible to proceed. In this short time Margaret and James saw each other daily, and by the time James had to leave they had fallen in love and made their decision.

The great-grandson continues his story.

> The American Civil War broke out early that year, it was wartime; that made for worries about the outcome, and complicated James's plans for traveling from New York to Virginia again. But to James this was merely a challenge.

In February 1861 James wrote to a member of the mission board, "How shall I go — married or alone? Having met 'the right one' and esteeming it as having 'obtained favor of the Lord' I know you will rejoice with me. Especially when she is what you recommended, 'a fine specimen of a woman,' at least in my estimation, and a devoted Christian and Missionary spirit [sic]. . . . ready to sacrifice everything . . . ."[6]

The great-grandson finishes the story.

The date of their departure from New York had been set, and in May
James traveled south again, this time to bring his bride-to-be from
Virginia to the north. They were married on a Sunday, and the next day
they left on horseback to catch a train in another town. It was quite the
honeymoon! Before coming south to marry the woman he had fallen in
love with James had to get a special permit from the Confederates, and
they had to travel through both Confederate and Union lines, but they
arrived safely in New York. Two weeks after their marriage, on 1 June
1861, they sailed for Japan.

It would be a journey of several months, and on board ship
Margaret began writing letters home. More than forty years later a
friend, who knew that these letters had been saved, persuaded Margaret
to publish them, not only for the sake of her own family, but also to
encourage young people's interest in missions. Margaret agreed, added
a few notes, and published the letters of her first missionary term under
the title of *Glimpses of Old Japan: 1861–1866*, covering the first years of
her life in Japan.

It was exciting to board the sailing ship, but not so easy to say goodbye.
Margaret and James traveled with three missionary families and three
single missionaries, and it seemed "beyond humanity" for all six men
to be asked to give a farewell speech to the many friends who had come
to the wharf to send them off. Margaret wrote, "I suffered to see my
husband suffer."[7]

Except for some seasickness, life aboard ship and the presence of
other missionaries was pleasant and informative. An older missionary,
returning to China, gave daily lessons in Chinese writing, for knowing
some Chinese characters would be helpful for the Ballaghs in their
future Japanese language study. After a few weeks Margaret noted that
they had learned a hundred of the difficult characters, and soon
afterwards, two hundred. She had fun and enjoyed the company of
James and the other missionaries. Yet there were moments of loneliness;
each day took her further away from home and nearer an unknown

future. "I do not often weep these days or even feel sad or lonely for I trustingly put my hand in my husband's, and I know he has put his in that of his heavenly Father," she wrote. But one day she went to their cabin for a good cry, and could not even speak when James entered. He then knelt beside her bunk, took her hand in his, talked gently, and prayed for comfort and a strengthening of Margaret's faith. This is but one example of James' prayerfulness, like that of his mother.

Japan was still a land of mystery for Westerners, but Margaret and James must have learned something of its history before they left home. The missionaries who were already there must also have had the opportunity to mail letters.

Until the 1500s Japan was made up of clans and feudal lords competing for control but, during the sixteenth century, three strong warrior-leaders emerged, warring to place the many clans under one central rule. Meanwhile, European merchants arrived, and with them came Jesuit missionaries who told the Japanese about other places in the world, places the Japanese knew nothing about. The Japanese were thrilled with the new items they received from the foreigners, and with the new ideas the long-nosed Europeans brought them. Trade with European merchants became popular. Thousands converted to Roman Catholicism.

At first the Jesuit priests had much freedom, but when Japanese leaders were told that missionaries would be followed by European soldiers they became afraid and tried to rid themselves of both European merchants and Christian missionaries. Foreigners were expelled and Japanese Christians were ordered under penalty of death to give up their Christianity. For some forty years Christians were harshly persecuted, and thousands of Roman Catholic Japanese heroically went to a martyr's death.[8] After this came a period of more than two hundred years during which no foreigner was allowed into and no Japanese citizen out of the country. Japan was a "closed country," although for practical purposes, some contact with the outside world continued via a minimal amount of trade with Chinese and Dutch merchants.

Americans finally pressured Japan into opening their country to outsiders; several treaties were signed, and in 1859 the first Americans came to Japan, both businesspeople and missionaries who had been waiting for the opportunity. The pioneer families of the Presbyterian/Reformed mission were those of Samuel R. Brown, an educator; James C. Hepburn, a physician; and Guido F. Verbeck, an engineer; they would soon be joined by Margaret and James Ballagh, the first evangelist and his wife.[9] They were restricted to two towns, one was Kanagawa, near Yokohama, the other was in northern Japan. They had to lie low because many Japanese still despised foreigners, and they were very limited in what they were permitted to do. They knew that any Japanese converting to the Christian faith would still be subject to the death penalty, and so the missionaries spent much time doing language and culture studies.

When foreigners first came to Japan in the 1800s they may not have been aware that rewards were offered by the government to anyone who reported the name of a suspected Christian, or that, throughout the country, there were notice-boards along the roads offering such rewards. And they did not realize that Japan itself was in ferment, that clan leaders were trying to return power to the group around the emperor, nor could they realize the consequences of the end of the long period of Japan's isolation.

Margaret Ballagh was young and it is interesting to note that she described things the way she saw them. She was not afraid of extremes such as, "... it is most glorious ..." and "... I have a most horrible idea ..," but she seemed always to have remembered that she was writing for the public and was trying to encourage support of overseas missions.

After twelve weeks at sea Margaret and James were glad to reach Shanghai, but found

> *When foreigners first came to Japan in the 1800s they may not have been aware that rewards were offered by the government to anyone who reported ... a suspected Christian.*

Margaret Ballagh. Newly married at age twenty, she was ready for "voluntary exile."

that they had to wait a whole month for a ship to Yokohama. When the time came to embark, and they boarded the small open boat they were horrified by the filth, "ants, cockroaches and rats scampering over and into everything; a little low, dark cabin, no deck, [even] a corpse on board, [and an] inefficient and small crew." She wrote: "I confess that my heart went down into my shoes at the first glance, but I try not to show it, and talk cheerfully to my husband of how nice we can fit up our room for I see that he is annoyed exceedingly, only on my account."

When they finally approached Yokohama Margaret was anxious and downhearted. She would have no way of knowing that many missionaries before and after her, though zealous and eager to be God's ambassadors, had similar experiences once they finally reached their destination. "What are my feelings in approaching this land," she reflected, "that it is a dreadful thing to live, a thing for many reasons more to be dreaded than death. And this new life on which I am about to enter crowded with responsibilities seems very heavy for me. All the future is shut away from me by heavy clouds." Comforting herself with the words, "We must live this life with a trustful faith, and all will go well," probably did little to cheer her.

The journey had lasted one hundred and twenty-one days when they landed in Yokohama. It was Margaret's twenty-first birthday, and, though young, she must have realized that she was pregnant. From Yokohama it was but a short trip in an open boat to Kanagawa, their destination. It was dark, cold and bleak when they arrived, but they were welcomed warmly by Dr. James Hepburn and the Brown family. Here they were ushered into the old Buddhist temple into which the

Hepburns had moved when they could not rent a house, and this is where Margaret and James lived for two years.

Mrs. Anna Hepburn was not at home; she had gone back to America to visit a college-aged son, and James Hepburn invited the Ballaghs to stay with him in the temple. When his wife returned to Japan the Hepburns moved to Yokohama, leaving the Ballaghs in the temple-home. Samuel Brown and his family lived in the priest's residence next to the temple. The third family of the Presbyterian/ Reformed mission was that of Guido F. Verbeck, who lived in southwest Japan, in Nagasaki.

Years later a fellow missionary wrote about these four pioneer missionaries. He noted that Hepburn became known for his excellent use of the Japanese language; Brown was the theologian who passed on much knowledge of biblical teachings; Verbeck was able to influence national leaders and was instrumental in having the notice-boards warning of the death penalty for Christians removed; but Ballagh was remembered for his humility and sincerity.[10] Hepburn was a physician, Brown was an educator, Verbeck was an engineer, and Ballagh was an evangelist. All of them were "mission-minded," but Ballagh was the only one trained as an evangelist.[11] During their many years in Japan each of these men made huge contributions in their area of specialty.

It was encouraging to be welcomed kindly by Dr. Hepburn and the Brown family,

Forty years later Margaret is a respected and seasoned missionary. Margaret's letters home tell of her experiences of the early years. She was resolute and able. Together with her husband she taught many young men of the upper classes who wanted to learn English. She also gave Bible lessons, and was always involved in evangelism. *Photos courtesy James Ballagh Moore.*

but the temple-home was dark and gloomy. The greens of the temple grounds were beautiful, but Margaret missed her friends. And when their belongings arrived and she unpacked her trunks she was sad when she saw the photographs of her friends. She was homesick, but fought it by thanking God for choosing her for the work of missions.

A week later Margaret felt worse.

> I am greatly distressed that I cannot feel. I seem as callous and indifferent to all the heathenish things done around me as if it were a matter of course and perfectly right; while my better judgment tells me it is perfectly wrong, and must not be allowed to go on. Seeing heathenism with all its revolting practices, I am convinced will either cause the soul to be deadened to the wickedness of it or will cause a deeper disgust and hatred of it because it is so displeasing to God. Now I am distressed that I do not hate it more; there is a morbidness about my moral nature that I had not suspected before, and in vain I try to put the knowledge from me by trying to account for my feelings (or rather, my not feeling) by laying the fault to the fatigues of the voyage, this dull weather, and my utter inability to do anything for this people.

Yet she adds that she has peace, for God has promised "I am with you, even to the end of the world." Perhaps no one told her that during early pregnancy many mothers-to-be feel depressed.

In her letters Margaret described her life in Kanagawa in detail. She wrote about the area, the people she met, the pony her husband bought for her, the temples, Japanese food, crows, bats, insects, dogs, temple bells and language lessons.

> First comes Mr. Ballagh's dignified, bald-pated teacher; their study is a little room off the verandah in front of the house; then Dr. H[epburn] has his stern, melancholy teacher in the center of the house, while I have my frisky little baldheaded priest at the back of the house. Any one to look in on us would be amused to see the various methods to which we severally resort, in pumping, and jerking and holding tight to the little

In her letters Margaret described her life in Kanagawa in detail.

we can get from these native teachers, who have no more idea how to teach us, or what we wish to learn, than my pussy cat which purrs softly at my feet. With no books as helps, and being able to speak but a very few words, it is wonderful that the poor creatures understand as well as they do, what we want to know.

Spring in Japan is beautiful, and in glowing terms Margaret told her friends about the beautiful blossoms, only to follow this with the sigh that it was troublesome to study the difficult Japanese language when nature seemed to be calling her outdoors. And when a missionary couple from Shanghai stayed with them for three months Margaret was distracted for a long time.

After four months in Japan Margaret was getting impatient, she longed for letters from home. She wrote her friends that even the beautiful ferns, vines and bamboo, and Japanese people around her were "not enough to bamboozle one out of the idea that a good fat letter from the homeland is a necessary article, at least once in six months." She wanted to receive mail, and was especially concerned about family members and friends because of the Civil War in America (1861–1865). She realized that war conditions might make it difficult to write and send letters, but she was anxious.

Finally, nearly a year after the Ballaghs left home there was a letter. "My first letter from home received last month, was a great event in my Japan life. I acted like a little child, running about the mission compound and reading to every one, 'authentic news from the South.'" Mail from the southern American states, where Margaret's family lived, could not easily be processed because of the Civil War. However, contact with the northern states, where James's family lived and where the mission board office was located, was probably possible during this time. We can assume that official mission correspondence and mission funds were received in Japan. Margaret was particularly interested in mail from her family and friends.

Margaret found that life changed totally once the "little pale-faced baby" joined her and James in their temple-home. Little Carrie brought much happiness to her mother, who tried so hard to look at life in a happy way. James Hepburn and the Brown family were present when the baby was baptized on James's thirtieth birthday, this surely was the first time a child in a Protestant Christian family was baptized in that part of Japan, and in a Buddhist temple.

It was summer, and hot. Because of the rats in the temple James rigged up a way to suspend the baby's crib, so no rats could get near Carrie.[12] Mosquitoes seemed to love the dark nooks and crannies of the temple, and Margaret could hardly keep them away from her little daughter. The mosquitoes were so thick that Margaret began to call their home the "Mosquito Temple."[13]

Margaret had a new realization.

> It seems to me I get nothing done these hot months but wash and dress baby and keep her as comfortable as I can. Babies make sad havoc of missionary aspirations. Why, I expected to have a parcel of little ragged children around me, teaching them by this time; but I have not looked into a Japanese book for three months. I was beginning to read the characters pretty well before baby came, but since I have been up, we have had so much company that I have had to take more than my usual share of the housekeeping.

And she still looked for mail which did not seem to come.

> Thus far, God has graciously sustained my faith, but each mail, as I hope for letters and receive none, my heart is becoming sick with "hope deferred." Truly the love of Christ constraineth me to be here, but the heart sometimes grows faint and the spirit weary; then the cloud of witnesses, and the multitude of promises, and the grace of him who is ever with his people renews and sustains the affections and the will.

A year had passed since Margaret and James arrived in Japan, and everything was very different now. Margaret's enthusiasm had changed to depression during the early months in Kanagawa, and then, after Carrie was born, she gradually bounced back to her former self. She writes that, when they arrived, she was a spectator, but a year later she felt that she was a worker. Looking back, she related that they had had three single missionaries and two families from China as houseguests, and that she began some new things as well as hoping and praying, "that I may be instrumental of adding many more to Christ's elect to the list of his redeemed."

After James Hepburn left the temple-home there was much to do for Margaret.

> With no servants, no cooking stove, and three young men to board, my time is quite taken up in housekeeping and attending to baby.... I mean to try to do something with the language this winter and prepare myself for future usefulness here. I seem on the threshold of the very kind of usefulness I have nearly all my life longed for, and I so ardently desire the honor of doing something for these poor people, gathering a few sheaves before I die. Yesterday P.M. [sic] I called with my husband on some of the people, and had a trial of our conversational powers. Oh! for more liberty in this tongue.

This probably encouraged Margaret to start studying again and, though progress was slow, she gradually improved.

> I went with my husband to call on several families again last evening; we were received cordially and treated to scalding hot tea, without sugar or milk, and a kind of cake made of gelatin and sugar. At another house I was invited to a seat on a box turned upside down, and a cushion placed on it; then I had offered to me the pipe, but on explaining that I could not use it, they laughed and chatted away to each other, no doubt commenting on our customs.... Mr. B[allagh] then attempted to speak some of the words of life, but it was with a stammering tongue.

It seems that, in all his years in Japan, James Ballagh never became totally fluent in the Japanese language. It was well known that, while Margaret was at ease with the Japanese language when she visited and chatted with people, James always used gestures to make up for what he could not express in words. In a mission history a Japanese Christian is quoted, "I did not understand his sermons, probably because he did not have a proper language teacher. Nor did we understand his prayers. But all were deeply moved by his great earnestness."[14] James Ballagh's gifts lay in personal evangelism, in prayer, and in kindness.

As they visited in the neighborhood Margaret and James visited the home of James's language teacher, Yano Riu, whom they

The two hundred year old *Jōbutsu* Temple in Kanagawa, where Margaret Ballagh and her family lived during their first two years in Japan. Margaret wrote that she had a hard time protecting their first baby from mosquitoes and rats in the old and dark building. *Photo courtesy James Ballagh Moore, one of Margaret Ballagh's grandsons.*

addressed as *Sensei* (Teacher). He was ill. James had asked his teacher to translate the Gospel of John into Japanese, for future evangelism, but also so that the teacher himself would learn about Jesus.

All this time the missionaries were severely limited in their work of evangelism. James Hepburn treated patients in his house, and made available what Christian literature was available, while he produced a dictionary which one hundred years later was still in use. Samuel Brown began to teach English language lessons when he found that there were Japanese who understood that it would be important in the future to be conversant in English. Sons of the *samurai* (warriors) whose lives changed radically during the political turmoil now turned to business or government careers. These young men were eager to study English, the missionaries were delighted to start classes for them and had high hopes of possible opportunities for evangelism.

Margaret also began to teach. As usual, little is written about women's work of this time, but it is clear that Margaret played an active role in teaching young men's classes, together with James. Some of these men would later become prominent leaders, such as the student who became a minister of finance.[15] All of their students would know that these Americans were Christians, and numerous students listened as the missionaries talked about their Christian faith. Some of them became believers.

There was a lady who came around selling eggs, and brought some fun wherever she went, and Margaret told her family about her. Little Carrie loved Baba to play with her. As Margaret watched the two she thought about it that Baba had little faith in idols and seemed interested in listening to Bible stories. If only Baba would become a Christian she would be a great missionary as she went from house to house with not only eggs, but also with the gospel.

Margaret wrote about *Sensei* again because his illness became serious, and Margaret and James went to his house nearly every day. Gradually, much against his will, *Sensei* said, he became convinced that the Christian gospel is true. James Ballagh later wrote that his first Japanese prayer was with Yano Riu, his teacher. "It was very lame," he wrote, "but I trust the Spirit of God accompanied it." When he visited his sick teacher James also prayed with the man's family.

When *Sensei* became a believer he "begged" for baptism. James asked his colleagues for advice, not only because he wished to be certain that *Sensei's* faith was genuine, but also because it was still illegal and very dangerous for a Japanese to be baptized. They agreed that he was ready, but wanted him to know how dangerous it was. When they reminded him that it was a crime for a Japanese to be baptized, *Sensei* replied that that was a small thing to him. And so, on the first Sunday of November 1864, nearly three years after the Ballaghs came to Japan, with the doors tightly closed

> *Little is written about women's work of this time, but it is clear that Margaret played an active role in teaching young men's classes.*

against possible spies, James baptized Yano Riu, his language teacher. *Sensei's* son had given his permission and was present.

The next time they called on *Sensei* Margaret was shocked at how ill he was. Before they left he lifted "himself up on his elbow and said, bowing his head to the floor, 'I must say my last "goodbye" to you. I am going to see Jesus, and when I see him, I will tell him all you and your good husband have done for me.'" Margaret wrote,

> Could I ask for anything more precious than to have my name mentioned to Jesus by a heathen convert? I consider it the happiest event in my whole life.... Until his death, I had not realized that heaven was as near Japan as America, and formerly felt that I must return home to die; but now that he has opened the gate, I feel that it stands ajar for me, even here....

And in James's words, "Can you conceive of a higher reward, or a greater blessing, than 'to be mentioned to Jesus'? My eyes fill with tears whenever I think of it." The funeral, which followed, was difficult for the Ballaghs.

> We attended the funeral, which had to be conducted by the Buddhist priests. The son tried to buy them off; but custom and law prevailed. The body was taken to the temple, and there we left it. I could not endure to be the spectator of such senseless rites over my dear Christian friend's body. I would have rejoiced to have committed his ashes to the grave; but we must be content to try and save the soul, and for the present let the priests bury the dead.

Clearly, Margaret had matured through a difficult time of adjustment to being wife and mother and missionary, and also to life in Japan. Two years after Carrie was born Margaret and James had another daughter; it is telling that they named her Anna Hepburn, after Dr. James Hepburn's wife Anna.

During these years there was political turmoil in Japan, and foreigners could not help but be affected by it. Margaret and James were robbed, and had to leave their temple-home when the government forced them to live in Yokohama, near other foreigners. Before long they had to move again. In 1865 Margaret wrote that the "disturbed and rather anxious life of the past two years is beginning to tell on our nervous systems . . . a speedy return to America seems probable." And that's what happened. The next year Margaret, who was pregnant again, James, Carrie and Anna took a ship to San Francisco together, and from there James returned to Japan while Margaret and the children continued to her home state, Virginia. Later that year, while still in America, Margaret gave birth to a boy. He was named James Curtis, after the Ballaghs' beloved senior colleague, Dr. James Curtis Hepburn. In October Margaret joined her husband again in Japan.

Two years later Margaret, James and the children returned to America, and the Ballaghs' first term of missionary service was finished. Margaret had left a serious, yet starry-eyed honeymooner, and returned with the experience of having served God, together with James, as cross-cultural missionary in far-away Japan.

Except for Margaret's letters, collected and bound in a book, not much is known about her. She is rarely mentioned in mission reports; she is one of the many missionary wives who quietly carved a niche for themselves in the work of evangelism, and made their personal contributions. We do see the names of daughters Carrie and Anna, when they were grown, as missionaries teaching at the Ferris Seminary in Yokohama.[16]

It was noted earlier that James H. Ballagh became known for his prayers. And that was one thing which attracted the men who were hired to spy on him. Spying was not unusual during this time when foreigners were suspected of being informants for their own country. James C. Hepburn also recorded that spies watched him and then reported to a government office.

The men who were watching James Ballagh noticed that he spoke aloud during the middle of the night, though there seemed to be no one to talk to. These spies had been told to study English, just to learn more about James, and when they knew enough to understand him they were totally surprised. They heard him pray during the night for others, for them, even by name, and for blessings on the nation of Japan. Then they knew that James Ballagh could not be a spy for America. This was what other spies said about the other missionaries, too.

When the first Protestant church in Japan was organized in 1872, in Yokohama, it began with eleven members. Two of them had been baptized earlier, and nine young men were baptized that day. Three of these young men had taken lessons from Margaret and James Ballagh. They may have been the three who had earlier been hired by the government to spy and report on the missionaries.[17]

Once more we find Margaret Ballagh's name mentioned. This time it is a death notice in a mission report.[18] Here she is described as "gentle in manner, quiet in spirit, and not given to demonstrations in her religious life or temperament. She believed in action rather than in words...." It is enough. Margaret lived in Japan for forty-eight years, and died there. James was a missionary to Japan for fifty-eight years; when he became ill at age eighty-seven he returned to the USA and died there a few months later.

We may believe that, when Margaret Ballagh's life on earth ended our Savior said of her, "She has done a beautiful thing for me."

During the 1850s the Mission Board of the Methodist Episcopal Church in America was not prepared to send a single woman in India as missionary to help found a Christian school for girls even though that woman had been invited by her brother, a missionary in India. It took a group of daring women to organize themselves into the Woman's Foreign Missionary Society, to appoint Isabella Thoburn (1840–1901) as their missionary, and to start gathering enough money to support her. They actively raised funds so that their budget might also allow financial support for Clara A. Swain, M.D. (1834–1910), another single missionary candidate. In time both women went to India, and spent their career years in educational and medical work.

Great Britain ruled India at that time, and there were political problems and revolutionary outbursts. Still, the missionary women were well-cared for by missionary colleagues, while the whole mission community was backed by the British government and its military.

Yet, there were many challenges. Education and medical care were nearly non-existent for the poor, and especially for women. Prejudices of the

Indian upper classes often prevented missionaries from associating with high caste people, and it was a known reality that male missionaries were unable to approach Indian women with either the gospel or medical care. Isabella Thoburn and Clara Swain had the tremendous advantage of being able to meet with women.

Today the Isabella Thoburn College in Lucknow, Uttar Pradesh, has undergone much growth and many changes, but it is the outgrowth of a class for girls which Isabella began a few weeks after she arrived in India in 1870. It was the first college for women in Asia. The largest as well as the oldest Methodist hospital in India today, located in Bareilly, Uttar Pradesh, is named the Clara Swain Hospital, the first hospital especially for women and children. Clara Swain began a medical mission in 1870, and the work resulted in the founding of this hospital.

This chapter tells about Isabella Thoburn and of some of the struggles and accomplishments in her life.

The Law of Service

Isabella Thoburn (1840–1901)

An Indian girl once asked her missionary teacher why she had left her relatives in America, thirty years earlier, to come to India. The teacher, Isabella Thoburn, did not need to think before she answered, "It was my mother. She made us feel that we must help those who need us most."[1] This simple and straightforward answer, remembered more than fifty years later, shows how influential Isabella's mother was in her family.

Isabella's parents were Scots-Irish immigrants who had settled on a farm in Ohio, USA. They were devout Christians and active in the Methodist Church. Isabella was the ninth of ten children, five of whom were girls. Isabella barely remembered her father, because he died when she was only ten years old, but her mother left a lasting impression. Decisive and courageous, she was an example of practical Christianity, and consistently taught her children about her faith. She used to tell them that they were on earth not to be served, but to serve others, as Jesus had come to earth himself to be a servant. This is what Isabella later called "the law of service," and she practiced it as her mother had done.

After public school Isabella had the opportunity to study for a year in a private high school for girls and then a year in an art school. At eighteen Isabella was ready to be a teacher. She taught for several years in area schools, and did not hesitate to open her morning classes with Bible reading and prayer even in the public school.

A significant event in her life was when her brother James left for India as a missionary.[2] She was interested in his work, and in his

99

stories when he returned some years later, but of course she did not consider a missionary career for herself, single girls just did not do that. Then came the letter which changed everything.

Isabella's brother James was widowed young when his wife died of "childbed fever" in 1860. James could think of nothing better to do for his baby son than to send him to America, to his family. Little Crawford was brought to America and was cared for by various relatives in turn while James returned to India. Some twenty-five years after his wife died, James, now Bishop Mills Thoburn, married Anna Teresa Jones, who was a medical doctor. They had several children, two of whom grew to adulthood.[3]

After several unsuccessful mission efforts James realized that he, a male missionary, could not reach Indian women with the gospel. Missionary wives did some evangelism among women, but many more female missionaries were needed. Who would teach the women in the church? James thought that a boarding school for girls would be a strategic mission work. He then wrote Isabella, explaining the situation, and added, a bit flippantly he later admitted, "How would you like to come and take charge of such a school if we decide to make the attempt?"

Much to James's surprise, Isabella's reply came to him in five months, the shortest possible time for mail to travel the seas in both directions. She wrote that she was willing to come as soon as possible. But that is where it stopped — for a while. Generally, American church leaders at that time were not ready to let single women go abroad as missionaries. Many male missionaries on the field were not eager to have female professionals join them, and most were not sure that they wanted mission dollars, if available, spent on girls' education. Besides, as someone wrote, "The notion of a single young woman turned loose on the subcontinent was enough to give a missionary secretary nightmares."[4] Methodist Mission Board members, all men, just were not prepared to accept Isabella's application, their strategy for mission did not yet include unmarried women missionaries. Perhaps disappointed, Isabella then responded to an immediate need in her home environment, and for the next year she cared for a sick sister-in-law and her three small children.

The church may not have been ready to send single women to the mission field, but some of the missionaries in India were convinced that women who could work full-time, without the responsibilities of a family, were desperately needed. Lois Parker, on the way home from India with her husband Edwin, visited Isabella to explain the needs of the mission work in India. Once she knew that Isabella was sincere, Lois wasted no time. She and another furloughing missionary wife talked to many women in their home state, Massachusetts. They planned and invited as many women as possible to a public gathering to discuss the needs on the mission field, and perhaps form a women's missionary society.

On the day of the scheduled event there was a heavy rainstorm, and only six guests arrived, but the women went ahead with their meeting. The missionaries gave their talks, the guests were excited about possibilities, and on that very day in the spring of 1869 the Woman's Foreign Missionary Society of the Methodist Episcopal Church was born. Men who wrote about the founding of this society vary a bit in detail and date, but the outcome was the same.[5]

The women organized their own sending agency, and began with an empty wallet. They were agreed on their goals, and when they heard that Isabella Thoburn was willing to become a missionary, one of the women is said to have jumped up from her chair and exclaimed,

> Shall we lose Miss Thoburn because we have not the needed money in our hands to send her? No, rather let us walk the streets of Boston in our calico dresses and save the expense of more costly apparel. I move, then, the appointment of Miss Thoburn as our missionary to India.[6]

All the women agreed, and the decision was made. The members of the new society busied themselves with fundraising and, although they had to borrow money to do so, in a short time they were able to send not only Isabella, but also another female missionary to India.[7]

The other woman was Clara A. Swain (1834–1910), a recently-graduated medical doctor, the first qualified woman missionary physician in the world to go to a mission field. She probably knew that most of the male medical missionaries in India objected to her coming, but went anyway, in the conviction that God called her. Today the oldest and largest Methodist hospital in India — the first hospital specializing in women and child care — is called the Clara Swain Hospital commemorating her groundbreaking work.

The two women traveled to India together. This was the year of the opening of the Suez Canal, which shortened travel time between continents drastically, and brought many changes to world transportation. The ship they were on no longer needed to round the southern tip of Africa and, traveling via the Suez Canal, Isabella and Clara arrived in India within two months, in January 1870. Some passengers on the ship had never seen a female doctor, but did not hesitate to call on Clara when there was illness. Clara wrote that she looked after five patients while aboard ship. After their arrival Isabella and Clara each went their own way, to the places to which they had been assigned. For Isabella that was the city of Lucknow, some 225 kilometers southeast of Delhi.

Lucknow was a regional capital in earlier days, and one of the largest inland cities in India before the 1857 War of Independence. Isabella, with an eye for beauty, soon learned to love the splendid old buildings with their elegant roofs, and the colors and shapes of the flowers, and the foliage of the different seasons.

Her mother had probably taught her to be flexible, for she said that she was never homesick. Isabella learned much as she observed her new environment. The new teacher knew that not all her colleagues were happy to see her. "It's not the right time," some said. "It's unwise," said others. Some thought it useless to establish a school for girls, since the converts to Christianity were nearly all of the lowest caste and it was thought that these girls would probably have little need to read. Others wondered aloud from where the funds for Isabella's work would come. But Isabella steadily plodded on; her personality was probably like that of her mother, once she made up her mind she no longer doubted nor — she said — was she ever homesick.

Even before she reached Lucknow, where the Methodists had made their center in one of the suburbs, and where Isabella's brother James was posted, she was introduced to some Christians, and saw some classes which other missionaries had begun. She noted that boys' education was more advanced than that of girls, and reacted with an observation she would often repeat over the years, "No people ever rise higher, as a people, than the point to which they elevate their women."[8]

Education for girls seemed just wasteful to many, and few Indian women had enjoyed the privilege of education. It was different for boys, for if they had an education they would be able to apply for jobs in government or business. Even after thirty years a census in 1900 showed that female literacy in India was only seven percent of that of boys.[9]

Among the many needs Isabella saw, she identified two which would drive her in all of her years in India.[10] She saw the needs of Christian women who were often ignored, because male missionaries were unable to minister to them and there were so few missionary wives and widows to evangelize them. She also noted the urgency of the need for girls' education, for who would help the young Indian Christian women to grow and develop, and to teach their own and the next generation? Who would help prepare them to become Christian wives and mothers, teachers, or pastor's wives?

Isabella, or Bella, which seems to have been her family's nickname for her, was not afraid to speak up when necessary. Soon after she came to India her brother James asked her to copy some letters for him. It was a tedious job to write them out by hand,

> "No people ever rise higher, as a people, than the point to which they elevate their women."

but Bella did it cheerfully. A few days later James asked her again to do some copying. This time she looked at him and said quietly that it would be very helpful for her, too, to have a copyist. He caught her message, and wrote, later,

> . . . I had to reconsider the situation and once for all accept the fact that a Christian woman sent out into the field was a Christian missionary, and that her time was as precious, her work as important and her rights as sacred as those of the more conventional missionaries of the other sex. The old-time notion that a woman in her best estate is only a helper and should only be recognized as an assistant is based on a very shallow fallacy. . . .[11]

Almost immediately, Isabella began to search for a centrally-located place where she could begin a class for girls, and she found it in a one-room building just off the market in the center of town. It seemed to Isabella that color and caste ought not to separate people and from the beginning she treated everyone with the same respect and dignity. One morning, within three months of her arrival in Lucknow, she taught her first lesson to six shy girls, with the brother of one of them standing guard by the door with a bamboo stick. After a few weeks the class moved to a room in the home of one of the missionaries, and still later a rented home was found.

The work of education had begun. Isabella did not forget that she had originally been called to work among the "secluded" high caste women. She helped with that work, and also with other evangelistic work, but she realized that the greatest needs had priority, and for her this greatest need lay in the area of education. Again, it was her mother's law of service.

Establishing the school was not easy, not only were there shortages, there were also personal and relationship problems among the students. Yet, the school grew. One great blessing came when a well-known evangelist, William Taylor, came to India and began his preaching in Lucknow. A revival began among Indian, Eurasian and

European Christians, and the girls' school shared in revival blessings. After two years there were forty students, it was time to look for boarding facilities, but there were no funds for this.

Meanwhile, in Massachusetts, the members of the women's missionary society supported the work with prayers and with work. They collected money which was always welcome, especially when the mission, quite unexpectedly, chanced upon a property for sale in 1872 that would be an ideal site for its new campus.

A group of Indian girls with their teacher. The Lucknow Christian School began as a small class which Isabella Thoburn organized in April 1870, soon after her arrival in India. In time the school expanded, and in 1895 it became a chartered college, Asia's first Christian college for women. Eventually it was known as the Isabella Thoburn College.

The beautifully kept property of nine acres was in a convenient location in Lucknow. It was called Lal Bagh, "Ruby Garden," and had once been the mansion of a royal treasurer. When Isabella heard that it was for sale she walked past the property and peeked in from the road, but seeing a residence so fine, with its pillars and spacious veranda, she felt certain it was too gorgeous and would be too expensive for a mission school. The home had been empty for some time. The owner, fearful he might not be able to sell the property, asked less than what the property was worth. It was a lovely place, just right for Isabella's purpose. The other missionaries encouraged her to buy the property for the mission, and to make it the center of the women's work which was being done in addition to that at the school. Isabella hesitated because of her intense dislike of debts, but then she agreed. The sale was arranged, two missionaries went to the bank and withdrew fourteen bags of a thousand rupees each, delivered the money, and Lal Bagh, "Ruby Garden," was ready for Methodist mission occupancy.

Lal Bagh became the center of work among women. From there many Indian women and girls went out to teach Sunday school, to visit isolated women of the upper classes, and to work in the villages, but it was primarily the place for the school. With its two large meeting rooms, six bedrooms and a storeroom, the property became the boarding school Isabella had been longing to have for a Christian girls' school. She reasoned that, while the classroom was the place for formal education, the dormitory gave many opportunities for teaching practical Christian living. The lesson which she really wished the girls to absorb was her "guiding principle in life — the supreme conviction that the only real bond of union in this world, among all classes, all languages, all races, and all nations, is that of being made one in Christ."[12]

Another building was used for teachers' housing, and later a classroom building and student dormitory were built. This new campus became home for Isabella, and here she happily and humbly lived the "law of service" for nearly thirty years.

In time Lal Bagh was the place where missionary families stayed when they came to Lucknow, and it was seen as the Methodist center of the region, even more so than the bishop's home. Isabella loved showing Christian hospitality, and, after ten years in India she said, "I have felt more grateful for the privilege of extending hospitality to the many people who have come to our doors than for any other one thing connected with the past ten years of my life."[13] Again, it was the spirit of practical Christianity which prompted her.

" . . . The only real bond of union in this world . . . is that of being made one in Christ."

With the added space more girls could enroll, and more teachers were needed. At first Hindu and Muslim teachers had to be hired because there were no Christian teachers yet. From the start, Isabella hoped and looked for girls who might become teachers, and join the school as faculty. Girls had to learn to read and write their own language first, and English was soon added, because girls had to learn English if they were to be well-educated. Isabella was grateful that the women in the USA subsidized the students' tuition and supplies to make their education possible.

For some time she commuted to Kanpur (Cawnpore), some 70 kilometers west of Lucknow, to help start a school there also. An experiment in co-education there failed, it was too early for this, and the school in Kanpur became a girls' school. As much as she could Isabella helped with other women's work too, but little by little the demands at Lal Bagh required most of her energy and time.

Isabella was involved in all areas of the school. She rang the morning bell, she visited the kitchen daily, she took time to talk with each girl, she taught difficult classes and dealt with problem students. She was strict, but the girls loved her. As the years passed she helped girls get ready for their wedding, and, in those cases when a student died, she prepared the body for burial. Frequently Isabella cared for sick girls in her own room, in order to be available to the patient during the evening and night. Fearless of contagion, Isabella did not hesitate to take her turn nursing the sick during a cholera epidemic in 1873, though she had no formal medical training.

Some time later there was a smallpox epidemic and one of the Indian lady evangelists who worked at the school became ill with smallpox. So many caught the dreaded disease that, at the cemetery, open graves awaited the death of patients because burial had to take place as soon as possible. It was impossible to hire a nurse, especially since the doctor gave no hope for recovery. Isabella then decided to be the emergency nurse, knowing the danger of being with the patient who had smallpox. Others tried to stop her, but all she said was, "If my mother were here she would go,"[14] and went to the sick woman's house to care for her in isolation. The woman recovered and Isabella went back to Lal Bagh as if nothing had happened. Again, it was the law of service.

Isabella spoke little about her inner thoughts. A woman who prized practical Christianity, she was pious, but hesitated to speak about her own spiritual experiences except when necessary. She was a very private person. In company she spoke little about herself, and when she was called upon to pray she used few words.

Most Methodist missionaries in India took a furlough after ten years, and Isabella Thoburn followed this custom, though rather reluctantly. When she returned to the USA she had to learn many new ways, because during her ten-year absence the world had changed much. One of the things she learned about was public speaking, something which she did not wish to do. She had told friends, before she left India, that she would refuse to speak at meetings.

Interestingly, she felt as her mother had felt. Isabella's mother had never wanted Paul's first letter to the Corinthians read during family devotions, because in this chapter Paul writes that women should be silent in the church, he even writes that it is disgraceful for a woman to speak in the church (I Corinthians 14:33, 35), and then repeats this teaching in his first letter to Timothy (I Timothy 2:11–12). Isabella's mother apparently did not agree with Paul, and neither did Isabella. Yet, she disliked speaking in public, and wanted no part of it herself.

She was somewhat taken aback when she was invited to speak at a Sunday afternoon mission meeting. And then, the request did not even come from a Methodist church, but from Presbyterian people! No matter how she felt about it, she could not ignore the request, and finally she agreed to sit in the front pew of the church, and to answer questions. Once there, the questions kept coming. It was difficult to be heard throughout the building while she was seated on the front pew, and soon Isabella was standing before the congregation, giving a one-hour talk on missions among women in India. Afterwards she joked that the Presbyterians were responsible for her speaking in church, and from then on she accepted many invitations to speak before church groups.

Back in India, Isabella took up her work as principal of the girls' school with its growing student body and accompanying needs. When the school was first opened, in 1870, there were many barriers, but now there seemed to be many more challenges. While the youngest girls entering the school were about six years old, others were young women, and had different needs. Isabella was always sad when students left school to be married, and was happy when others continued, and enrolled for high school courses. But where to get teachers and supplies?

Lilavati Singh, a gifted, high-caste Indian young woman, had already had some education when she met Isabella Thoburn. Isabella encouraged her to do further study and helped make collegiate classes possible for Lilivati and others. These classes were the beginning of the women's college. Lilivati became an accomplished teacher of English literature, and remained a professor at the Isabella Thoburn College until her death in 1909.

Soon after Isabella's return from furlough a mother and her daughter came to Lal Bagh. Theirs was a moving story. The mother was born into a high caste orthodox Hindu family, and her father had actually allowed her to study. She was married, had a daughter, and then her husband died. While she and her daughter lived with her father, she met some female missionaries and received a Bible. She could not really understand this book, but it fascinated her and she wanted to know more. She was around thirty when she came to Lal Bagh, and there she was called Mrs. Chuckerbutty. Both she and her daughter Shorat enrolled in the school. They were part of the reason why, from the mid 1880s, the school included a complete high school course.

After a few years Mrs. Chuckerbutty became a believer. Her father tried to dissuade her but when she persisted he allowed her to be baptized, as long as it happened in a far-away city. Mrs. Chuckerbutty was eager to learn, and soon she and her daughter Shorat were ready to go to college. Shorat wanted to become a physician. Isabella was overjoyed — this had been her dream, to see Christian Indian women as professionals! On the other hand, it was disheartening, for where could Shorat go?

On a trip to Calcutta Isabella investigated. She visited the only Christian school where girls had completed college requirements, but the lady in charge, a Scottish missionary, told Isabella that her supporters in Scotland did not think it important for girls to get advanced education, and without their support she could no longer offer the course. The only place where Shorat could get her college training was at the newly opened University of Calcutta, a state university where female students were accepted. Mrs. Chuckerbutty knew the Hindu pressure on students in this school, and she had told Isabella, "I wish Shorat could finish her education, but I would rather she never knew anything than to be taught to doubt the truth of Christianity."[15]

Isabella wrote a note to Mrs. Chuckerbutty to report and to say that she had been disappointed, and that she wished a Christian women's college could be founded in Lucknow. Immediately Mrs. Chuckerbutty sent Isabella a letter, "If you open a college here I will be the first contributor towards it, and will give five hundred rupees." No wonder that Isabella wrote the women in the USA immediately, and enlisted their help in the establishment of the first Christian women's college in India. At the same time she began planning for college courses for Shorat and two other girls.

She saw that the mission needed . . . a college, where Indian women might be educated to be qualified professionals who could then lead their own people to lives of Christian service.

It would be costly to establish a college, and Isabella shrank from dealing with a large debt, but there seemed to be no choice. In the end Isabella followed the advice of the leading elder Edwin W. Parker, later Bishop

Parker, and went ahead. Even before actual collegiate classes were taught, the cornerstone for this new venture was laid in 1885. When the building was completed Isabella still felt burdened. She had always been against going into debt, and this was the first time she had taken the responsibility to deal with a large debt.

Isabella was overwhelmed by the numerous challenges she faced, and did some thinking about the work Methodist deaconesses were doing elsewhere. This movement had its beginning in Germany, and by it women, who could not be ordained as clergy, could be "consecrated" to the ministry of being a deaconess. They lived communally, and followed a simple lifestyle of service. This idea appealed to Isabella as she faced mounting needs in her mission work. She saw that the mission needed more than a high school, it needed a college, where Indian women might be educated to be qualified professionals who could then lead their own people to lives of Christian service. She needed Indian women to help in the mission work.

She did not consider herself a public speaker, nor a writer, and Isabella Thoburn wrote only one published paper, a tribute to a much-loved and successful student, after the girl died. Still, she worked for some twenty years on a small Hindi periodical. In the 1880s an American lady visited Lucknow and, seeing the need for Christian reading material, gave Isabella a very generous gift of $5,000 to start a magazine for Christian women in India. Later another $20,000 were raised to help shoulder expenses for this expensive venture. Isabella had frequently spoken about the need for Christian literature for, she asked, what could Christian women read, once they had become literate? *The Woman's Friend*, written in Hindi and Urdu, was intended for the whole family, and was published twice monthly. It had articles for mothers, for children, stories for the whole family, Bible stories, articles about household affairs and stories about other places in the world. Isabella was the editor, and managed this magazine from its beginning.

At about this time Isabella Thoburn became seriously ill and, though she protested, she had to take a medical leave. She sailed for the USA in 1886, together with her brother James, who was also ill, and

Soon after she began to teach girls and women in India, Isabella Thoburn began to wonder how she could advance Christian education for church workers. She then concluded that, if she was to teach future deaconesses she needed first to become one herself, and to model the life of a deaconess. During her second furlough to America, Isabella Thoburn trained to become a deaconess. She began then to wear the uniform of a deaconess and continued to do so for the rest of her life.

his second wife, Anna, and their child. This leave was to last nearly five years, but it would give her a new vision for opportunities for Christian service in India.

As she recuperated Isabella looked more carefully into the deaconess movement, and she and James and his wife wondered if they might start a deaconess home in Calcutta, where James and his family then lived. Isabella was always active, and as soon as her health permitted, she became a deaconess and enrolled in a regular nurse deaconess training. From this time until her death she wore the Methodist deaconess uniform, a simple, floor-length black dress with a white collar, and a cap. Wearing plain and inexpensive clothing was one of her ways of showing practical Christianity.

She helped out at new deaconess homes which were being started in the USA, and led in the training of deaconesses for work with the poor and the sick. This work inspired her, for she was convinced that, by bringing the Methodist deaconess movement to India, she could teach Christian women "the blessedness of service to the sinful," to do work for which there existed only a minimal budget. Later she would tell her Indian students, "If you once get the taste for this service nothing else will satisfy you."[16] The ministry of deaconesses seemed closely related to the work of Christian women's education, for it opened another avenue for teaching life-enriching courses.

Not long after Isabella Thoburn left for her medical furlough she received money in the USA for the collegiate training which would prepare high school graduates for university education, and more courses were added to the school in Lucknow. As of 1887 the school became officially known as the "Girls' High School," and some college courses were offered, as a forerunner of what was expected to become the Lucknow Women's College.[17]

There was urgency, for as yet there was no Christian college for women in India. The woman who substituted as principal during Isabella's furlough continued on a small scale with the courses, and in 1888 Isabella could send good news to her supporters: "Last week's mail brought the news that the first three students sent up for university examination had passed so creditably that they have received government scholarships to enable them to continue their studies."[18] The Annual Education Report of the Government of the year read,

> The Lal Bagh school takes the highest place among the native girls' schools of Upper India. One candidate was sent up for matriculation in the Calcutta University, and passed. Two others were sent up for first arts, and passed. If the school continues to pass such candidates, it will have to be classed as a college.[19]

All this time Isabella was busy with her deaconess work and with public speaking, raising funds for the college, and getting stronger physically for her return to India. Finally she received her doctor's clearance, and she was back in India early in 1891 for a term which lasted some eight years. This period would be significant. By now Isabella and her work were well-known in northern India, and she hoped to prepare the budding college to be recognized by the government. Not only that, she looked forward to having opportunities to help in many different situations.

Isabella felt rich when she returned to Lucknow because she had received a generous gift of $13,000 from the Woman's Foreign Missionary

Society for the new school. However, costs had soared. Digging the foundation had proved to be more difficult than expected, and actual construction costs were much higher than estimated. Then, after unusually heavy monsoon rains, it was discovered that the beams and flooring of the beautiful old house of Lal Bagh were being eaten by termites and needed to be replaced. A few years later Isabella received another $10,000 for the college, and again Isabella thought it might be enough, but again there were more needs. All the money was spent even before the construction project was complete, and none was left for furniture and educational needs.

At the Third Decennial Missionary Conference in Bombay, in 1892, Isabella Thoburn spoke on "Christian Women." She did not hesitate to speak before this large group of people, for she had much to say. She talked about the need for evangelism among Indian women, so that they might become vibrant Christians, and leaders of their people. But the only way for such evangelism to materialize, she said, would be to educate Christian girls and women, so that they could become such leaders. The work of mission is circular, she emphasized, for evangelism leads to education which, in turn, leads back to evangelism.

It was encouraging when, in 1895, the government gave full recognition to the college. It would be called the Lucknow Women's College, and the college became affiliated with the University of Calcutta. From this time girls who had completed the Christian high school course would be able to enroll in a Christian college course which, when completed, would give them access to the university. It was the first Christian women's college in India. Later the college became affiliated with other universities as well.

Though she was very busy during these years, Isabella continued to be anxious about the enormous budget needed for the school property. And then, suddenly it seems, she was given peace. She told one of her senior students that she no longer worried about it. Still, the problem was there, and it was a matter of much prayer.

Isabella Thoburn was ninth in a family of ten children. In 1899 the seven living siblings gathered for a reunion. Isabella is standing at the center of back row, while her brother, the well-known Methodist missionary-bishop James M. Thoburn, is seated at the far right. *Photo courtesy Crawford R. Thoburn, great-grandnephew of Isabella Thoburn.*

Finally, at the annual mission meeting of January 1899, when they discussed the matter of finances, the other missionaries suggested and agreed that Isabella should travel to the USA again, this time to raise funds. When she left there the last time Isabella had not planned to ever return to America, and she had said her goodbyes expecting to stay in India for the rest of her life. But this was not a furlough, it was a working trip. And so she went, two months after the decision was made.

Years earlier she had traveled with her brother James, his wife Anna and their child; that was when both Isabella and James were going to the USA for medical reasons. This time Anna traveled with Isabella because Anna, the physician, was sick. Anna was fifteen years younger than Isabella, but the two got along well, and Isabella was hoping that Anna would take her place some day. But this was not to be. Anna died soon after she arrived in America, and never returned to India.

The Woman's Foreign Missionary Society in the USA faithfully collected money for missions. The women who had organized this society, thirty years earlier, supported not only Isabella Thoburn and Clara Swain, they now had many mission projects, even though it was not always easy for them to meet their commitments. Not long after she arrived in the USA Isabella was joined by Lilavati Singh, one of the three young women for whom the initial college classes had been organized.

The women traveled far and wide across the country, always speaking to groups and individuals about mission ideals and needs in India. The response was warm and generous. Both women made an impression on their audiences, the deaconess Isabella Thoburn, a rather stout and aging person with thirty years experience in India, and Lilavati Singh, the young Indian Christian, elegantly dressed in her sari, who spoke English beautifully with a soft voice.

In one of her speeches[20] Isabella observed that, in India, higher education is usually only for men. She recalled that Alexander Duff, the missionary educator who became famous in North India, once said, "You might as well try to scale a wall fifty feet high as to educate the women of India,"[21] and added that it ought not to be so. Advanced education should be available to women too, for they are as intelligent as men, she insisted.

At all levels, Isabella emphasized, education "should be full of Bible teaching. All through the courses of study the supreme object for which missions are founded should be kept in view, as though the schools were special training institutions for that one purpose — the evangelization of the country in which they are situated."[22] And then she explained how an "educated womanhood" might serve God and the people. More missionaries were needed to reach this goal of female Indian Christian leadership, she said, and as she challenged women she often affirmed, "We want your best."

The generous reaction to the American women's efforts were heartening, and in May 1900 Isabella and Lilavati returned to India. Back at Lal Bagh Isabella was soon absorbed in her work again, but some people noticed a subtle change in her when she spoke about the future. It seemed as if she sensed that her task on earth was nearly done.

Later that year Isabella acquired new neighbors; she had known Edwin W. Parker and Lois Parker for many years. Lois was the woman who had come to talk with Isabella about becoming a missionary, long ago. Lois had worked hard to help start the women's missionary movement, and she was the woman who spoke to the few women who turned out that rainy day in Boston, in 1860. Since then her husband had become bishop, and the couple now moved to Lucknow, near Lal Bagh.

Bishop Parker was ill, and Isabella helped his wife take care of him. There seemed to be little hope for recovery, and some missionaries suggested to Isabella that she go to the cemetery to find a suitable burial place, as in India the funeral always takes place as soon as possible after death. Isabella went, and reported that she had chosen the best spot in the cemetery.

One morning soon after, Isabella herself did not feel well, and did only some light gardening and baking cookies for the school girls. That evening she hosted a birthday dinner for one of the missionaries, then excused herself, saying she had work to do. During the night she called for Lilavati, who had become like a daughter to her. When Lilavati suggested they call the doctor Isabella said that that would not be necessary, she only had indigestion. But Lilavati knew the symptoms; she could see that Isabella had the dreaded cholera, and did indeed call for medical help. Isabella had fierce stomach cramps, holding Lilivati's hand tightly so she would not groan aloud. She became confused and, in her suffering, spoke only Hindi. The next day she died.[23]

While Isabella's body was still on her bed it was covered with flowers by people who had loved her. She had asked, much earlier, that her body be buried without a coffin, to show her bond with the poor, who could not afford one. But this was not permitted by the cemetery authorities, and a simple white coffin was chosen for Isabella's funeral. There was a brief ceremony at Lal Bagh and then many mourners followed to the cemetery, ironically to the spot which Isabella herself had selected for Bishop Parker. There were Hindustani, Europeans, and Eurasians among the people present at the committal service.

Isabella Thoburn was an extraordinary woman. One of her students said of her, "Her real, and practical, and quiet and beautiful Christian life among us appealed to us even more than her words."[24] And Isabella's words left no doubt as to their meaning, they were always direct, brief and to the point. The sight of this woman in her deaconess uniform was itself a picture of practical service, a reminder of her belief in the law of service. In 1903 the Lucknow Women's College was renamed the Isabella Thoburn College, and afterwards it became the Women's College of Lucknow University.

We may believe that when Isabella Thoburn's life on earth ended our Savior said of her, "She has done a beautiful thing for me."

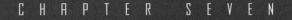

Until a little more than a century ago very young girls in India were often married to older men. When the husbands died, their widows were often still children, and these child-widows were doomed to a life of humiliation and shame. If the wife had not born her husband a son she was considered "worse than a demon," Pandita Ramabai wrote.

Ramabai Dongre, born in 1858, was taught to read and write by her enlightened father. He was a Hindu scholar who broke with tradition when he and his wife taught their daughter the ancient Sanskrit, the language of classic literature, and encouraged her to read and memorize large portions of the holy writings. This opened her eyes to thoughts and ideas women were not supposed to know.

When she was a young woman, Hindu scholars were so impressed with Ramabai that they honored her with the title "Goddess of Wisdom," thus making her a *pandita*, a scholar-teacher. While in her twenties Pandita Ramabai married, became the mother of a daughter, and was widowed. She met many people, read many books, studied religion diligently, and had compassion for the thousands of child-widows in her country.

All this time God worked in Pandita Ramabai's heart. He opened her eyes and her mind to the Christian gospel and enabled her to believe it. She was to become a devout Christian woman, and Pandita Ramabai spent her life helping child-widows and other destitute women and children.

Today Indians remember Pandita Ramabai whose Christian social efforts and school for widows and children still flourish.

A Woman's Voice in India

Pandita Ramabai Dongre (1858–1922)

After their parents and elder sister died during the famine of 1876–1877 Ramabai and her brother continued their family's pilgrim existence wandering across India for more than three years. They visited holy places, bathed in sacred rivers and worshiped the Hindu gods. Sometimes people gave them food and sometimes they went hungry; in some villages they were allowed to sleep in places where pilgrims were welcome, otherwise they spent the nights outside under a bridge or a tree. They had no blankets or thick robes to keep warm during cold nights and one evening, beside a river, it was so cold that they dug two pits, lay in them and covered their bodies with sand.[1]

Ramabai and her brother were very poor, and experienced intense hardship. They had been brought up to value the Hindu religion and the holy life more than physical comfort, but it was difficult to being cold and hungry. Because they were of a high caste Brahmin family it was below their dignity to beg, and they could do no menial work.

Ramabai's father was a Brahmin priest, a Hindu scholar, and though he was orthodox, he was open to new ideas. When he was young and still a student, he once heard the voice of a princess repeating the words of the Puranas. That was a shock. The Puranas were Hindu texts, written in Sanskrit, the sacred language of Hindu learning. Everyone knew that women and Shudra (also Sudra), low caste people, were never permitted to learn Sanskrit. How strange to hear these words from a woman's mouth!

Ramabai's father never forgot what he had heard. Years later, when he was a widower and forty-four years old he married a nine year-old girl. This was not unusual, many older widowers took a very young girl for a wife. What was unusual was that, even knowing that he was not permitted to do so, he began to teach her Sanskrit. She learned readily and, though she continued to do the wifely tasks at home, she became well-read in the ancient literature. When others heard about this they, of course, reported him to the religious scholars, and Ramabai's father had to appear before a council of priests. He knew the ancient books so thoroughly that he could quote all the texts which stated that it was not wrong to teach women and Shudras the Sanskrit literature of the Puranas. The council could find no fault with him, but traditions were law. There was much opposition to Ramabai's father, and though he was not forced out of his high caste he was driven away from his hometown.

He built a home in the forest near a mountain top, close to a sacred place where pilgrims gathered. In time many came to the house to listen to his lectures. His wife became so learned that, when her husband had to be absent, she lectured for him. Ramabai's father believed that it was important for him to offer hospitality to travelers, and by doing this continually for thirteen years he used up most of his resources. He had always been interested in pilgrimages, and from this time he and his family became pilgrims.

Ramabai's parents had six children of whom three lived to adulthood, Ramabai was the youngest. She was six months old when her mother placed her in a basket, and a man carried the basket on his head as the family left their mountain-top home to begin their wanderings.

By the time Ramabai was twelve years old she could recite 18,000 Sanskrit verses.

From the time Ramabai was eight until she was fifteen Ramabai studied with her parents. By the time she was twelve years old she could recite 18,000 Sanskrit verses. They must have spent much time

Ramabai, a toddler, second from left, with her Hindu scholar-parents, two sisters and brother. When Ramabai turned eight her parents began to teach her sacred scriptures. She learned to read and memorized lengthy portions of Hindu literature. When she was fifteen Ramabai joined her parents and siblings in the public reading of *puranas,* holy writings. This was unheard of in India at that time, where few girls were even allowed to be educated.

together! As they traveled about she also learned the indigenous local languages of three other Indian regions.

As far back as Ramabai could remember the family moved from one holy place to another, visiting temples and sacred rivers, staying in each place only a few weeks or months, always trying to do what they believed would please the gods. For years her father and mother, and after some time the children also, read Sanskrit Puranas in public places. The Puranas were Hindu writings intended for the common people to listen to, they were poetic and popular. People who read them in public believed that this was a good work by which they earned religious merit, and listeners usually offered the family food, coins, fruit, clothing, or even just flower petals. It was considered an honorable profession to read Puranas, even though the listeners could not understand the language and the readers usually did not explain what they had read. Hindu priests were generous to Purana readers and offered them hospitality in the temple.

Being public readers gave the family sufficient income to live on, but this changed when there was an economic turn for the worse. When a famine occurred in India the family discovered that Hindu priests no longer were kind to them. The family became poverty-stricken, and Ramabai's father became blind. Ramabai saw the horrors of people dying of starvation, and watched her own parents and elder sister weaken. Later, remembering this terrifying time, she wrote about her Hindu father,

> Though his blind eyes could see me no longer, he held me tightly in his arms, and stroking my head and cheeks, told me, in a few words broken by emotion, to remember how he loved me, how he had taught me to do right, and never to depart from the way of righteousness.... "Remember, my child, you are my youngest, my most beloved child. I have given you into the hand of our God; you are his, and to him alone you must belong and serve him all your life."[2]

Ramabai also could not help but notice how badly women in Hindu society, especially widows, were treated. She knew that her own experience was an exception to the norm for young women, for her parents had educated her. Women were not normally educated, and many were maltreated. She observed that very young girls were often married to older men, for it was usually the widowers who married young girls. Frequently these child-brides who were married to older men were widowed at a very young age, sometimes before they were ten years old, and then they lived lives of shame. Heads shaven, wearing drab clothing, without any jewelry and having to fast regularly they lived without hope of change in their lot. Hinduism taught that widows could never remarry, and that widows were simply receiving their punishment for crimes committed in previous lives.

It was very unusual that Ramabai's father had not arranged a marriage for her when she was young, for most high caste girls were married between the ages of five and eleven. When her parents died Ramabai was sixteen years old, well beyond the normal marrying age. Her father had contracted a marriage for her older sister at an early age, and the boy to whom she was married did not grow up to be a good man. Ramabai's father always regretted having contracted that arrangement, and though he was criticized for not arranging a marriage for his youngest, he left his Ramabai free. He had even promised that she would have something to say about a choice of husband when the time would come to marry.

Pandita Ramabai did her best for India's widows and orphans. When she had opportunity to study in England she took her young daughter, Manorama, with her. She then went to the USA to study and made plans there for the founding of a school for women in India.

When Ramabai and her brother were orphaned they decided to continue the life their parents had taught them, and so they traveled about, reading Puranas and visiting holy places. However, it troubled them that though their parents had lived the life of pilgrims, and had been very devoted, still they had not found happiness — rather, they had starved to death. And, though Ramabai and her brother had followed their parents' example for three years, they had found only bitterness. When Ramabai and her brother eventually reached Calcutta, where they hoped for good opportunities to earn a livelihood by public reading, they were totally disillusioned with the Hindu faith to which they had so carefully devoted themselves.

Word spread about the young woman who could read Sanskrit and was well versed in Hindu teachings, and Ramabai and her brother were invited to meet with some *pandits* (scholars). These were Brahmins, high class Hindus, who were reform-minded, and they were altogether surprised to see the young woman's knowledge of Sanskrit and of the Puranas. A group of them listened to her, tested her knowledge and discovered that she was indeed a learned and witty young woman. They then conferred upon her the title *Saraswati* (Goddess of Wisdom); this title made her a *pandit*, scholar-teacher, like the scholars who had tested her. The word *pandita* is the female form of *pandit*, and from this time Ramabai became known as Pandita Ramabai. No Indian woman before her had ever received such great honor.

The Calcutta Brahmin scholars were fascinated by Pandita Ramabai's knowledge, and asked her to research ancient scriptures to find teachings on the duties of women. In order to do this Pandita Ramabai would have to study the sacred books which not even her father had dared teach her. But she was on a path of no return. She followed the suggestion of one of the modern liberal scholars who advised her to read the sacred scriptures reserved for the *pandits*, and studied the *Dharma Shastra*, which was said to have been divinely created, and to hold the sacred laws and customs for society. These scriptures prescribed the rules for society. By doing these studies Pandita Ramabai cut herself off from the orthodox Hindus, the branch of Hinduism to whom her family had belonged.

Years later she wrote that, though the learned men and the ancient writings frequently disagreed, they agreed on two things.[3] First, they all claimed that women were evil — even worse than devils. Secondly, they taught that women could never be delivered from their low position, unless they were reborn thousands of times at higher and higher levels, and would finally be reborn as a high caste man. And in order to be reborn at higher levels women had to worship their husbands. No matter how much of a criminal a husband might be, to the wife he must be her god. Women themselves, like all Shudras, low caste people, were not allowed to study the sacred Hindu writings which held the keys to deliverance from this life. Their only way to improve their lot was by becoming lifelong slaves to their husbands.

A good wife had to be the mother of sons, for no man could go to "heaven" if he did not have sons. And it was believed that, if a woman learned to read and write, her husband would die.[4] Pandita Ramabai wrote,

> My eyes were being gradually opened; I was waking up to my own hopeless condition as a woman, and it was becoming clearer and clearer to me that I had no place anywhere as far as religious consolation was concerned. I became quite dissatisfied with myself. I wanted something more than the *Shastras* could give me, but I did not know what it was that I wanted.[5]

Her sympathy for uneducated women who were kept in ignorance, and the sad state of child-widows had moved Pandita Ramabai along, but now her thoughts began to crystallize and she felt that she must do something to raise the standard of living of women. During the year she lived in Calcutta she lectured widely and became well-known as a Hindu scholar.

Once she and her brother were invited to a meeting of Christians. They were not certain whether or not to accept, but one of her new liberal Hindu friends suggested they go, so they went. This was a new experience, in a home with "chairs and sofas, tables and lamps," things they had never seen. The Indian people present at the meeting wore western-style clothes, and Pandita Ramabai and her brother were shocked to see that these upper class Hindu Indians ate bread and drank tea with the British. It seemed very wrong to Pandita Ramabai and her brother, being the caste-conscious Brahmin Hindus they were.

At this meeting someone read from a book, but Pandita Ramabai and her brother understood none of it. When they grew up their parents had shielded them carefully from western ways and anything which was not part of the life of devout Hindus. After a while the people knelt by their chairs and spoke with their eyes closed. Someone explained that they were speaking to their god, but Pandita Ramabai saw no images and wondered if the chairs represented the gods of these Christians. Before they left the house someone gave her a Sanskrit Bible. She liked the book's appearance, and tried to read it, but did not understand it at all.

When Pandita Ramabai was twenty years old her brother died. Now she was the only one left of her family. She received several marriage proposals from Brahmins but refused each one, instead marrying a friend of her brother, a Bengali lawyer. This man was a Shudra, low caste, and by marrying him Pandita Ramabai further alienated herself from her Hindu acquaintances. She went with her husband to his home in Assam and learned Bengali. Together they talked about opening a school for widows. They were delighted when they became parents, and named their daughter Manorama, "Heart's Joy."

Living in her husband's home, Pandita Ramabai made a find which really interested her. Her husband had been educated in a mission school, and had a Gospel of Luke in his library. Pandita Ramabai still had her traditional Sanskrit Bible, but it meant little to her. Reading the Gospel in the Bengali language was easier, and she was happy when a Baptist missionary visited their home to talk about the Christian faith and to explain more about the Bible. She found the book of Genesis appealing, it was so different from what she had learned as a Hindu. Her memoirs read,

> Having lost all faith in my former religion, and with my heart hungering after something better, I eagerly learnt everything which I could about the Christian religion, and declared my intention to become a Christian, if I were perfectly satisfied with this new religion.[6]

This is when her husband became uncomfortable. He did not want to be called a Christian, nor did he want his wife to become a Christian and to be baptized, because Christians were scorned by society. He told her that he would no longer allow the missionary to come to the house.

They had been married less than two years when her husband became ill and died. Now Pandita Ramabai was alone again, though with the responsibility for her toddler. She was a widow, but worse than that, she had no son. However, if she had been low caste and poor she would have been like the destitute, despised widows, but she still had some standing and income because of her scholarship.

Pandita Ramabai was now twenty-four years old. She took her baby and traveled to Pune (Poona), the capital of her home state, Maharashtra, in western India. There she lectured on the ancient Hindu literature, but also spoke more and more frequently about the need for education for women. She was not the only one committed to this, prominent liberal Hindus were promoting this idea, and welcomed her cooperation.

To further publicize her ideas and ideals Pandita Ramabai helped organize the *Arya Mahila Samaj*, the Aryan Women's Society, a society which was established to develop women's education and social reform, and was especially aimed at eliminating prejudice against widows. She pleaded for opportunities for Indian women to get medical education, because women were not permitted to be treated by a male physician. One of her distant relatives went to the USA to study medicine, a course which Pandita Ramabai herself would have liked to have taken up.[7]

It is said that reports of Pandita Ramabai's efforts on behalf of Indian women's health eventually reached Queen Victoria. She entrusted the wife of Viceroy Dufferin, about to embark for India, with the distribution of funds for the training of nurses in maternal care. Some of these funds, sent to India and Myanmar (Burma), made possible the development of the so-called Dufferin hospitals and of medical care and education for women.

Pandita Ramabai helped organize the Arya Mahila Samaj, the Aryan Women's Society, a society which was established to develop women's education and social reform, and was especially aimed at eliminating prejudice against widows.

One day a Brahmin widow, twelve years old, was brought to Pandita Ramabai.

> She was very dark, had cross eyes and was very unattractive in many ways.... She had been given in marriage when five years old, but the boy husband died a few days after the marriage was performed. Her mother-in-law would not look at her. She said the girl had eaten up her son and was a great demon.
>
> As I looked at that little figure my vague thoughts about doing something for my sisters in similar conditions began to take shape . . . I began to place [before my countrymen] a plan for starting a Home for Hindu widows and to ask for their help.... I tried my best to get help, but could not.[8]

It was now clear to Pandita Ramabai what she must do. It was her guess that, at that time, there were some 23 million widows in India, fifty-one thousand of them below age nine, and ten thousand of those under the age of four.[9]

In Pune she met missionaries of the Church of England, one of whom gave her English language instruction and also taught her the New Testament in Marathi, Pandita Ramabai's first language. Later she wrote that she was sometimes more interested in the Bible lessons than in the English language instruction.[10] She wanted to know more. She was speaking and writing, and had earned enough money to accept the invitation of a sisterhood of the Church of England in Great Britain. She traveled there with little Manorama and enroled in the Anglican college, hoping to follow a medical course. However, because she had a hearing impairment she was not accepted in the medical program. She did learn much about the Christian life and about other academics.

Once, on a trip to London, she saw the work of the Anglican sisters among the prostitutes and was amazed. She had always been taught that "fallen women" were to be despised and were beyond compassion. Pandita Ramabai began to see a radical difference between Hinduism and Christianity. She asked one of her sister-teachers why they reached out to "fallen women." In reply the sister read the story

A widow herself, Pandita Ramabai had compassion for widows and orphans, and loved to tell them about Christ. She never tired in her evangelistic work at the Mukti Mission. *Photo courtesy Mukti Mission*

of Jesus and the Samaritan woman in John 4, and explained that Jesus did not despise sinners, but loved them.[11] Pandita Ramabai's response was,

> I realized . . . that Christ was truly the Divine Savior He claimed to be, and no one but He could transform and uplift the downtrodden womanhood of India, and of every land.
>
> Thus my heart was drawn to the religion of Christ. I was intellectually convinced of its truth . . . and was baptized in the Church of England in the latter part of 1883, while living with the Sisters at Wantage. I was comparatively happy, and felt a great joy in finding a new religion, which was better than any other religion I had known before. I knew full well that it would displease my friends and my countrymen very much; but I have never regretted having taken the step. I was hungry for something better than what the Hindu *Shastras* gave. I found it in the Christian's Bible and was satisfied.[12]

During her stay with the sisters Ramabai was baptized with the name Mary Rama; her daughter Manorama was baptized the same day. Pandita Ramabai was satisfied with the religion that taught a concern for all people, including widows and prostitutes. She continued to study Christianity, but became confused by the numerous Christian groups and denominations. Pandita Ramabai disagreed with some academic arrangements at Wantage, and she could not accept some of the Anglican church positions, yet she kept the faith.

About a year later, when her distant relative, the girl studying medicine in Philadelphia, was about to graduate and invited her to come, Pandita Ramabai and Manorama went to the USA. The planned short visit there stretched into three years, because Pandita Ramabai was fascinated by kindergartens. Hoping to apply what she learned in the USA to the situation in her homeland, she studied how American kindergartens functioned and were administered.

While she was in the USA Pandita Ramabai lectured and wrote extensively about the desperate needs of Indian women and girls, and began to draft plans for the education of child-widows in India. Interested people in Boston, Massachusetts, established the Ramabai Society to support the project. A board was set up, and its trustees represented several Protestant church groups, Unitarians, and wealthy private sponsors. They promised to support the school to be established with $5,000 annually for ten years.

Pandita Ramabai had been away from India for five years when she returned in 1889. She said that when she arrived in Mumbai (Bombay) she fell on her knees, committed herself to the care of her living Heavenly Father and then set up the *Sarada Sadan*, "Home of Wisdom," beginning with two day-students. While still in the USA she had agreed with her sponsors that the home-school would not include religious education. The Indian school board included liberal Hindus who championed for women's education, and Pandita Ramabai wanted to cooperate with them rather than work separately. And so there was no objection to students continuing their Hindu way of life when they enrolled in the home-school. Pandita Ramabai herself continued her Christian lifestyle, and insisted that the door be left open when she and Manorama had their daily devotions. Religion was not taught in the school so that liberal Hindus would feel free to send their daughters, and Hindu writings were side by side with the Bible in the library.

The students must have been impressed by their school mistress, a short woman with shining grayish-blue eyes, which was an unusual eye-color in India, a straight nose, wavy black hair, wearing a simple white sari and shawl,[13] and always ready to listen to them. After a while some of them asked about the Christian faith, and then some of the girls wanted to become believers. This angered the Hindu board members intensely, and newspaper articles publicized these conversions widely.

Fearing that something might happen to the girls Pandita Ramabai moved the *Sarada Sadan* with its eighteen widows away from Mumbai to the city of Pune. But even here Hindu opposition was bitter, and soon Hindu board members resigned from the school, while twenty of the fifty-three young women were taken out of the school by their angry parents.[14]

This was a trying time for Pandita Ramabai, not only because of the burdens of the school and the opposition, but also because of personal inner turmoil. She now had a school for child-widows, but her former Hindu friends looked at her as one who, having been influenced by the West, had forsaken her Indian heritage. She herself had many questions, and felt quite distant from numerous church issues and from European thinking. She pondered about her life, her work, and her future. As a result of her struggles she realized that there was much she did not understand, and came to the conclusion that her reason for being attracted to Christianity had been its attitude to women, and the way it seemed to fit so well when she was searching to find a way to relieve women's oppression. She saw that she had studied and read about the Bible, but not really the Bible itself, and now she began to read the Bible

> *She came to the conclusion that her reason for being attracted to Christianity had been its attitude to women, and the way it seemed to fit so well when she was searching to find a way to relieve women's oppression.*

regularly. This reading resulted in a renewal within her. "I came to know after eight years from the time of my baptism that I had found the Christian *religion*, which was good enough for me; *but that I had not then found Christ, Who is the Life of the religion*, and 'the Light of every man that cometh into the world.'"[15]

She compared herself to the blind man of John 9, who was blind for forty years and then received the gift of sight from the Lord Jesus, and she wrote that she felt like the man who heard the words, "In the name of Jesus Christ of Nazareth, rise up and walk," and he "entered the temple walking, and leaping, and praising God." This was Pandita Ramabai's experience as she reflected on the new knowledge that she, a woman who had always been taught that there was no deliverance possible except after thousands of rebirths could, in fact, be delivered from misery in this life. She now knew that

> . . . no caste, no sex, no work and no man was to be depended upon to get salvation, this everlasting life, but God gave it freely to anyone and everyone who believed on his Son. . . .
>
> The Holy Spirit made it clear to me from the Word of God, that the salvation which God gives through Christ is present, and not something future. I believed it, I received it, and I was filled with joy.[16]
>
> I found it a great blessing to realize the personal presence of the Holy Spirit in me.[17]

It must have been welcome news for Pandita Ramabai and her friends, when the Government of India passed the Age of Consent Act in 1891. This raised the age of consent for girls in India to the age of twelve, and made it illegal to consummate a marriage with a girl younger than that. The laws permitting marriage to a younger girl were kept intact. It was heart-warming to know that other reformers were speaking out in the effort to raise the standard for women; this law was a breakthrough.

The *Sarada Sadan*, Home of Wisdom, had been in operation for three years when twelve child-widows were baptized. Although Pandita Ramabai's former friends, the liberal Hindus, were furious, she had peace, and now felt free to change the "no religion" practice in the school to one of Bible teaching in class. She changed the school's constitution to include religious instruction. The group of students who had been baptized was just the earliest beginning of years of revival during which hundreds of young women became believers.

Stories of Hudson Taylor (in China), John G. Paton (in the South Pacific) and George Müller (in England), all of whom had done great mission work and totally depended on God to supply their needs, inspired Pandita Ramabai to do the same. Until now her funds had been limited mainly to what American supporters sent her, and still the school had so many needs.

She decided to broaden her work and to trust God to provide. She then bought a hundred-acre farm in Kedgaon, outside of Pune, and prayed. Unsolicited from people, but in answer to the prayers of many, the money did come. Wells were dug, fruit trees planted, vegetables seeded, housing built, and soon the community counted some two hundred and twenty-five girls. The people worked hard. Somehow needs were always met. Pandita Ramabai wrote,

> I feel very happy since the Lord called me to step out in faith, and I obeyed. To depend upon Him for everything; for spiritual life, for bodily health, for advice, for food, water, clothing, and all other necessities of life, — in short, to realize by experiment, that the promises of God in Philippians 4:6, 19 and in other parts of the Holy Scriptures are true, is most blessed.[18]

Sarada Sadan had been a school for Brahmin child-widows only, for it was unthinkable that people of different castes would eat, study and live together. This changed in 1896, during a severe famine in Central India. The memories of hunger, and of scavenging for food when her family suffered and her parents died, must have haunted Pandita Ramabai. With her helpers, she went around the countryside and invited six hundred needy widows and children to come to her home. She had temporary huts put up to house the refugees, there were gifts from overseas, and the farm yielded enough food and water.

With so many people living on the farm much organization was needed, and the numerous tasks were divided among them. One half of the day was usually scheduled for studying. Girls who had learned to read and write became teachers for the younger children, and others took care of those who had special needs. The second half of the day was spent working. Cooking, laundry, needlecraft, weaving, carpentry, baking, shoemaking and other jobs were all taken care of by the women. It was good that Manorama had grown and become a young woman; she was a great help, and her mother was hoping that, some day, Manorama would take over the responsibility of the community.

Pandita Ramabai's work did not go unnoticed by other Christians. Already several Christians had offered their support and encouragement for the opening of *Sarada Sadan* in 1889, and she had friends among women missionaries in India. One of these, a Methodist deaconess, was Minnie Abrams, who had been sent to India by the Methodist Episcopal Woman's Foreign Missionary Society. This was the women's organization which was founded in 1869 and had sent Isabella Thoburn and Clara Swain, M.D., to India as their missionaries. Minnie, like Ramabai, was inspired by the idea of depending wholly on God to provide what is needed, and that of spiritual revival. Minnie joined Pandita Ramabai in her work when the Mukti Mission was opened.[19]

Each year more space and more buildings were needed, and soon Pandita Ramabai bought a piece of land of twenty-two acres across the road for her expanding "family." Especially during the famine, with so many women crowding in the settlement, there were hundreds of conversions and baptisms. Prayer meetings, Bible studies and revival were part of life, and after one revival meeting Pandita Ramabai named the community *Mukti Sadan*, House of Salvation.

Pandita Ramabai thought big. In 1899 a church was built on the *Mukti Sadan* property, a church large enough to seat two thousand people. The building also served well during times of crisis, when extra shelter was needed. Its cornerstone reads,

> Praise the Lord. Not by might, nor by power, but by My spirit, saith Jehovah of Hosts. That Rock was Christ.... That our sons may be as plants grown up in their youth; that our daughters may be as cornerstones, polished after the similitude of a palace.
>
> September 1899.[20]

The next year there was another serious famine, this time in western India. Again Pandita Ramabai went out into the country and brought back women and children by the hundreds, most of them low caste people. These people, rejected by the world, found a warm (and crowded!) welcome at the *Mukti Sadan,* House of Salvation. During this year the home had some two thousand residents. There were always numerous needs, and countless prayers for help were lifted up. And God always provided.

One time, when more than one thousand seven hundred famine refugees at the compound needed clothes, and Pandita Ramabai had prayed that she might help them, someone sent a large amount of clothes. They were spread out on the floor of the church, and as people were given what they needed, Pandita Ramabai reminded the people that, "The young lions do lack and suffer hunger; but they that seek the Lord shall not be in want of any good thing" (Psalm 34:10, *Updated NASB*).[21] As the various works of mercy became more numerous they were organized into one umbrella organization, called the Mukti Mission. Today the Mukti Mission continues to care for orphaned children and abandoned women, and is offering non-denominational Christian care for the poor in other places in India as well. Child-widows are rare now, but the three schools of the Mukti Mission have more than a thousand students, and special education is available for the blind and for mentally challenged children.[22]

The Mukti Mission not only received support from overseas, gifts also were sent from Mukti to other places, such as the China Inland Mission. Pandita Ramabai kept up with Christian work elsewhere, and prayed for conversions throughout the world.[23]

In 1905, she wrote that she felt led by the Lord to begin a prayer-circle. Each morning about seventy women gathered to pray for an outpouring of the Holy Spirit everywhere. This was the time of a widespread revival which began in Wales, and reached many countries, including India, and it flourished in the Mukti Mission. After six months five hundred and fifty women met twice daily for prayer. After nine months Pandita Ramabai said that tongues "were given for a sign for unbelievers among us, that they may see and hear of God's wonderful works and repent of their hardness of hearts . . . a deep spiritual work began in our midst."[24]

Together with Minnie Abrams, the woman who had joined her a few years earlier, Pandita Ramabai felt heartened by the manner in which the Holy Spirit moved among the people in the mission. The spiritual renewal and Pentecostal revival which began here in 1905 was the first of its kind in India,[25] and would spread to other places as well.

Many stories have been told of renewal, of speaking in tongues and of Pentecostal type experiences at the Mukti Mission. Pandita Ramabai encouraged the revival, though apparently she herself did not speak in tongues.[26] She wrote about the mission's spiritual experiences in English as well as in Marathi. She praised God in her life, and her writings bubble with the joy of knowing that she was a child of God.

Pandita Ramabai had experienced hearing problems already when she was in England, and they worsened as she became older. For years she could do her work, and was at her post of administrator-teacher many hours each day, but the time came when conversing became difficult. Yet, even when she could no longer hear what was said in church services she slipped into a pew to be with other worshipers.

She was a controversial person. Today people still measure the life and achievements of Pandita Ramabai with either criticism or praise. And yes, looking closely, there are questions one may ask. There are questions about her theological arguments; about her intellectual probing, and her struggles with the doctrines of the Church of England; about her railing against British traditions and customs when she was prevented from teaching co-ed classes; and, from the Indian perspective, about her becoming a Christian and for receiving funds from overseas to fund her many works of charity. But these things seem to matter little when we catch a glimpse of this small, courageous woman who could have led a life of admiration and friendship of scholars, a life of ease in high society traditions. Rather than choosing that, she determined to minister to the outcastes and the dispossessed, women who could never begin to repay her.

Pandita Ramabai still had the Sanskrit Bible which was given to her many years earlier, and which, though she could decipher the difficult language, had meant so little to her. She thought much about the new believers in her community who did not have Scripture in their own language, and was deeply concerned. These young women were taught to read, but how would they ever read the Bible if there wasn't one in their own language?

Her deafness had increased, but Pandita Ramabai, in her late forties, felt challenged to begin the huge project of Bible translation. However, before she could translate, she had to know Hebrew for the Old Testament, and Greek for the New Testament, and so she studied both. Now she knew seven languages.

Having studied the biblical languages, Pandita Ramabai began to translate the whole Bible into Marathi, her mother tongue, which was spoken in the Pune area. She used very simple language, so that even poorly educated women would be able to read and understand. She had help from others, and it took fifteen years, but eventually the translation was completed.

Pandita Ramabai had learned bookbinding in England. This enabled her to teach the women at the Mukti Mission to typeset, print and bind. In this way, even while she was still translating Bible portions, the women were already preparing them for publication. The Gospels were completed in 1912, and the entire New Testament the next year. In 1920 the whole Marathi Bible was finished.

It was another historic first, because never before had a woman translated the whole Bible. Pandita Ramabai's version of the Bible received mixed reviews, but undoubtedly it was a blessing for the people for whom she had spent these fifteen years preparing the simple Marathi translation. This Bible version was revised in 1958, the year of the centennial of Pandita Ramabai's birth.

In the midst of her administration of the Mukti Mission and of her translation project, Pandita Ramabai's daughter Manorama died. Manorama's background, her influence and her western education would have been a great help if she had followed in her mother's footsteps, but it was not to be. Her death caused tremendous sorrow, but her mother did not abandon her translation work.

More than one hundred thousand copies of the Gospels were translated, printed and distributed by the workers of the Mukti Mission. Pandita Ramabai was then hoping for fifty thousand copies of the whole Bible. The girls were already printing some of the early portions, and she was still working on the final part of the translation when she became ill. She knew that she could not live much longer, and prayed fervently that God would spare her till she completed her proofreading; the night after she had checked the last page proof she died in her sleep. She was sixty-four years old.

When she died in 1922 the *Times of India* called Pandita Ramabai one of the "makers of the modern India," and she continues to be acclaimed by many, especially for her work in women's education. In 1989, one hundred years after Pandita Ramabai founded the *Sarada Sadan*, Home of Wisdom, the government of India issued a commemorative stamp with a photograph of Pandita Ramabai's face "in appreciation of the work of P. Ramabai for the advancement of Indian Women." An accompanying brochure elaborates that she was a "social reformer, a champion for the emancipation of women, a pioneer in education, and a Sanskrit scholar," and adds, "Deeply impressed by her prowess, the Sanskrit scholars of Calcutta University conferred on her the title of 'Saraswati' and 'Pandita,'" followed by further details of her work, including her Bible translation.

We may believe that when Pandita Ramabai's life on earth ended our Savior said of her, "She has done a beautiful thing for me."

Lillias Stirling Horton Underwood did not give in easily to physical problems, even though she struggled with health issues most of her life.

She was known to have a buoyant spirit, and was headstrong; once Lillias determined that she should become a physician to help in medical missions she let nothing stall her. While she had earlier been too squeamish to take her younger sister to the dentist, she now studied medicine and nothing was too gruesome for her. Later, in Korea she was to treat repulsive sores and wounds of people who walked into the clinic from the street, and perform delicate surgery procedures. She also became the official physician to the queen, and, dressed in fashionable gowns, met with high government officials dining with them in the palace.

Much of this ended when her arthritis crippled her. One day a guest at her home was horrified when, at dinnertime, she saw Lillias carried to the table by her husband.

This little frail woman let no pain stop her. When she could no longer carry out a physician's work she helped her husband with translating tasks, and turned to writing. She was delighted when their only child, Horace Horton Underwood (1890–1951), followed in his parents' footsteps in becoming a missionary to Korea, thus carrying on the effort in which his diminutive mother had played a significant role. The Underwood family is still represented in Korea today.

One does not need to be strong and powerful physically to be a strong and powerful witness of our Lord!

Chapter Eight

Physician to the Korean Queen

Lillias S. Horton Underwood, M.D. (1851–1921)

In Korea the name Underwood will always be known as that of one of the pioneer Presbyterian missionary families. From the time Horace G. Underwood began his missionary career in 1885 until the present day the family has been represented in Korea. Five generations of missionaries have chosen to serve God in Korea, and have conducted evangelistic, medical, educational and social work. This chapter tells the inspiring story of Lillias Stirling Horton Underwood, the wife of the first Underwood missionary to Korea.

Lillias Horton was born in Albany, New York to devout Christian parents. As she grew up she often heard about missions. Her mother had earlier regretted not becoming a missionary, and dedicated Lillias, while still a baby, to God. As her daughter grew up the mother urged her to think of becoming a missionary to India, but Lillias showed absolutely no interest — she was interested in enjoying life in the USA. Yet even as a child Lillias was devout, she was a spirited person with a great imagination. While she had health problems from childhood, she never gave in to them. During her teens the family moved to Chicago, and Lillias and her sister had many opportunities to enjoy the things their well-to-do parents provided for them. However, when it was time to go to college her mother was afraid that Lillias might leave the Christian faith, and at the last moment she did not permit her daughter to go.

Lillias was still young when she spoke with a woman from England who said that she hoped to become a medical missionary to India. She added that, since medical education for women was not available in her home country she had come to the USA to study. As the woman spoke about the miserable condition of many women in India, Lillias became interested in the missionary challenge and in the possibility of joining the medical mission there. Suddenly Lillias saw her opportunity and, coming home, announced, "She told me such awful stories of the condition and needs of women there that I have decided to study medicine and go there too!"[1] Her decision had been made and that was it.

There was no stopping her, though illness had kept her from completing high school. Her sister Leonora described Lillias as yielding only to a stone wall,[2] and Lillias managed, with extra studies, to prepare for the College of Medicine. Her family was amazed that Lillias, easily frightened, not strong physically and fussy about anything unclean, could study about the human body, work with blood and wounds, and finally graduate with honors from medical school. She was thirty-seven years old when she was ready to become a medical missionary to India — she applied to the Presbyterian Board of Foreign Missions, and was accepted.

At about this time the Board of Foreign Missions received a letter from Horace Allen (1858–1932), a newly-arrived missionary in Korea, that the queen there had requested him for a female physician. The queen had heard from Mr. Allen about female doctors; this was something new to her. Korean tradition prevented a male doctor from treating women, and when she heard that there were women in America who were qualified physicians, she asked for one to be sent to serve her and the court ladies. The Presbyterian mission board members considered this an unforeseen blessing for their budding mission effort in Korea, and immediately searched for a female physician. Lillias Horton's application came just at this time, and she was asked to go to Korea, rather than to India. She agreed. It gave her mother, hesitant to see Lillias go to a far country, more things to prepare for the daughter's outfitting, and an opportunity to have some formal gowns sewn for her, so that she would be well-dressed when she had to meet the queen.

Lillias Horton arrived in Seoul in March 1888 as a Presbyterian medical missionary. She was the first female physician in Korea. With characteristic gusto she began her new task, perhaps not even noticing Horace G. Underwood, a bachelor eight years younger than she was, but she certainly caught his attention.

The history of Korea is a fascinating one, especially the history of mission. Out of fear of foreign exploitation Korea had earlier shut itself off from the world and become a "hermit nation;" Roman Catholic Christianity came to Korea via Beijing in 1784, and Protestant Christianity entered the country in the early 1880s via ethnic Korean Christians in what was then Manchuria, the area northwest of Korea.

After an attempt on the life of a Korean prince, Dr. Horace Allen provided medical treatment and the prince recovered. (Dr. Allen was officially the American government physician, and formerly a Presbyterian missionary doctor in China.) The king then became interested in Allen and his work, and permitted him to begin a western-style medical work in Seoul. This project became a hospital, and this is where Lillias Horton was put to work, in the women's department.

This hospital was the first modern hospital in Korea, for in Korea medical practices differed greatly from those in western countries. An early traveler in Korea described the traditional Korean apothecary:

> On the floor sits the old doctor surrounded by his assistants who prepare the medicine, grind the powders, and fill the prescriptions. The doctor himself is a jolly old man and enters into conversation heartily. He has been in the business many years, knows his art well, his dispensary is well stocked with the multitudinous herbs and preparations in use. Above us are many paper bags filled with dried herbs, barks, and powders some of which have been brought from China, the rest from his own hearth. Each bag is labeled on the bottom with the name of the drug in Chinese.[3]

When Lillias Horton arrived in Korea she immediately noted how unsanitary the general conditions were. She wrote home,

> All sewage runs into filthy, narrow ditches, frequently stopped up with refuse, green slimy pools of water lie undisturbed in courtyards and alongside of the road, wells polluted with drainage, soiled apparel washed nearby, quantities of decaying vegetable matter thrown out and left to rot.... Every imaginable practice which comes under the definition of unhygienic or unsanitary is common.[4]

Such conditions caused much sickness and helped epidemics to spread rapidly. Among the main ailments which people suffered were indigestion, malaria, and the much-dreaded cholera, as well as smallpox, fevers, and other diseases. Conditions in Korea then were much like those of Europe some two centuries earlier, and it seemed impossible to bring a change.

> How hopeless looked the task we had before us in those days. A little company of scarcely a dozen people, including our Methodist brethren, many of us able to stammer only a few words of the language as yet, attempting to introduce Christianity into a nation of fourteen or more millions of people, in the place of their long-established religions; and beginning with a few poor farmers and old women.[5]

Besides the challenges of working in a foreign country, where Lillias must learn the language, and have only limited medical resources available, she soon experienced that conservative Koreans refused to be treated by women. Even ten years later Dr. Mattie Ingold, Southern Presbyterian medical missionary, was working in a small town, but was not permitted to treat the sick because she was a woman and not tolerated by the local residents. Instead, she was relegated to supervising men workers — a delicate task! Almost daily a nearby missionary without any medical training came and stood beside Dr. Ingold, repeating everything she said. Then, following

Lillias soon experienced that conservative Koreans refused to be treated by women.

Dr. Ingold's instructions, the male workers followed Dr. Ingold's directions and treated the patients.[6] Even some male missionaries were still hesitant to work with female physicians. And then there was the issue which was discussed for decades on nearly every mission field: evangelism versus medical work. Not everyone considered medical work a legitimate aspect of mission work, for a long time some believed that mission meant teaching Bible lessons and preaching exclusively.

Life for Korean women was difficult during the centuries when Confucian teaching was the official doctrine for daily life. Confucius, the ancient Chinese teacher of ethics, taught men to be respectful and unconditionally obedient to their parents, and to worship their spirits after they died. This obedience was said to be the filial duty of a son, and it included fathering one or more sons. The greatest wrong one could do, Confucius taught, was to not provide an heir for the family name, for that meant that the family name would not continue.

The duty of women was clear, and they were not given much recognition. They were just a necessary part of a man's life. For centuries Korean women were taught three obediences: to the father when a child, to the husband when married, and to the son when widowed. It was so important for women to become the mother of sons that baby girls were unwelcome, brought up uneducated, often barely tolerated by the father. Many girls were given the name, *Sup-sup-haby*, "sorrowful."[7] These were the women whom Lillias Horton and other missionaries served. What a challenge!

The mission hospital in which Lillias practiced was small. It was the outgrowth of Dr. Allen's pioneering, some three years earlier. Lillias was assigned to work in the women's section, where women workers were indispensable, as male physicians were unable to practice in that department. Foreigners had to tread carefully and local customs had to be observed. Only four years earlier foreigners had not even been allowed to enter Korea. Her letters home described her life as missionary doctor. Her sister reported,

> She was kept busy every minute by people with every known ailment who wanted help. She did things she didn't know she was capable of and we could hardly believe she had done; she operated for cataract

and it was successful! She pulled an ulcerated tooth! She who shuddered at the sight of false teeth and turned pale when she took me to the dentist! There were other things perhaps worse, ulcers, distressing sores and wounds, but she treated them all and repeated to them the sentences she learned in Korean of Jesus' love.[8]

Lillias was one of a committee of missionaries sent into a rural area to assess just what were the greatest needs of the people there. After all, the mission work was young, and careful plans had to be made for the most efficient use of missions personnel and funds. While carrying out her part in this assignment Lillias made some rather startling discoveries about her fellow missionaries and also about herself. In her sister's words,

> . . . she wrote of her surprise at finding being a missionary had not cured her faults. She had always had such an exalted opinion of missionaries, she had felt they were so far removed from the failings and spiritual feeblenesses of other people, and without reasoning about it at all, she believed she must have thought that setting foot on [sic] Asia she would find she had left all her own badness behind. Certainly she was sick enough on the Pacific, she said, to have parted with all innate sin, but no, here on the mission field she was just the same old tiresome sinner she had always been.[9]

After Lillias had been in Korea for a few months she was invited to meet Queen Min. The Queen was intrigued by the foreign doctor with whom she could speak face to face. It was a high honor for Lillias to be the Queen's official physician, it was also a great responsibility. Until she could speak Korean, she communicated with the Queen via an interpreter who stood hidden behind a screen. Men were not permitted in the Queen's presence. In the olden days, when the Queen needed a physical exam, one end of a long cord was tied around her wrist and the other end of the cord brought to a nearby room. Then, holding only this cord as a point of contact, the male doctors examined the Queen from the next room. And when they checked her tongue she had to stick out her tongue through a narrow slit in a screen so they could see and investigate. At least Lillias could personally be with her patient. Nevertheless, on the day that she saw that the Queen had a boil, and wanted to lance it, her attendants were horrified and the king promptly forbade her to give this treatment.[10]

The Queen was the same age as Lillias, and once Lillias had learned to speak Korean and could talk with her, the two found that they shared several interests. The Queen was fascinated by stories about other places and events. On special occasions she showered Lillias with presents, such as fans, lacquerware, rolls of silk, bags of nuts, and packages of beef and fish. Being a royal, her world was very small, she lived in near isolation and rarely left the palace. She often asked Lillias to come and asked about western customs, other countries, and world events.

One December the Queen asked Lillias to come and tell her about the "great festival" of Christmas. Before she went Lillias asked her colleagues to pray that she might explain clearly, and then went and told the Queen the Christmas story. It took wisdom to tell it in a way which would not antagonize the Queen. She also decorated a Christmas tree in the palace so that the king and queen could see a tree, but was disappointed when the royals would not wait for it to become dark, and so the candlelight did not give the atmosphere of intimacy for which Lillias had hoped.[11]

Politically, Lillias and her colleagues lived in Korea during a disturbing period in its history. Shortly before the first Protestant missionaries came several nations had coerced Korea to open up to others, and the missionaries' arrival was one result of a treaty to which Korea had to agree. There was rebellion, murder and intrigue. Queen Min was murdered in 1895, and King Kojong was forced to abdicate in 1907 in favor of his son. This coronation was not celebrated with joy, because the Koreans were well aware that their country had become a protectorate of Japan. For many years the Protestant missionaries were rather unwilling participants in Korean political matters.

One December the Queen asked Lillias to come and tell her about the "great festival" of Christmas.

When Horace G. Underwood, the first ordained American Protestant minister to come to Korea, arrived in Seoul on Easter Sunday of 1885 he was a young man of twenty-five. Like Lillias, he was born into a Christian family, and his parents were sincere believers. Horace's mother died when he was only six years old. He and a brother were sent to a boarding school in France for two years, and later moved to the USA with their father.[12]

When he was just four years old Horace had decided to become a missionary, and planned his studies with that in mind. He became engaged while in seminary, but his fiancée decided against becoming a missionary wife, and broke off the relationship. Thus Horace was still a bachelor when he left home as a Presbyterian missionary, though he knew that future colleagues, and especially mission board members, wished he were married. He was told time and again that he needed a wife. Church leaders considered it important for a male missionary to be married, and Koreans thought it unnatural for a man to be single, they had their suspicions about bachelors.

Horace seems to have wasted no time in showing Lillias that she charmed him although she was some years his senior. He helped her with her Korean language lessons, took her horseback riding, hovered around her, protected her on the road when there was danger, and sent her flowers on a rainy day when he knew Lillias felt homesick.[13] He called her by her family nickname, "Lillie," and she began to call him "Captain." Before long they surprised family and colleagues by announcing their upcoming marriage, and when Lillias had been in Korea for a year, they were married. She was then thirty-eight, and he was thirty. Neither of them was tall, he stood at 5' 8" and she was a petite of less than five feet. Lillias ordered her wedding dress, trimmed with lace, from the USA. Her mother knew her measurements, had the dress made, and sent it to her with a veil and other wedding fineries. Because the family would not be present at the wedding, they wondered how to celebrate the wedding. Finally her parents decided on a grand reception in the Chicago hospital where Lillias had done her internship. Flowers in every room, a festive wedding dinner for all the patients and staff, and an orchestra for the occasion made for a joyous celebration of Lillias and Horace's wedding, thousands of kilometers away.[14]

Before the wedding Lillias and Horace planned carefully for their honeymoon. When they heard about it, the other missionaries were alarmed, for the couple planned an in-country journey. It was unsafe in rural areas where few Caucasians and certainly no white woman had ever been seen and where potential illnesses, anti-foreign individuals and robbers lurked. Still, Horace was able to get a passport for in-country travel, on the condition that he would neither preach nor baptize. Looking back years later, Lillias wrote, "It seemed to me that no honeymoon so rich in delight could ever have been planned before, and I looked forward with the greatest pleasure to a journey through a lovely country, to be filled with blessed service."[15]

And so they packed blankets, food, medicine, and Christian literature and arranged for helpers and packhorses; they had eleven companions on their honeymoon! The morning after their wedding they set out for two months of travel which would cover more than a thousand miles, and reach as far as the Chinese border, visiting village after village. During this trek Lillias would treat more than six hundred patients, and together they mingled with thousands of Koreans who crowded around them, wondering about these white people's ways and their stories.

Horace traveled mostly on horseback. Lillias walked whenever possible, but usually traveled in a traveling chair carried by two men. It was unacceptable for women to be out during the day, only women "with reputation" did that. The "chair" was actually a bamboo box with carrying poles, with the top and sides of the chair covered with oiled paper, and the front flap open only when there were no other people nearby. Riding in the chair, Lillias sat

> Lillias wrote, "It seemed to me that no honeymoon so rich in delight could ever have been planned before, and I looked forward with the greatest pleasure to a journey through a lovely country, to be filled with blessed service."

on pillows, and was isolated from the outside. As the carriers walked along she swayed back and forth, except when there was a ditch or uneven terrain, or when they went through a rice field, then she bounced around very uncomfortably.

The two months were filled with adventure and excitement. They slept in inns along the way. When they stopped for the night they asked for clean roof thatch for the floor of their room, so they would not need to sleep on dirty mats which might have been used by people sick with contagious diseases. They never had privacy, for curious people were always around, poking holes in the oiled paper windows and doors to watch them. Each morning Lillias attended the sick, and Horace helped to prepare and dispense medications. In the afternoon Lillias told Bible stories to women, and taught songs to children. She admired Horace for the gentle and friendly way he talked with whomever he met, and his ability to speak easily with people about the Christian faith. Soon they ran out of medicine and Christian tracts and had to order more from Seoul.

Once they met "twenty or thirty wild-looking men with fierce, blood-shot eyes" who took all their belongings and companions, and gave them such a hard time Lillias feared that her new husband would also be taken away. How relieved they were when the local people protected them and, when they sought help from government officials in the next town, those men retrieved the Underwoods' companions and belongings.[16] They were astounded to meet some people who had already heard about the gospel of Jesus.

When Lillias and Horace reached the area near the Chinese border they found that Korean Christian workers had been there, and some people who had already become believers asked for baptism. After prayer and careful discussion they were convinced that thirty-three men were ready for baptism. Remembering the conditions of his passport they crossed the river into China. Here Horace G. Underwood felt released from his promise to the Korean officials. He baptized the thirty-three men and altogether they celebrated the Lord's Supper.

Many years later Lillias heard about a woman who had met the Underwoods during their visit to her area of the country and told her town mates all she knew. Then, when a Korean Christian bookseller came, they were ready to listen to him and to read his tracts. Many of them became believers and were baptized, and some years later there was a congregation of some seven hundred members in that town.[17]

What a honeymoon they had! In spite of the joys they experienced when people asked them to tell more about the Savior, they must have been happy to return to Seoul safely, to be

Lillias S. Horton Underwood, missionary physician, and her husband Horace, pioneer missionary, held daily medical clinics and numerous evangelistic gatherings during their honeymoon in 1889. During their three months of travel in remote areas of mountains in North Korea they covered more than 1,500 kilometers. *Photo courtesy Jean W. Underwood, whose husband was a grandson of Dr. Underwood.*

in their own home and to finally have privacy. Their house was not very different from others, for during the first few years they lived Korean style in a mud house with oiled paper windows and doors. Lillias described how, soon after their marriage, the Presbyterian mission board secretary and his wife visited from the USA and stayed with her and Horace. One night there was a strong wind and a downpour which tore holes in the paper windows and leaked through the roof, making it necessary to put up umbrellas in the house. The next morning, Lillias wrote, the mission board official "reprimanded us for our carelessness, warning us that missionaries were too expensive commodities to be so ill protected."[18]

Eighteen months after their marriage, in 1890, Lillias gave birth to Horace Horton, becoming very ill soon afterwards. Her old rheumatic fever, which had never left her, acted up again and she became crippled with arthritis. The Underwoods were urged to take a medical leave, and they left for the USA. Lillias wrote, "I can never tell with what regret, shame, and pain I left Korea, to go *now*, *a failure*, to leave my work scarcely begun, perhaps never to return was bitter. But more bitter still was the thought that I was dragging my husband back from a life of usefulness."[19]

When they arrived in the USA the family was shocked to see Horace carry Lillias off the train.[20] During their furlough Horace did much to promote the work in Korea, while Lillias regained her health and strength. They were delighted to be able to return to Korea two years later.

The story of the early Protestants in Korea is a wonderful story, it is one of a kind. Years before the pioneer missionaries arrived in Korea two Scottish missionaries in China had befriended a Korean who had no employment. This man was willing to teach them the Korean language. After some time he became a Christian and was baptized and then helped the missionaries to translate the Gospel of Luke and, later, more Scriptures.

They were soon joined by another Korean who became a believer and helped to prepare these booklets. Both of the men then went around Korea to spread the Good News and to distribute the gospels, thus becoming missionaries to their own people.[21] One of the Scottish missionaries in Manchuria traveled into Korea where he met people who had become believers and who asked for baptism. Because these early Korean believes had been missionaries to their fellow Koreans, the honeymooning Underwoods met people who had already heard the gospel, who wanted to know more, and who wanted to be baptized. No matter how many reasons for the many conversions are cited, it is nothing short of amazing how the Spirit of God worked in Korea.

It was a time of opportunity, and usually the missionaries were shorthanded. The incredible response of Koreans to the gospel, with many new believers themselves evangelizing their surroundings, resulted in an inordinate amount of work for the missionaries. In 1887 Horace G. Underwood organized the first Korean Presbyterian congregation with fourteen members.[22]

Lillias Underwood was deeply touched by the medical needs around her. She noted that people who became ill with contagious diseases were usually sent away by family members, who were afraid that they would also catch the disease. Then the sick became street people for whom no help was available.

Thanks to a generous American donor Lillias was able to open a small hospital in 1893 which she called The Shelter, complete with a clinic where Bible classes were held.[23] All medical work done by the missionaries was accompanied by their witnessing and Bible lessons, in fact, it was simply viewed as part of the whole evangelistic venture.

Two years after The Shelter opened a fast-spreading cholera epidemic occurred and, in spite of heroic efforts by many, hundreds of Koreans died. The entire facility of The Shelter was made available for cholera patients. But there were no Korean medical workers. Horace G. Underwood then appealed to the members of the small congregation he was pastoring. The response was unbelievable. Scholars and high-class people who never worked with their hands turned out to do the most menial work to help the sick.[24] While generally in the city sixty-five percent of the patients died, in The Shelter sixty-five percent of the patients recovered. Of the one hundred and seventy-four patients who were treated there one hundred and twelve survived.[25] Throughout the city of Seoul most volunteers who aided cholera patients, thereby risking their own lives, were Christians. This made an impact.

The missionaries faced an immense task. There were not enough workers to deal with the large numbers of Koreans who wanted to join the church, there were not enough buildings and money, and the political situation was tense. Korean leaders battled to keep their nation independent under the growing threat of international warfare. Several missionaries, especially the medical workers, broke down under workloads which were too heavy.

Lillias did what she could. Once she became a mother, her involvement in medical missions lessened, and later she was frequently housebound because of illness.[26] Her arthritis disabled her and made medical practice impossible. Gradually she began to spend more time supporting Horace in his work of Bible translation and education. She wanted to help him. Perhaps she had heard the testimony of missionary colleague who was challenged by an old and devout Korean man. The Korean had put his hand on that of the missionary, and said, "Brother, you have told me the gospel, be careful lest translation work and the like should take you away from telling it to others also."[27] More and more Lillias applied herself to writing, and her publications became important sources of information about Korea, her people, and the Protestant mission work done there.

In his thirty-two years in Korea Horace served in almost too many areas to name. Among the many tasks he accomplished were: pastoring a church; founding the Chosen Christian College (which later merged with the first hospital to become Yonsei University); helping with the organizing of the Korean YMCA; opening an orphanage, and, in the beginning, serving as unofficial advisor to the king. Horace was scholarly, he translated Scripture and hymns, taught at the seminary and wrote several books. Then he made numerous evangelistic trips into the country, averaging more than a thousand miles on foot a year for several years.[28]

It was great joy for Lillias and Horace when, in 1912, their son Horace Horton joined them in mission having completed his studies and now a young man. It was a particular blessing to them that he was even assigned to his parents' station.[29]

Lillias was concerned when her husband, fifty-five years old and too involved in his work, became ill. As they had both aged a great deal and were struggling with their health, their son Horace Horton accompanied them when they traveled to the USA. Horace Horton helped take care of his father until Horace G., the father, died a few months later. Horace Horton and his fiancée Ethel Van Wagoner changed their earlier plans to marry in Korea. Instead, Ethel traveled from Korea to the USA where they had a small wedding. Lillias then returned to Korea with the young couple, and lived with them. She continued her correspondence and writing until she died in 1921 at the age of seventy.

A few years ago Koreans asked for Horace G. Underwood's bones to be brought to Korea. There they buried them, beside Lillias's grave. On the tombstone, in a cemetery in Seoul, Horace's name and accomplishments are listed. His name is shown in the *hangul* Korean script, but apparently Lillias never had a Korean name, she was simply known as the wife of Dr. Horace G. Underwood.[30] Her tombstone says, in Korean, "The grave of 'Ho Don,' wife of Rev. Won Doo Woo of America." It also shows four dates: Lillias's date of birth, the date of her arrival in Korea, the date of her death and the date of the erection of the memorial stone.[31]

It seems that, even today, Dr. Lillias H. Underwood is one of those women whose life and work is not well remembered by either the people of her own country or by those in Korea. One of the grandsons of Lillias and Horace, also called Horace G. Underwood [#2], and also a life-long missionary in Korea, died in Seoul in January 2004 at the age of eighty-seven. Several publications mentioned that this Horace G. Underwood [#2] was the grandson of the pioneer missionary Dr. Horace G. Underwood [#1], but were silent about Dr. Lillias Horton Underwood, the grandmother who was a trailblazer in women's medicine in Korea, and a courageous pioneer missionary. Obviously, the Chosen College–Yonsei University connection between the two men is clear, for the senior Underwood founded the school, and the junior Underwood was a professor there until his death; yet one wonders how it is that Dr. Lillias H. Underwood, grandmother of Dr. Horace G. Underwood [#2], and one-time physician to Queen Min, was not mentioned with her husband in either newspapers or memorial tribute.

Lillias would certainly agree that the amount of praise given a person is not important. Nevertheless, this chapter was written so that today's Christians may remember something of how she lived her life and what she achieved as the first female physician to Korea, her attempts to tell Queen Min about Jesus, and her many varied and helpful writings.

We may believe that when Lillias Stirling Horton Underwood's life on earth ended our Savior said of her, "She has done a beautiful thing for me."

Until they heard the news of the defeat of the Spanish navy in Manila Bay on 1 May 1898 most Americans knew little or nothing about the Philippines. The USA was at war with Spain and when that war was settled in the Treaty of Paris, signed on 10 December 1898, one of the American demands was that the islands of the Philippines would be ceded to the USA. There was, and still is, controversy over this treaty; nevertheless, it began a new chapter in American history as well as in that of the Philippines.

Suddenly Americans were interested in the Philippine Islands, and wanted to go there. In a short time there were hundreds, then thousands, of Americans in the Philippines, each for his or her own reason. Government leaders deliberated, then made decisions on how to rule the people, many of whom did not want to be ruled by Americans. Scientists explored the forests and the lowlands to learn about flora, fauna, and natural resources. Educators thought it a choice opportunity to teach English and western interests to Filipinos. Adventurers roamed the Islands, learning about Filipino culture, or just enjoying themselves. Businesspeople scrambled to start successful enterprises, while others investigated how they might line their pockets without such strenuous undertakings. And yes, there were also missionaries among the newcomers to the Philippines.

The Philippines had been colonized by Spaniards for more than three centuries, and most towns had a large Roman Catholic church at its center, a church built by Filipinos. Yet, the majority of Filipinos had not heard the gospel.

Most Spanish Roman Catholic church leaders left the Philippines during the early American Period soon after the turn of the century and Protestant missionaries from America arrived in the Philippines. Protestants had been trying for decades to enter the Philippines, but had been kept out by Spaniards, for the Bible was a forbidden book. One Spanish priest began to preach biblical homilies after reading a stealthily purchased Bible, and was sent back to Spain, never to return. Now, with the Americans a new wind of religious freedom came to the Philippines.

Early Protestant missionaries soon realized that, if they were to evangelize throughout the Islands and avoid conflict among themselves, they must spread out. In a comity arrangement, spelled out in 1903, they agreed that each Protestant denomination would work in a chosen area and not interfere in places where others had chosen to evangelize. Except in the Manila area, where any group might have its headquarters, the Protestant missionaries dispersed through most of the nation.

Dedicated Christians, some with their families, left home and friends in the USA to lead lives as evangelists, teachers, medical practitioners, or in some other capacity. The stories of most of these people remain untold, though even today tombstones of many of them reveal their names. Whether because of modesty, on the part of the missionaries, or just our own lack of interest in remembering and preserving the record, most of these individuals are no longer known.

This chapter is about one of these brave and hardy pioneers, S. Rebecca Parrish, M.D., the Philippines' first female physician, who came to the Philippines in 1906. Unfortunately not much has been written about her, only a ten-page biography of her life and a few letters can be found in the Methodist archives. Yet, Dr. Parrish left a legacy. Her life and activities have been interwoven in the lives of many Filipinos, and make up a part of a chapter in Philippine history.

Healing Among the Poor in Manila
S. Rebecca Parrish, M.D. (1869–1952)

Sarah Rebecca Parrish (known as Rebecca, rather than Sarah) was born on a small Indiana farm in the USA and was the eldest of nine children. Throughout her life she remembered her childhood as one filled with love, and even wrote a small book about her memories of life on the farm.[1] Life in the rural area circled around local affairs, but Rebecca's mother subscribed to a magazine which widened their horizons and gave mother and daughter pleasure. This was *The Heathen Women's Friend*, a missionary magazine from which Mrs. Parrish read to her young daughter.

Rebecca was fascinated by the stories, and especially those about medical missions. She knew when she was still very young that she wanted to spend her life doing that kind of work. One day she said, "Mother, how would it be if I should be a missionary when I grow up?" Her mother replied, "Why, I think it would be fine!" and Rebecca's wish to become a missionary doctor became the secret of mother and daughter.[2]

Rebecca's desire was clear, but it would not be easy for her to become a missionary. Both of her parents died young and, though she was not physically strong, Rebecca had the responsibility of taking care of her eight brothers and sisters. She managed to follow a teacher's course and taught school for seven years. During these years she acted as parent as well, and still was busy with family duties when she enrolled in a medical course. Later she said that, during her studying years, she often had no time to walk, but had to run between chores and assignments, and she often studied until after midnight.[3] Without sufficient nourishing food and rest she became quite sickly and yet, when she graduated from medical school, she stood in fourth place in a class of forty-seven students.

By this time her siblings were grown, and Rebecca was now free to follow her dreams. She applied for a missionary physician appointment, but because she had become ill again she was not accepted. She then worked as assistant physician in a hospital for four years, always hoping and praying to go into medical mission work.

And then, one April day in 1906, while she was in the hospital recuperating from yet another bout with illness, Rebecca received a letter with the words, "You are appointed to medical work in Manila, Philippines, to sail October first." Her first response was a despairing remark, "I look like going to Manila, or anywhere else, don't I?" but then she felt that the Spirit of God was moving her, and she added, "God willing I *will* go, October first!"[4] During the next six months she did become strong, and in October she traveled to Manila. What joy to finally be commissioned by the Woman's Foreign Missionary Society of the Methodist Episcopal Church. She was to say, later, that from this recovery until the end of her stay in the Philippines she was a healthy woman.

When Rebecca Parrish arrived in Manila she faced a volatile situation. Politically there was peace, but reminders remained of the three hundred and thirty-three years of Roman Catholic Spanish rule, as well as the Philippine Revolution against Spain which had followed, and now Filipino voices opposed the American government. Protestantism had come to the Philippines with the Americans in 1898; Rebecca's Methodist Episcopal

When Rebecca Parrish arrived in Manila she faced a volatile situation.

Church had already sent several missionaries as medics and teachers, but Rebecca was their first female missionary physician. Indeed, she was the first female physician with modern medical training in the Philippines.

There was great need all around Rebecca. She was moved by the prevalence of disease, the lack of hygiene, the social conditions, superstition and suffering, and her compassion was matched by her determination to help the sick in service of the Great Healer. She was especially distressed when she saw poor women and sick babies who were not getting proper care. She was told that more than fifty percent of the children died in infancy,[5] and Rebecca desperately wanted to help the people around her.

Within two months Rebecca was ready to see patients in her new clinic. She was allotted the use of a room in the new Harris Memorial Training School (now Memorial College). Three years earlier the Woman's Foreign Missionary Society of the Methodist Episcopal Church had commissioned a teacher from Missouri to start a training school for young Filipinas in Manila. This school began with a class of six girls in an old Spanish mansion in Manila. It was intended to be a deaconess training school for young Filipinas.[6] Methodist leaders reasoned that deaconess training would be for future deaconesses what theological education was for future pastors. The school had grown quickly from six to twenty-five students, and needed more space. When a Chicago man, Norman W. Harris, offered money for a more permanent place a building was put up near the earliest Methodist church building in Manila, today's Knox United Methodist Church, on Rizal Avenue. The girls' school was moved to the new location and renamed the Harris Memorial Training School. In 1906 the building was new, and there was room for Rebecca's work.

Rebecca placed a sign, *Dispensaria Betania*, "Bethany Clinic," above the door. Memories of that room always include its often cited contents, "one chair with a crooked front leg, a desk, a blue enamel basin, and a pitcher." The next year she could report to the Methodist missionary conference that her inventory included "a fair stock of drugs, a small

From left to right: Rose Dudley, Gertrude Dreisbach, Dr. Parrish, four Filipino nurses. From the beginning Dr. Parrish knew that she'd need to train Filipino nurses to help in the work of medical mission, and she had already begun to teach basic medical skills to some Bible students while she still operated from the clinic. She was overjoyed when an American nurse joined her during the next year, and then another one. The women worked hard, and were proud to train some of the earliest Filipino nurses. *Photo courtesy Myrna Velasquez, M.D.*

quantity of dressings, one large dispensing case, a desk, a few miscellaneous articles such as enamelware, and five chairs."[7]

The clinic quickly became a popular place. No one was turned away, and Rebecca always found time to listen and help. The room became too small, and Rebecca was happy to receive use of another room. When ten bamboo cots were brought in, the clinic changed into a hospital. There were as yet no trained Filipino nurses, and three of the Harris Memorial Training School's students, young girls, were assigned to help Dr. Parrish. These girls became her first student nurses.

The next year an American nurse, Gertrude Dreisbach, joined the work in the small hospital, soon another nurse, Rose Dudley, joined; that was a great help, but there were always more people needing medical care than Rebecca, the nurses and the girls could give. Rebecca and her assistants made many home visits during these early years and they treasured the opportunities to speak of the Savior to their patients and their families. It was not long before Rebecca realized that, regardless of culture, all people share basic needs. She commented, "It is nonsense to say, 'East is East and West is West and never the twain shall meet,' for 'In Christ there is no East or West, in him no North or South.'"[8]

The young Filipinas probably found their clinic work difficult at first, but they persevered. Classes were started for them, and soon three more girls joined for a complete nurse's training. What satisfaction it was in 1911, when the first group of girls, six of them, graduated as full-fledged nurses!

Walking, riding, even coming down the coast by boat, people arrived from far away to be helped at the clinic. There was so much suffering and so little could be done, it seemed. Rebecca said later, "Did we heal them? Oh, not all. But from the opening day, December 10, 1906, the sick have been faithfully referred to 'The Great Physician' who healeth all their diseases — for that is why the medical work was established."[9]

Her growing love for Filipinos was evident when she communicated with Christians in America. In an article for the *Michigan Christian Advocate* she explained that she had joined a weekend trip to a village across Manila Bay. The pastor of a small group of Christians there was also a student at the seminary in Manila. Rebecca was stunned by the many needs of the fishermen's families in this village. She wrote that a communion service had been planned, but because of heavy rains the mud floor of the chapel was wet, and there was no dry place to kneel. The people had brought in two banana trunks, laid them parallel to each other, and then placed a broad plank across the two trunks, to improvise an altar. She commented, "Well, my heart was stirred. I sat there on the little bamboo platform, and desecrated time and place by trying to figure out in my mind whether I could, from my already overtaxed salary, squeeze out $13 required to put a floor in this chapel; the poor people ought to have a place to kneel."[10]

It soon became clear that more space was needed for Rebecca's medical practice than the *Dispensaria Betania* could provide. Filipinos in Manila had an interest in this and began to solicit funds. They collected between $5,000 and $10,000. In 1907 Rebecca was overwhelmed when she learned about an offer which an American real estate man had made. Daniel B.R. Johnston was grieving the death of his wife Mary, who had been active in promoting the cause of missions. He had decided to build some kind of memorial so that the world would remember her. As soon as members of the Woman's Foreign Missionary Society heard about this their secretary visited Mr. Johnston and told him about Rebecca Parrish in Manila and the needs of medical missions there. She then asked him frankly to have a hospital built in Manila as a memorial for his wife. This spoke to him, he promised to help, and soon he sent a gift of $12,500. He offered the money in memory of his wife, and only requested that the hospital to be built would be named after her.[11] Rebecca wasted no time in recommending that land be bought in Tondo, a crowded, depressed area of Manila, near the waterfront. This was done and early in 1908 the cornerstone was laid.

That year a two-storey facility with room for fifty-five patients was built and the Mary Johnston Hospital for Women and Children was officially opened in August. Rebecca Parrish left the Bethany Clinic and moved her work from there to the new hospital, which would specialize in maternity and child care. It was the only Protestant hospital in the region, and served as a powerful witness in the work of Christian mercy.

> That year a two-storey facility with room for fifty-five patients was built and the Mary Johnston Hospital for Women and Children was officially opened in August.

Both local and overseas Christians donated money toward hospital expenses. Groups in the city frequently solicited funds for the hospital, and Rebecca Parrish was invited to speak at social gatherings about its achievements and needs. She would attend these

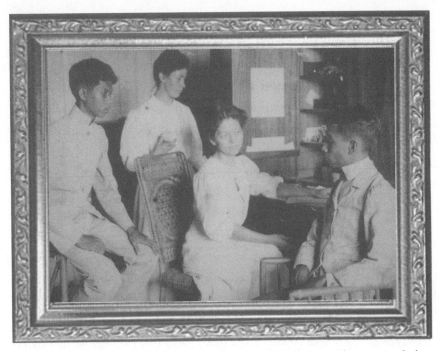

Rebecca Parrish, M.D., was the first female physician in the Philippines. She was moved when she saw the countless needs of the sick, especially the pregnant and nursing women and their babies. From the small *Dispensaria Betania*, Bethany Clinic, she moved into a new hospital building, the Mary Johnston Hospital, in 1908. Dr. Parrish, seated, is consulting with a patient while a companion and the newly arrived American nurse look on. *Photo courtesy Myrna Velasquez, M.D.*

affairs and in her kind yet direct way she would present the challenge at concerts, and church and community gatherings. Sometimes they received outright gifts, such as when the Masonic Lodge provided for a ward for crippled children and later expanded this ward, thus helping to continue the work.

From the beginning it was difficult to make ends meet, and many prayers went up in times of crisis. Once there were only sixty-five cents left after the day's food had been purchased, and the wards were full of patients. What to do? Dr. Parrish decided to speak to the Methodist bishop, who called a meeting of friends in the city, and within an hour they contributed $850. Rebecca's comment was simply, "It was a test of faith."[12]

It was a big disappointment when this first hospital building burned down only three years after it had been erected, and the hospital had to be closed for four months for reconstruction. A destructive fire would blaze again later during World War II. On 5 February 1945 there were numerous fires burning in Manila. As fire approached the hospital both staff and patients were able to escape to the nearby Manila Bay; they must have been disheartened as fire scorched and consumed the buildings of the area. Then, after the fire, when workers found the sign "Mary Johnston Hospital" intact, they took that as a sign of a bright future. And yes, more funds came in and the new hospital was more spacious and more complete than ever before.[13]

As the years went by more and varied projects were initiated, a maternity ward, a clinic, and a milk station where malnourished infants and toddlers were given milk all became a part of the hospital. Anyone could ask for help and not be refused. Word had it that all one had to say was "*May sakit po ako* (I am sick)" and Dr. Parrish would listen attentively. She never tired of helping, and once admitted, "Hundreds of days — thousands of days, I worked twenty hours of the twenty-four among the sick, doing all that was in my power to do my part, and hoping the best that could be had for all."[14] Filipinos loved her, and liked to call her "Dr. Rebecca." When the next generation grew up many called themselves, "Dr. Parrish's children." Former patients returned to visit her, and many people who had been inspired by her example became volunteers themselves, helping the poor and treating the sick.

For Rebecca Parrish her medical expertise was only one way to help show God's love. She complemented her already full-time work with her evangelical activities. She insisted that the medical standards of the hospital were high, and that workers were involved in its evangelistic program. Every day there were vesper services in the hospital, and in its clinic there were daily Bible lessons. Rebecca Parrish saw to it that there was always a poster with a Bible text in a prominent place near the front gate, and each day she replaced it with a new one, so that people passing the gate could read it.

Finally the effects of the gratifying but strenuous work began to show as Rebecca's health gave way. She developed a serious anemia which would not heal, and it became time for Dr. Rebecca to rest. In 1933, after twenty-seven years in the Philippines, Dr. Rebecca Parrish returned to the USA. She remained active for many years as she lectured in many places about medical missions, and wrote articles, letters and stories. She affirmed that as a young missionary candidate she had confidently said, "I believe God will care for me," and after many years of intense work she simply acknowledged, "He has!"[15]

Dr. Rebecca Parrish was eighty years old when the Civic Assembly of Women in Manila honored her with a gold medal awarded by the President of the Republic of the Philippines. She was unable to come to Manila, and the medal was handed to a representative. The medal read,

> The blessings of health and of social welfare which the Philippines enjoy today have been inspired by the pioneering effort of this sincere and determined American missionary doctor, who came a long way across the sea, bringing Christian love, healing, and enlightenment, and a better way of life.

Rebecca Parrish lived for two more years. A Filipina who visited her shortly before her death related that she found a "frail little" woman lying on her bed, weak but alert and interested in people and events in the Philippines, and especially in the work of the hospital. She always hoped to visit the hospital once more, but that was not to be. Dr. Rebecca Parrish died in her sleep.

As part of the fiftieth anniversary festivities in 1958 the hospital was planning a new maternity wing which was to celebrate Rebecca Parrish's dedication and vision when she opened her one-room clinic. When the news of Dr. Parrish's death came all activities stopped as people remembered her in a thanksgiving service. Then they continued working feverishly, as more gifts arrived in honor of Rebecca. The day of the anniversary came, and the new and complete maternity section was dedicated as the "Rebecca Parrish Pavilion," with the wall plaque,

Rebecca Parrish Pavilion
In Appreciation of Her Years
of Sacrificial Service for
Mothers and Babies of
The Philippines

Today the Mary Johnston Hospital is one of the main hospitals in Manila, and is well-known for its Christian care. Its literature states that it "continues to pursue the mission of Dr. Parrish, which is to reach everyone with the message of life in Christ."[16]

We may believe that, when Rebecca Parrish's life on earth ended our Savior said of her, "She has done a beautiful thing for me."

It was 1945, World War II had ended, and Tena Holkeboer was on her way back to China, where she had been a missionary teacher for more than twenty years.

Four years earlier, Tena had been one of the American missionaries who had been advised by the American government to leave her mission post for a furlough because of the war. After her furlough ended war still raged and usual travel routes were blocked. When she learned that she would have to travel in a round-about way from her home in Holland, Michigan, USA, to Gulangyu (Kulangsu), in Southeast China this news did not stop her. She decided to go ahead, as she was anxious about the people she had left behind in China and wanted to help.

Along with other missionaries who were on their way back after the enforced furlough, Tena was delayed first in Portugal, then in Africa and again in India. Here she stayed at her church's mission and utilized her waiting time by teaching in the mission school. Waiting month after month was discouraging, and Tena followed the international news impatiently, looking for a way to return to her post at the girls' school in Gulangyu.

When news came that she'd be permitted to fly to Shanghai on a military plane Tena quickly put her belongings together. Shanghai was still some 200 kilometers away from Gulangyu, but at least it was in China. Excitedly Tena boarded the plane, not realizing that she was embarking on an agonizing journey of some fifteen days.

At last Tena reached Gulangyu, China. She had been so anxious to return to her mission community and her work; however, she soon found that conditions had changed for the Chinese as well as for Christian missionaries. Life was very different from pre-war days and Tena would need to make adjustments to mission work with a new focus.

"She Became the Tiger of the School!"
Tena Holkeboer (1895–1965)

The story of the earliest Protestant missions to China is fascinating, and a significant part of the whole story of western Protestant missions to Asia. With few exceptions, Protestant missions did not begin until nearly two hundred years after the Reformation in 1517. Little by little, as European explorers reached Asian areas where they could buy spices, and eventually colonize people, European Christians developed an interest in bringing the gospel to faraway places. William Carey, an English Baptist, read and studied the world map and was a trailblazing pioneer in Protestant missions to Asia. When the Dutch colonized what is now Indonesia they established the first Protestant church in the "Spice Islands" (the Maluku Islands) simply by removing the statues from a small church which Roman Catholic Portuguese had built and initiating Protestant worship services. But China?

Well before the year AD 1000 Christian missionaries had accompanied Nestorian merchants from Syria and West Persia along the Silk Road, and attempted to evangelize the Chinese. Another group of missionaries, Roman Catholic Jesuits, had reached Beijing via a different route around AD 1600. However, though they worked heroically, they impressed the men at the imperial court more with their knowledge of mathematics and science than with their Christian faith.

Traditionally the Chinese government was aloof, and only tolerated foreigners who were willing to perform the *ketou* ("kowtow"), the repeated prostrating before the emperor. But Europeans who came to China during and after the 1700s were unwilling to play the role of humble barbarians. And, though there was some limited international trade, officially China wanted no part of it.

When traders of the British East India Company discovered that there was a valuable market for high quality opium in China they transported it from Bengal (Bangladesh) to China and sold it at great profit. The Chinese government tried unsuccessfully to keep both opium trade and foreigners away. Only the Portuguese were permitted to stay on Chinese soil in the small colony of Macau, and they lived under strict Chinese rules governing their commerce and travel.[1]

Unscrupulous British traders brought so much opium to China that this illicit trade had become huge by the 1800s and became a tremendous problem. A shrewd local Chinese leader then fought back. He forced foreign merchants to give up their shipments of opium and ordered his men to throw them into the river. Next he burnt British warehouses in Guangzhou (Canton) where thousands of cases of opium were stored. Great Britain struck back, and the first Opium War was on. The British "won" this war and, under the Nanking Treaty, signed in 1842, China was forced to allow foreigners to live and work in five southeastern coastal cities. Xiamen (formerly called Amoy), the place near which Tena Holkeboer lived for many years, was one of these cities.[2] This city known as the "Elegant Gate," is located about 650 kilometers north of Hong Kong and was known for its deep harbor. As difficult as it was for China to make these concessions to foreign nations, more were to come, later.

For decades Protestants had waited eagerly to enter China with evangelistic work, and the first missionary to arrive was the Reverend David Abeel, who represented the Reformed Church in America. He arrived on 24 February 1842, even before the Nanking Treaty to end the Opium War went into effect.

David Abeel traveled first to Guangzhou (Canton) in 1829, and spent several years doing mission work in Southeast Asia. He saw the pitiful condition of many Asian women and became passionate about helping to provide an education for girls and women in the hope that this would improve their standard of life. He helped found the *Society for Promoting Female Education in the East* in England, and wrote five books on the subject. Undoubtedly his presence in Xiamen (Amoy) helped to start the educational mission there.

In a letter home, dated 1 March 1842, and sent from Xiamen, Rev. Abeel explained that, when he came to China, it had taken seventeen days to reach Xiamen from Hong Kong, a distance of some 500 kilometers. When the ship arrived in Xiamen it docked at the opium market — not a safe place for a white foreigner so soon after the Opium War! He immediately went to the British consul's office, for he knew that the consul's wife was a Christian, and he was warmly welcomed. Xiamen was a dangerous place for foreigners, and the consul helped Rev. Abeel to find a house on a nearby small rocky island, Gulangyu (Kulangsu), less than a kilometer from Xiamen. This island had been "taken over by the British army" and offered more safety. The existing buildings on the island had been badly damaged during the war, but Rev. Abeel wrote, "We only feel profoundly grateful and our hearts burn with fervor."[3]

Gulangyu was the island on which Tena Holkeboer would live and work years later. David Abeel was in poor health, he returned home sick after two years and died of tuberculosis in 1846. Though he did not see one new believer, he helped lay the foundation for future Christian work.

Within two years some English missionaries arrived and joined the Americans. Soon there were baptisms, a community of believers came into being and a church building was in the process of being constructed, the first Protestant church in China. The missionary in charge of the building project went to Hong Kong to purchase lights for the church building. On his way back the ship he was on was wrecked, and he drowned. Thus the dedication service of the new church building became, at the same time, a memorial service for the man who lost his life buying lights.[4]

It is a testimony to the faith of those early Christians that, at a time when there were as yet a mere two believers, they designed a church building large enough to accommodate five hundred.[5] As more people became Christians a second congregation was established, then a third. This third congregation was on Gulangyu island, where Tena would live, years later.

The evangelistic workers were joined by missionary teachers and physicians who came to Xiamen and Gulangyu to teach at schools and to treat the sick at clinics and hospitals, all newly established. By the time Tena Holkeboer came to Gulangyu at the end of 1920 the Amoy mission had several outstations with schools and clinics. The Chinese in the area who could afford it sent their children to the mission school for a western-style education, while patients, most of them poor, crowded the hospitals and medical clinics. There always seemed to be room on the mission compound for poor students and patients, and many received help.

When Tena Holkeboer was born in Holland, Michigan, USA during a stormy January night in 1895 nobody could have guessed that this baby girl would grow up to live in Asia for some forty years; that she'd fly in an army plane and be so cold that even the seven dresses she wore all at once could not warm her; that she'd be aboard a ship attacked by pirates; or that Bob Pierce, founder of World Vision, would say one day that he considered her one of the greatest missionaries of the century.[6] Yet all these became true.

Tena was the first of eight children in a Dutch-American home where the parents taught their children the Christian life. "It was in the family's genes to be a Kingdom worker," a cousin said of her.[7] While she was a student Tena joined the school's mission club. She loved studying, graduated with honors from prep school, taught school, and helped the family with her salary. It was good that Tena had opportunity to become a teacher because, as one of her sisters quipped, she seemed to have little talent for housework.[8] Tena was known for her spellbinding story telling, and for being an excellent speaker. A century ago few women spoke in public meetings, but Tena preached sermons in evangelistic meetings, even in church services.

Years later Tena wrote that, while she was teaching, she struggled with the idea of becoming a missionary. She wrote that, while reading her Bible,

I came upon the passage about loving father and mother more than God. I stopped, and asked myself if I loved him more than my parents. I knew that I loved them, but how could I know who was first in my life? I could not answer for a long time.... It was two years and then finally God's grace enabled me to say, "If it is thy will I'm willing to go."[9]

One day she was personally challenged to become a missionary. Having listened to a guest speaker at school about God's call to mission, she approached the speaker and talked with him about her thoughts. He encouraged her, and even offered to pay for her studies. This was an exciting proposal, and Tena talked about it with her parents. Her father, with a typical Dutch attitude, said that, if she really wanted to become a missionary, the family would somehow manage to bring up the money for her studies. This was Tena's signal to move ahead, and she resigned from the school where she had been teaching for three years.

It was a wonderful surprise when, the very next day, one of her sisters landed a job, and her father was also given a pay increase. The family was overwhelmed with thankfulness when they discovered that the salary which Tena's sister would earn, and her father's pay increase totaled exactly what Tena would have earned during the next school year.[10] Father and sister were willing to help, and Tena happily enrolled in college.

When Tena was nineteen years old her father died of a rare kidney disease. Because her mother had eight children, and the youngest was not yet ten, Tena doubted that she would be able to stay in school, but the family managed. Both Tena and a brother were able to complete their college studies. After graduation in 1920 she was ready to go. The Reformed Church of America was looking for teachers for China. As her own church, the Christian Reformed Church in North America, did not have a mission program in China at that time, Tena joined the mission team of the Reformed Church in America (RCA), and was appointed to the "Iok Tek Amoy Girls' Middle School" in Gulangyu

(Kulangsu), near the city of Amoy (today's Xiamen), in Southeast China. This was the third girls' school to be established in China.

It seemed harsh for Tena to leave home. After all, her mother was a widow, and could use the help of her eldest. Yet, when others asked, "How can you let her go, you need her!" Tena's mother always replied, "If the Lord needs her, I'll let her go."[11]

It was September 1920, and the train whistle announced that it was time to leave. Her younger sister Chris clutched Tena's hand tightly, reluctant to let go. Her mother was stoic, and cried only after Tena could no longer see her. But Chris remembers that, sitting by the kitchen stove at night, her mother would cry, and Chris would say, "Why, mother, why did you let her go?"[12]

There were several considerations involved in the huge undertaking of going to China. For a young woman, it meant that she'd probably never marry. Tena did some thinking about that before she left home and indeed had opportunities to marry. A nice, jolly neighbor boy, also a Hope College student, seemed to like her, Chris said. Tena had marriage proposals from others, but did not accept. Tena reasoned that if she were to marry she'd have children, and she'd have to stay at home. She was convinced that she ought not to burden herself by marrying, for she wished to be able to devote herself completely to mission work.[13]

The journey to China lasted four weeks. First there was the train trip to California, then the ship, via Honolulu, Yokohama and Shanghai, to Hong Kong. From there another ship would take her and Jean Nienhuis,[14] a new missionary nurse with whom she traveled, to Amoy.

Tena's mother kept all the letters the family received, the envelope of the first one is marked that it was written aboard ship on the way to China, and mailed in Honolulu.

> *There were several considerations involved in the huge undertaking of going to China. For a young woman, it meant that she'd probably never marry.*

It begins, "Dear, dear mother, brothers and sisters, I thought that I had always keenly appreciated my home and think I did too, but never has it seemed quite so precious as now."[15] Three days later another letter, in the same mail packet from Honolulu, is also optimistic, but has the request, "Be sure to give me glimpses of home when you write." And in the seventh letter, still aboard the ship, "Don't fail to have someone write each week."[16]

Tena knew that God was sending her on her way to China to be a missionary, and went with enthusiasm.

Dr. Tena Holkeboer, long-time Christian educator in China and Southeast Asia. This likeness of her hangs in a hallway of Hope Christian School in Manila, which she helped to establish. *Photo courtesy Cecilia A. [Holkeboer] Mereness, niece of Dr. Holkeboer.*

Though she must have tried to learn what she could about China before she left home, she had no idea what would await her, or that her life would take many unexpected twists and turns. She probably knew something about Xiamen, and its neighboring Gulangyu, a tiny island only a five-minute ferry ride distant, where she would be living. However, when she arrived in China her first impressions were quite different from what she had expected.

Tena's letters home tell of the warm welcome she and her companion received from the other missionaries in Xiamen, and how they were assigned a place in a house where there already were some single missionary women. This made for "instant family." As for all missionaries, the first months were spent mostly in studying the language, and in learning about her new environment. She wrote that she was happy to be invited to share the house with her new acquaintances.

Tena learned to speak Chinese fluently, both Mandarin, the national language, and Amoy, the language used in the Xiamen area. Nearly seventy years later several of her former students remembered this about her.

Tena had been appointed principal of the Amoy Girls' Middle School, as well as teacher. It took little time to learn to love the people around her, and she cared deeply for the girls. She knew that the Chinese are a disciplined people, thrifty and hardworking, and that suited Tena, for this was her own background as well. The Chinese also recognized Tena as an excellent teacher and a fascinating speaker. Tena loved doing evangelistic work, and did her best in the school's chapel and in talking with the students, most of whom came from non-Christian homes. In line with Rev. Abeel's thought, she hoped to educate girls to develop their talents. Trusting that at least some of the girls would become Christians, she hoped to train them to be evangelists ("Bible women"), pastor's wives, or to lead other useful lives as Christian wives and mothers.

The mail carrier regularly took birthday cards to Tena's nephews and nieces in the USA. Although she lived far away they were dear to her, and she took souvenirs for them when she went home on furlough. She also showed her consideration to her mother, organizing a big family birthday party once, when she was in the USA.

At the same time she could be painfully candid. One of her nieces remembers, "At times Aunt Tena made sharp remarks about things such as people's habits or even the color of their wallpaper, and sometimes pushed others away by her abruptness."[17] Her words could leave an indelible memory, such as when she visited a friend and frankly asked how the friend's spiritual pilgrimage was. This friend's young son, about eight years old, felt awed by this question, and was stunned when Tena Holkeboer turned to him and said, "Edward, you will be a missionary."[18]

Tena's first furlough, in 1924, gave her definite, planned opportunities to tell people in the USA about China and the challenges there. She told the people that, though life might be comfortable for the wealthy and old established families, missionaries saw different things in the countryside. The first "big road" of some 45 kilometers, from Xiamen to the provincial capital of Zhangzhou (Changchow) caused excitement in the 1920s, although bus travel was still arduous for travelers as they bounced about on the wooden seats. River travel was more comfortable, but it required a whole day to go downstream to Zhangzhou, and two days to return upriver to Xiamen.

Poor people lived in mud houses. Women led burdensome lives, were often maltreated, and had few options in life. Children had sicknesses that were left untreated. And yet it was said that "the pursuit of wisdom and passion for beauty are the two poles of the Chinese mind." The Chinese did not know the Lord of the Bible, and wisdom was understood to be that of the ancient teachers, such as Lao Zi of Daoism, and Confucius of Confucianism. Pioneer preachers, who had studied the classics before they became Christians, often quoted sayings of the sages as they explained Bible texts.[19]

Tena herself remembered the decade after her first furlough as a difficult time, with "an atmosphere which was definitely hostile to the gospel."[20] And yet, though the Amoy Girls' Middle School was clearly a Christian institution, enrollment grew to more than two hundred and fifty girls in 1935.[21] Besides her work at school Tena often helped by preaching in various mission outreaches, but there were few visible results during these years.

After the important international Jerusalem Conference in 1928 the National Christian Council of China resolved to make a concerted effort to double church membership in the country over the next five years. Everywhere in China Christians were asked to pray, "Lord, revive thy Church, begin with me." However, in spite of fervent prayers there was only a modest response, and both Chinese and foreign Christians were disappointed.

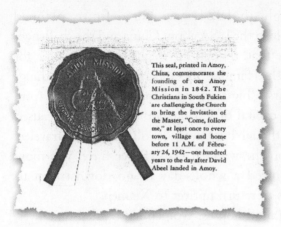

This seal, printed in Amoy, China, commemorates the founding of our Amoy Mission in 1842. The Christians in South Fukien are challenging the Church to bring the invitation of the Master, "Come, follow me," at least once to every town, village and home before 11 A.M. of February 24, 1942—one hundred years to the day after David Abeel landed in Amoy.

In spite of war conditions Chinese Christians responded to the challenge of the church, and were encouraged by it. The seal shown here symbolized the call to local Christians to bring the good news to the entire area of South Fujian province as part of their celebration of Protestant Centennial. Most of the missionaries, including Tena Holkeboer, had been evacuated from the area when the Centennial Celebration took place in 1942. *Photo courtesy the Western Theological Seminary Collection at The Joint Archives of Holland [Michigan].*

Then, during the year after this movement ended the Lord answered the many prayers, and sent revival in the province of Fujian (Fukien), especially after 1934, when John Sung came to speak at a series of meetings. Evangelical Christians throughout Southeast Asia know the name of this spirited young preacher, a man who spoke with conviction and charisma.

Born into a poor pastor's family and helped by missionaries to study overseas, John Sung earned high scientific academic honors, but wandered away from the Christian faith and returned to the faith after a harrowing experience and determined to preach Christ from then on, becoming a tireless Christian speaker. John Sung only lived to the age of forty, but used his years as preacher to lead thousands of people to Christ, first in China, then throughout Southeast Asia. Wherever John Sung went people turned or returned to Christ. He often held "One-month Bible School" sessions. These consisted of thirty days of teaching, in which he taught from the beginning of the Bible to the end. Each day he spoke three times, at least two hours at a time. His unflagging enthusiasm for the gospel became his trademark, though his relentless schedule was at times a challenge to his listeners.

He first came to Xiamen in 1934. For some time he returned annually, and spoke to large audiences. Each visit was welcomed, and resulted in numerous opportunities for Tena to do follow-up work among her students. She described the resulting blessings among the students as the "miracles of grace."[22]

Tena Holkeboer herself attended one of John Sung's conferences, and was one in a crowd of more than one thousand five hundred people. She wrote her supporters that she experienced her greatest personal spiritual experience when she saw groups of Chinese from all areas of Fujian province and Southeast Asia introduced to the audience, and then heard each group sing a favorite hymn.[23]

At school Tena was busy with her Bible classes, chapel talks, personal conversations with students and administrative duties. Yet she always found time to preach in mission churches, to be the leader of the Sunday school program, and to single out those who needed some encouragement.

Fourteen years after the class of 1936 graduated Tena Holkeboer visited Manila. Several former students who had moved to the Philippines gave her a party. Tena asked about the alumnae of 1936, mentioning both family and first names of the girls. At that same party, speaking with one of her former students, Tena was not afraid to be candid. Knowing that this former student, now forty years old, had left the Christian faith, Tena kindly but openly, said, "Have you ever thought about where you will go after this life? Go home and think about it." The woman went home, thought about Tena's words and returned to her previous Christian ways.

In November 2000 several of Tena's former students met together, now senior citizens and residents of Manila. Seven ladies remembered Miss Holkeboer from her Gulangyu years. Speaking freely on condition that, to protect their privacy, their names would not be mentioned, nearly all mentioned that Miss Holkeboer was very strict. One day some thirty girls were to take a government exam, but ran away from school when they were frightened by other students. Later each one was confronted and reprimanded by Tena, and all of them were marked down for their behavior on their next report card. "She easily earned both the fear and respect of the students." She was also loving. One alumna recalled that, because of many responsibilities at home, she slept in one day and was late. Running into school, who should she see standing in the hallway but Miss Holkeboer! The teacher understood the situation and gently helped the girl enter her classroom without getting into trouble.

These alumnae appreciated it that Tena spoke to students privately when there was a problem. She knew that Asians lose face when scolded publicly. It was evident that she cared not only for the girls' spiritual and academic welfare, but also for their daily interests. The alumnae recalled Tena's able teaching. She could explain the Bible lessons clearly and was eager to bring up the girls as "worthy Christians."

Her memory was remarkable. Not only was she fluent in Mandarin and Amoy but, like the educated Chinese, she could quote from the classical sayings. She was "humble, always wanting to learn."

Once, before she went on furlough, she helped two boys to obtain a study grant in the USA. She introduced them at her church in Holland, Michigan, and told the congregation something about the mission work in Gulangyu, not even mentioning herself or the part she had in it. "She was truly humble and modest."[24]

The women chuckled as they recalled Tena's nickname: Miss Ho. The name "Holkeboer," when pronounced in a Chinese manner, becomes "Ho Ko Po," and when students said just the part "Ho" in a slightly different way, it sounded like the Chinese word for "tiger." Laughingly, one of her former students said, "She became the tiger of the school!" For years students called her that, "Miss Ho, Miss Tiger." "Upon meeting her one might think she was like a tiger. But really, she was so kind and good."[25]

Already in 1935, in her letters home Tena mentioned growing political tensions. Many Chinese in the Xiamen area feared a Japanese invasion, even occupation. Perhaps these tensions added to the response to the Christian work, but the current spiritual renewal caused Tena to tell her friends that this time was for her "the happiest period of all the years spent in China."[26]

The name "Holkeboer," when pronounced in a Chinese manner, becomes "Ho Ko Po," and when students said just the part "Ho" in a slightly different way, it sounded like the Chinese word for "tiger."

Two Chinese women became lifelong friends. Carol Chen was a friend already in the early years. She became a teacher, and Tena was able to arrange a study leave in the USA for her. Earning a master's degree, Carol later replaced Tena as principal of the Amoy Girls' High School. Christina Wang was another dear teacher friend. Tena and Christina worked together for many years, and Christina accompanied Tena when the Communist government made Tena leave China.

The Sinkoe Church, the first Protestant church in China, merged with two other pioneer churches in 1931 to become the Xiamen Christian Trinity Church. This photo shows the foundation stone of the new building, completed in 1934. *Photo courtesy Amanda Shao Tan.*

Throughout the 1930s Chinese Christians in South Fujian province faced great hardships from Communists. They were forbidden to worship publicly. Yet, some of the faithful met in small groups. A missionary report of 1934 reads,

> It was with mixed emotions that I faced the group of Christians on Sunday morning in their meeting-place, an old ancestral hall. They had come in from the villages, some as far as ten miles, to attend the services. In the back seat sat the Bible Woman. She it was who had remained at her post during the years of terror and had brought comfort to the more timid souls and, when threatened had borne this brave testimony: "You may do with me as you will, but I belong to Jesus." Chiang Ho, the deacon, was also there. Lands and fields were his no more. He knew what it was to sit behind Communist prison bars and to feel the smart of their rods. There were many others whose faith had been sorely tried. They were as those who had come out of 'the great tribulation' and had remained faithful.[27]

Japan did invade South China and occupy Southern Fujian, and its army occupied Xiamen in 1938. Many of the residents fled, as did Pu

Life seemed hopeless for Jin-gi and his widowed mother before someone introduced them to a kind Christian. Thanks to help from Tena Holkeboer and other missionaries Jin-gi went to school and learned about God. He became a believer and later a pastor. In March 1941 he, his wife and children posed with his benefactor. *Reprinted with permission from Tena Holkeboer: God's Bridge, or the Story of Jin-gi, 2nd ed. (Grand Rapids, MI: Wm. B. Eerdmans, 1945), frontispiece.*

Hai and his family (see the story of Tong Tjien Nio in chapter 12), thousands of them to Gulangyu. After the bombing of Pearl Harbor on 8 December 1939, the Japanese sequestered the Amoy Girls' Middle School for some time.

Already before this, the American government had "urged that all whose presence in China was not essential should return to America." Because of this Tena Holkeboer, together with several other missionary families, left Gulangyu in 1941. Late that year communication between Gulangyu and the mainland was cut off. Some of the remaining missionaries were interned by the Japanese for some time, and in January 1942 the Japanese government took over the entire mission school compound.[28]

Partly to be helpful to the author, partly to publicize life and missions in China, Tena Holkeboer edited and rewrote the life story which a student gave her. In the little book *God's Bridge, or the Story of Jin-gi*[29] she gives the true account of a sickly nine-year old boy, Jin-gi. The story begins after the death of the boy's father when the boy and his mother have been turned out of the house of his wealthy grandfather, who wants nothing to do with his son's widow and her ailing little boy.

They are destitute. A traditional woman with bound feet, the young mother prays to the Chinese gods that there will be a bridge prepared so she and Jin-gi can cross it and live. In God's providence the mother and son meet a Chinese Christian, become believers, and after the boy is given opportunity to study, he decides to become a pastor. Having become a Christian, and received help in raising her son, the mother is happy as long as she lives. Soon after the Japanese come and occupy Xiamen in the late 1930s, Jin-gi, now a young man, graduates, marries and becomes a father. For a while he works as a hospital chaplain, then he accepts the request to be the pastor of a church in Xiamen. At this point in the young man's life the book ends. The story is true to life, and the flyleaf of the book shows a photograph of Jin-gi and his wife and two children, together with Tena Holkeboer.

Soon after Jin-gi entered the ministry the Chinese church of the region celebrated its centennial, and Jin-gi was asked to research and record the history of the church from the time the Rev. David Abeel arrived in Xiamen. In the history which Jin-gi wrote he explained why he accepted the call to be pastor of the church in these words, "At this war time, the ministry of our church is more than ever important, but the workers are few. Although I am a useless man, yet if God will use me, how can I decline it. I will offer myself as a living sacrifice for the ministry of God."[30]

Tena was eager to get back to China, though the war had not ended, but she had to wait for permission to return. She expected to receive her travel document in August 1943, but did not get it until 2 December 1943, and then traveled with others who were trying to go back to their mission posts. The wait from August to December was only the beginning of numerous delays, frustrating and difficult. She knew that war meant hardship for the Chinese, and was impatient to go back and do what she could to help. The day before she left Michigan Tena sent her supporters a proposed schedule which would bring her back to Gulangyu three months later. In fact, it took a whole lot longer before she reached Gulangyu. Wartime travel was nearly impossible!

Tena's regular letters to her family and supporters gave many details of her experiences. They began with a boat trip to Lisbon, Portugal, because Portugal was neutral during World War II. Here she met other missionaries who were waiting to travel further. It was difficult to be patient, especially when, as Tena wrote, "My heart is much with my colleagues in China."[31] From Lisbon the group traveled to Portuguese East Africa. After another wait, three months this time, then a train took them to Durban in South Africa, and from there Tena sailed to Calcutta, India. Not having heard from home for six months, it was refreshing to receive mail — even if it was five months old.

What a disappointment it must have been to hear that the American consul was not permitting women to travel to China. Tena had to bide her time. She contacted RCA missionaries in South India so she might use her time well and work at the mission school there temporarily. Tena was anxious about the people in China. It was so frustrating to meet people who had been forced to leave war-torn China and were on their way home.

Tena enjoyed her work at the school in India, but was always prepared to return to China. She wrote less often to her "friends in the homeland" when, after one and a half years she was still in South India. She did not know then that she'd be there for another year and would only leave India in December 1945. By then World War II had ended, but there was still much unrest, travel was hazardous and irregular.

Suddenly a travel permit came from the military authorities for Tena to fly to Shanghai on a military plane. Good news! It was a cold trip across the Himalayan Mountains, then to Guangzhou (Canton) and finally to Shanghai. Anticipating the cold, Tena decided to wear all seven of her dresses, one over another. The trip was long and arduous, but Tena was overjoyed to have covered "at least 3,000 miles in less than twenty-four hours."[32] She wrote,

> Always when I dreamed of the moment when I would once more set my foot on China's soil, I was sure I would be just thrilled with gratitude. But the first hours were not thrilling at all. My whole attention was centered, on the one hand, on my cold body — my very blood seemed to be congealed — and, on the other hand, was the need of finding a place to lay my head for the night.[33]

At last she was in China!

Traveling from Shanghai was another harrowing experience. Plans were for the ship to go as far as Fujian's provincial capital, Zhangzhou. Tena's bunk on the ship was eighteen inches wide, with two men sleeping in the somewhat wider bunk above her. The six days on this stretch of the journey included a fire aboard ship, a storm worse than Tena had ever encountered, a shootout with four pirate junks and then a four-hour sailboat ride to Foozhou, where the sailors had decided to drop anchor, rather than continue to Zhangzhou. The last leg of this trip was an hour's rickshaw ride which brought Tena to the mission hospital, where she knew she could stay. Tena was cold, had not eaten for three days, and not undressed for six days. As she entered the mission hospital she noticed Christmas decorations. Suddenly she realized that it was Christmas Eve.

A warm welcome, a hot bath and dinner, and the sound of missionary colleagues in the mission hospital singing Christmas carols were magnificent aids to her recuperation from the experiences of the past week. Tena wrote her friends that her greatest comfort during the distressing days of travel had been that of remembering the many hymns she had learned at home. While she could not recall many songs from school and church, she remembered the words of nearly all the hymns her family used to sing, and knew this to be a valuable heritage. "Please remember to teach your children the songs and hymns," she urged her relatives.[34]

Covering 30 to 40 kilometers a day in sedan chairs, followed by another boat ride, Tena and her companion covered the 200 kilometers to Amoy in six days. They continued to Gulangyu, and arrived there 9 January 1946.

The war was finished, and Tena soon noticed that many changes were taking place.

"At last I am back in my China home — after an absence of four years and nine months!" sighed Tena in a letter from Gulangyu.[35] She noted that the people on Gulangyu island had suffered much during the war.

There was not enough food and no oil for fuel, but tremendous tension. Numbers of people were imprisoned, some were tortured by Japanese soldiers, and many had escaped out of fear that they would be killed. Tena also heard many stories about God's care during those troubled times.

After the war ended food and supplies became more easily available and people began to regain their strength. Tena saw that nearly all mission buildings had been damaged, looted or destroyed. Fortunately for Tena, some of her friends had removed a few belongings from her house early on, and now returned her bed and bedding, some chairs and a few odds and ends. Three Taiwanese families had occupied her house; they had kept rabbits, goats and chickens inside, and when they left they took most of Tena's furniture with them, leaving the house nearly bare and a mess. Tena ends this letter,

> It has been a long hard road back to Amoy, but I can today thank God for every step of the way in which he has led me. Having known trouble, fear, and uncertainty, I can better understand and sympathize with those who have known fear, uncertainty and disappointment for four long hard years. Had my path been easy and prosperous, I should not have been fit to take my place here. He knew what I needed and led me back to his place for me — and all the way thru his presence and comfort never failed.[36]

There were countless challenges in re-opening the mission school and hospital on Gulangyu island. During the nine years of wartime church and mission supplies had dissipated; inflation forced many church workers to earn an income elsewhere, so that they were less involved in the church; many people were still malnourished; there was not even one physician who could do major surgery; and cholera and the plague were rampant. While other missionaries were still away Tena was assigned regular pastoral duties at one of the mission stations in the Amoy area. Her days were filled with teaching, evangelistic meetings, youth conferences, retreats and church services.

An American visitor who came to Gulangyu in 1947 to observe the mission work saw that Tena stretched the mission budget to the utmost, as well as her own strength. While he was at her house the doorbell rang. Tena answered and when she returned he was baffled to see a crying infant in her arms. An orphan had been left with her. In her typical direct way, she deposited the child in the visitor's arms and said, "What are you going to do about her?" The visitor replied, "All I have on me is five dollars." Unruffled, Tena said, "That's fine," and added, "When you get home, send me five dollars every month. I promise you I'll take care of this child." And she took the child back in her arms.

The visitor kept his promise, so did Tena. The visitor was Bob Pierce, and this happening eventually led to the founding of World Vision, the Christian worldwide relief and development organization which today brings relief to millions of people living in dire conditions.[37]

Inspired by a Chinese government wartime program, Tena had an idea. At the start of the war Chinese young people were recruited by the government, and set to work in rural areas. They used nationalistic songs, speeches and drama to encourage people to be loyal to their country. This had proved to be very helpful in maintaining morale during the difficult years of war. Tena wondered if this same idea could not be used in the church.

Her new venture, called "Bible Institute," began small. Tena and two women workers went for one month to a village where there was a small church. In the daytime they held literacy and Bible classes in the church, and visited homes. In the evening they taught the Christian faith, Christian family basics, hygiene, and other topics. Throughout their month in the village they tried to start classes in Christian living for everyone, and to train potential leaders. After a month Tena and her colleagues moved to another village, and did the same there for a month. They planned to return to each village three years in a row, spending one month each time. They prayed

> *An orphan had been left with her.*
> *In her typical direct way,*
> *she deposited the child*
> *in the visitor's arms and said,*
> *"What are you going to do about her?"*

that the villagers would be strengthened in their faith by this support and inspired to raise their own volunteers to reach out to others.

Tena did this work for a year. Carol Chen, the principal of the Amoy Girls' Middle School, then went to the USA for further studies, and Tena became acting principal on Gulangyu. Little did Tena realize that there was another bend in the road ahead.

The next year Tena was in the USA again for a furlough, and was able to take along the two students for whom she had secured a study grant at her alma mater, Hope College, in Holland, Michigan. One of these, Wesley Shao, later spent many years as a pastor in the Philippines, and worked with Tena there. He remembers her with great admiration and respect. While in Holland, Michigan, Tena was given a great distinction by Hope College when she was awarded an honorary Doctor of Laws degree.

Dr. Tena Holkeboer's personal papers include a diary of this furlough, and it shows that she had two hundred and thirty-one speaking appointments during her months in North America. It is interesting to see that she copied both English and Chinese poems into her diary. Her relatives remember that she commonly spoke Chinese with her friend Jean Nienhuis, with whom she had traveled to China back in 1920. The women always spoke Chinese together, and when the words came rolling out of Tena's mouth, especially when she was in telephone conversation, her relatives chuckled and laughed out loud to hear her converse in Chinese.[38]

In South Fujian Province meanwhile, conflict between Communists and Nationalists escalated. For some weeks there was heavy bombing, usually at night. Finally, in October 1949 the Nationalists in Xiamen and Gulangyu surrendered to Communist rule, and Chinese Christians became a target for severe persecution.[39] It was not long before open Christian missions in China came to an end, and all missionaries had to leave.

Wesley Shao stressed that one reason why the Amoy Girls' Middle School was pivotal was that the school's graduates spread throughout

Southeast Asia.[40] The school had been founded to help the future of the Church in China, but during the 1930s and 1940s countless Chinese left their country. Numerous graduates of the school had made a new start in Malaysia, Singapore, Taiwan, Indonesia and the Philippines, and established churches there. The Girls' School graduates had opportunity to give leadership in these new communities. When Tena realized that she'd have to leave China, she wondered what her next task should be. Soon she began to see the challenge of visiting former students and other Christians who had moved to other Southeast Asian areas, to encourage them. Of course there were other missionaries in those places and they had studied local languages, but they did not master the Chinese language. Tena was fluent in both Chinese and the dialect of South Fujian, and was ideally suited to give spiritual guidance to overseas Chinese Christians.

Tena Holkeboer and Christina Wang were warmly welcomed by Chinese friends in the Philippines and in Indonesia, in 1951 and1952. The people especially appreciated Tena's Chinese preaching in the churches and her personal visits with the elderly, with whom she interacted in a personal way.

As she could not return to China Tena found another new challenge. She received several offers and requests, and decided to work in Manila, where Chinese Christians were about to establish a Christian high school. Tena's experiences in administration in the Chinese community were significant, and she gladly helped, even naming the school "Hope," after her alma mater Hope College. By 2005 this school has grown to a student body of about one thousand three hundred students. Christina Wang became the principal of the high school,[41] while Dr. Holkeboer was the dean and taught English. This is where she earned the reputation of being the "tiger of the school," because of her strictness. Her former students cannot forget this part of Tena's personality.

For ten years Dr. Holkeboer worked in the Philippines, and was active in education and evangelism. Her enthusiastic letters to friends gave many details of her work and the people around her, but she rarely wrote about herself, or her own struggles. Yet, during this time, she was thousands of miles away when her mother, whom she loved dearly, and her youngest sister, the family's darling, died. She herself went to the USA temporarily for surgery because of breast cancer. These were matters which were rarely mentioned, and Tena's nieces hardly remember that their aunt was sick. People just didn't talk about these things, they insist, once the surgery was over and done with, it was never mentioned again.[42] Tena did write about the plight of the Christians in China, who often risked their freedom when they openly spoke of their faith, and of whom several fell away from the Christian life.

Another thing people did not talk about was that in the Philippines Dr. Holkeboer was involved in freeing several girls from white slavery.[43] These girls came from impoverished Chinese migrant families, were taken by ruthless slave dealers, and sold as prostitutes in the city. Dr. Holkeboer cared for several of these girls who found their way to her home, begging for help. She herself risked physical harm when she appeared in court on their behalf.

Dr. Holkeboer did write about one of these girls in detail when she asked her friends for special prayers. This girl had been one of Tena's students in Gulangyu. She was brought to Manila and put into a brothel. Trying to escape, she was recaptured, suffered starvation, beatings and cruel punishments and, when she was found to be pregnant, she was even given some poison, but did not die. Months later, when she was about to give birth, she was in such dangerous condition that her keepers, who feared troubles with the law if she were found dead, brought her to a small hospital. Here a church worker found her, but no Chinese in Manila dared help her, for fear of the brutal white slavers. Dr. Holkeboer saw no way but to take the girl and her baby into her home. They received round-the-clock police protection for some time. Christians helped support the girl and her child, and eventually a family cared for them. Her ordeals had disturbed the young woman emotionally so much that she had lost her ability to speak and to walk, and she needed frequent hospitalization. Overwhelmed with the girl's misery Tena committed her to a hospital for mental care, and then asked friends around the world to pray for the young woman.

In 1959 Dr. Holkeboer thanked her friends for their prayers and was able to report that the young woman had regained the ability both to walk and to speak, and was trying to earn a living for herself and her child. Dr. Holkeboer again requested her friends to pray that the girl would become a Christian believer. In this letter she asked that this woman's story not be published, as the white slavers were still active. Now, nearly half a century later, the family has given permission for this story to be told.

Exactly forty years after she first left home for Asia, Dr. Holkeboer returned to the USA to retire. But before leaving her beloved Chinese people she again traveled around Southeast Asia to encourage the Chinese in various countries to live fruitful Christian lives. For two months she visited Chinese churches and former students in Vietnam, Singapore, Malaysia, Thailand and Burma while she spent time with believers, gave counsel and preached. Following that she traveled to other areas where she had worked in the past.

In her last letter to her friends Tena explained that she was thankful for having had the privilege of bringing the gospel to the Chinese people, then added, "Needless to say, I leave a big part of my heart on this side of the world, but the work must be passed on to younger hearts and younger hands."[44] Then she journeyed to Holland, Michigan, and moved in with her sister Gertrude who was equally gifted. Gertrude had focused her career on her immediate environment, and had worked hard as she taught, preached and evangelized in her home area during the years Tena was away.

Dr. Holkeboer continued her interest in and concern for Chinese Christians during her retirement. She corresponded with friends, and was familiar with the sacrifices many of them made for their faith. She traveled to Asia once more to encourage her former students and friends. Everywhere she went she was received with open arms, flowers, words of thanks and an outpouring of love. She was seventy years old now, and it was time to rest. She returned to Holland, Michigan.

One evening Dr. Holkeboer went to her room to read her Bible and to pray. When her sister heard a noise and entered the room she saw that Tena had quietly died in her chair, her Bible had fallen on the floor.

We may believe that when Tena Holkeboer's life on earth ended, our Savior said of her, "She has done a beautiful thing for me."

The great majority of Indonesians are Muslims, though the nation's basic philosophy of *pancasila,* "five principles," offers freedom of religion. In every town and village there is a mosque for the faithful Muslims, but other faiths are also practiced. Actually, Islam is a latecomer among Indonesia's religions.

Long ago there was little writing and we know few details, but it is clear that Indonesia's earliest religion was animism. The people believed that spirits dwelled in the unseen places of nature, and had great powers. These guardian spirits, ancestors' spirits and many other forces in nature must be appeased with gifts. The *dukun* (the medicine man) conducted mysterious rituals at which sacrifices were made. A *slametan* (a sacrificial meal) was often held when one wished to remember and honor a loved one who had died, or when one began to build a house, or went on a trip. Ancient Javanese taught their people and entertained themselves with *wayang* (shadow puppets) who represented deceased ancestors. Everything religious was thought to be mysterious, and this idea has continued on Java to this day.

Around AD 400 Indians traders began to come to Indonesia, and brought Hindu ideas with them. Indonesians then began to assimilate Hinduism into their religion. Three hundred years later Indian merchants added Buddhist thought to religion in Indonesia, and there was more assimilation. *Wayang* presentations were artful and the ancient stories, with both original Javanese and Buddhist–Hindu teachings, were a powerful means of education. Architectural masterpieces were built in Central Java in the 800s. The Borobudur, a Buddhist structure with an abundance of Buddhist statuary, and the Prambanan, a skillful example of Hindu themes, are still visited daily by tourists who marvel at the artistic ability of so long ago.

Another religion came to Java in the form of Islam, in the 1300s. It, too, was incorporated into Javanese faith. Muslim *sufism* and mysticism harmonized with the Javanese ideas of the supernatural, and were incorporated in local religion. This is how native Javanese religion is today — a syncretism which includes concepts of animism, Hinduism, Buddhism, Islam, and even some other ideas.

Christian missionaries found many religious barriers to their message when they began to arrive in the 1600s. Christian concepts of love, humility and salvation earned on the Cross did not seem to fit with existing faiths. And yet, by God's grace, there were those who responded, and Christian churches came into existence. As happened elsewhere, Christian missionaries made mistakes; yet their preaching, medical, educational and social contributions, but perhaps even more notably, the exemplary lives of many of them, made an impact.

This was the world to which Dr. Geertruida J. Dreckmeier came in 1920.

Chapter Eleven

"Do it! Do it! Do it!"

Geertruida J. Dreckmeier (1895–1992)

It was always a delight when my mother allowed me to look at the family picture albums. I'd sit on the floor and I'd be very careful as I turned the pages with photographs of a time I could not remember, and of the place where I was born. The village in which we lived when I was a child, in the northern part of the Netherlands, looked so different from what I saw on the pictures in the albums.

Three of the photographs were my favorites. I often turned to the page with the picture of my missionary parents in Javanese dress, taken in the garden of their home in Indonesia.[1] The second one I liked was one showing three people in front of a house: My father in his tropical white suit, and my mother and another woman, both wearing broad-rimmed hats and light dresses which reached nearly to their ankles. The other woman was holding a baby, and I never tired of my mother telling me that I was that baby, and that the photograph was taken on the day I was baptized, when I was three weeks old. Then there was the photograph of the woman standing beside an empty bed, a woman in a plain dress with a lace collar, a woman with a stern face. That was our family doctor. Mother told me that this woman came to our house the day I was born, to help her.

Because I was very young I never questioned the fact that the doctor was a woman, though I was born in the mid 1930s, when female physicians were not so common. I had no idea that she lived through the historical eras of the end of the Dutch colonial age, Japanese wartime detention camps, and the Indonesian struggle for independence.

Many years later my mother explained to me that this physician, Dr. G. J. Dreckmeier, was an exceptional woman.

Geertruida Johanna Dreckmeier[2] (she was nicknamed Truus, with the "uu" pronounced like the German ü, as in "für") was born in the Netherlands near the end of the nineteenth century, and was the second daughter in a family of five girls and one boy. Her parents' Christian faith was stressed in the home, and they were interested in worldwide missions. At one time her father had been a follower of John Nelson Darby and the Plymouth Brethren,[3] and the family had been Darbyists before they joined the *Gereformeerde* (Reformed) Church. Both parents were keenly involved in mission activities, and three of their six children later went overseas as missionaries.

Truus related once that, during her elementary school years, she had a teacher who taught Christian songs, and who was especially kind to those children who had difficulty learning. This impressed her. A few years later there was an elderly pastor who inspired her with his sermons. He presented the gospel as a message for the whole person, one which "integrated the vertical and horizontal aspects of life inseparably."[4] Once, while listening to a sermon, it seemed to Truus that Jesus spoke to her and called her to give herself to his service. That was when she made her decision.[5]

The family was not well-to-do, and obtaining a high school education would be problematic. Would Truus have to do what was common in that day: stay at home to help her mother, rather than study? Unexpectedly a study grant became available for her to attend the local Christian high school, and it was here that Truus developed a vital interest in missions. Reading articles in a mission magazine and helping to collect funds for a mission hospital to be built in Indonesia developed that interest and, while still a high school student, Truus

Would Truus have to do what was common in that day: stay at home to help her mother, rather than study?

began to focus on a career as missionary physician. This was unheard of at that time. A woman doctor? Besides, how would the years of studying medicine be financed?

Her parents were not against the idea, but a local pastor suggested to Truus that it would be much more practical for her to enrol in a teacher training course. After all, there were women missionary teachers in Indonesia and there

Her years as director of the mission hospital in Magelang were her most fulfilling, Truus Dreckmeier said. Dressed plainly, with her usual serious facial expression, she was loved by many. Here she is in the early 1930s. *Photo courtesy Laninga family.*

were always opportunities for employment. Others also encouraged Truus to turn her mind to becoming a teacher, but Truus had little interest in this, and she kept dreaming.

During her last year in high school a missionary who had just spent seven years in Indonesia came home on sick leave. He had lived on the island of Java in Purworejo, the town where the mission hospital for which Truus had helped collect funds, was going to be built. Her father urged her to have a talk with this missionary. When Truus did that and explained to the man that she felt a desire to become a missionary physician he encouraged her to follow her dream. He added that, in his opinion, women on Java especially needed female physicians, because in Javanese culture it was improper for men to enter the world of women. Foreign male missionary physicians could do little to treat sick Javanese women.

When she was elderly, Truus Dreckmeier still recalled that the missionary had said to her, "Do it! Do it! Do it!"[6] With his urging, she no longer wavered, her mind was made up. The financial need was still very real, but through two friends who offered student loans Truus was enabled to enrol as a medical student at the university that year.

During her medical studies Truus became acquainted with several missionaries, and found much encouragement in a Christian student organization which she joined. Mingling with Christian students and with missionaries inspired her, and throughout her life she treasured some of the relationships made during her university years. She learned much about Indonesia. The *Gereformeerde* (Reformed) churches in her region supported the mission work on central Java, so that it seemed natural for her to anticipate working there.

When she heard that someone who had lived on Java was giving introductory language lessons to a young woman who was planning to travel there, Truus asked permission to join those classes and began to study Javanese. Following those basic language sessions she took a course in tropical medicine, and upon graduation from medical school in 1919 Truus Dreckmeier was ready and qualified to go overseas as a medical missionary. But were the mission directors of her church ready to blaze a trail and send a female physician to Indonesia?

Dutch explorers, traders and colonizers began coming to Indonesia around 1600, but they had little interest in missions. The Protestant Reformation, European religious wars and a budding sense of Protestant missions seemed far removed from the allure of spices, textiles and other exotica of Asia. When Indonesia became a Dutch colony, and was called the Dutch East Indies, some missionaries were sent out on company trade ships, but these men were intended to be pastors for the Dutch seamen aboard ships and the settlers in Indonesia. It was nearly two hundred years later that the first general Protestant mission organization was founded in the Netherlands.

Gradually Christians in Holland became convinced that they had a spiritual task in the colony. They began to send evangelists, who soon saw that Indonesians needed more than words; they began to dispense some medicines, but found this small service totally inadequate. Remembering that Jesus helped not only with words but also with deeds, Dutch Christians then began to organize medical help and limited social services. This was a new idea, and not all Christians supported these new ventures; some believed that the missionaries' task should be limited to evangelism.

As missionaries became familiar with the Indonesian culture they observed that, socially, men and women led separate lives. They observed that Indonesian women were reluctant to speak to men, and that even medical missionaries had very little access to women who were ill. Women workers were badly needed in both evangelistic and medical work. In the mid 1800s pleas began to come from missionaries for women to come and help, but for a long time the Dutch considered it unnecessary and even improper for a woman to go overseas as missionary unless she were married. And where to get married female medical workers? Shortly before 1900 two Dutch young nurses were active in collecting funds for a mission hospital to be built and, when it was ready, these young groundbreakers were permitted to go to Indonesia to work in the newly opened hospital. But a female doctor?

Truus, now Dr. Dreckmeier, contacted the mission leaders of her church, and they forwarded her application to the physicians of the five mission hospitals on Java which the mission supported. All of them had openings for physicians, but when the reply came, it stated that all but one of the missionary physicians on Java were opposed to hiring a woman for the position of missionary doctor. And yet, the mission hospital in the city of Yogya, for instance, had only one physician on staff, and was in need of two doctors.

The mission directors in Amsterdam explained this to Truus, telling her that, though there was no applicant yet for either position in the Yogya mission hospital, the missionaries there were waiting for men to fill these posts. Only if and when the second and third positions were filled by men, she was told, would Truus be offered the position of the fourth physician!

Truus was furious, and declined the offer. Angrily she left the meeting and walked the streets of downtown Amsterdam to cool off. In a conversation in her later years, Dr. Dreckmeier recalled that dark day when the evident unwillingness of men to allow a woman to join them in medical missions had come crashing down on her sense of calling, her hopes and ambitions, and had so angered and disappointed her.[7]

Only Dr. J. C. Flach, director of the mission hospital in Purworejo, the hospital for which Truus had helped raise funds during her teens, responded positively. Though his words must have been demeaning to Truus, who had worked so hard to become a physician, he wrote the mission directors in the Netherlands, "Yes, just send her."[8] Dr. Flach had worked in Purworejo for several years, and knew that Indonesian women were hesitant to go to a male physician. He hoped that, if there were a female physician, more women would come to the new hospital.

Added to the humiliation she experienced, Dr. Dreckmeier must have felt belittled when she learned that Dr. Flach's wife had been so benevolent as to say that she had no objections to her husband working with a woman! Nevertheless, this was the opportunity Truus had waited for. In February 1920 Dr. Truus Dreckmeier was appointed to become the second physician at the Purworejo mission hospital with its one hundred and twenty beds, a clinic, and outreach work in the village.

Usually there is a commissioning service in the church before a newly-appointed missionary leaves, but even in this Truus was to be disappointed. Though the mission directors in the Netherlands had appointed Dr. Dreckmeier, they did not really consider her a missionary! First, she was a woman, the first female missionary physician to Central Java. Then, in the minds of many, her work as a medical missionary would not really be considered on par with that of evangelism.

The authorities seem to have forgotten to prepare for Truus' departure. It was only at the initiation of a neighbor that a commissioning service was planned, and it was not held in the church but in a rented hall! Interestingly, many people attended this service to bid Truus farewell. Since she was being sent as a medical missionary rather than as an evangelist, and was a woman besides, it was highly unusual that she was given the opportunity to address the congregation.

She chose to speak about Acts 1:8, "But you will receive power when the Holy Spirit comes on you; and you will be my witnesses in Jerusalem, and in all Judea and Samaria, and to the ends of the earth." Her biographer wrote that Dr. Dreckmeier emphasized that witnessing is not merely a command or duty; rather, it is something which cannot be separated from the Christian life. Besides, witnessing is to be done by all believers, not only the clergy.[9] No one seems to have bothered about helping Dr. Dreckmeier to send her luggage, for her father accompanied her and her baggage to the port city from which she sailed.

After fifty years of medical missions Dr. Dreckmeier reflected on those difficult days, and remarked that the disappointing lack of interest of church leaders did have one positive result. It strengthened her conviction that she was called to this work not by people, but by the Lord God himself.[10]

In August 1920 she arrived in Indonesia, in the town of Purworejo, then a city with a population of some twenty-five thousand on Central Java. She was warmly welcomed by the family of Dr. J. C. Flach, and lived with them, at first. She'd been promised a home, but this was not completed until five years later.

There were many patients in the two-year old hospital and Dr. Dreckmeier immediately took up her responsibilities in the crowded women's ward. Very soon she also became involved in evangelism and in the training of Indonesian girls as medical workers. It was evident that, in addition to physical healing, Dr. Dreckmeier would emphasize spiritual healing, and the education of Indonesian female workers. While some church leaders in the home country distinguished between the work of evangelism and that which was considered a helping part in missions, this distinction did not exist for Dr. Dreckmeier. The

In addition to physical healing, Dr. Dreckmeier would emphasize spiritual healing.

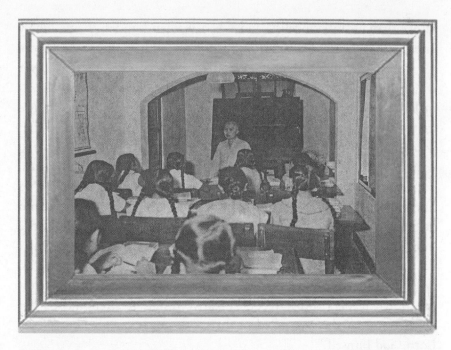

Ibu Sutirah was one of Dr. Dreckmeier's earliest students to be trained as evangelist for women's wards in the hospital. Later she herself trained future evangelists and then became the Javanese director of the SPWK School for Women in Magelang. Here she teaches a class. *Photo courtesy Uitgeverij Boekencentrum, Zoetermeer, The Netherlands.*

indivisible relationship between horizontal and vertical aspects of each person, about which the elderly preacher had spoken when she was young, was ingrained in her being as she sought to bring healing for both body and soul.

One of Dr. Dreckmeier's goals was to transfer knowledge. Young boys and girls, at first as young as twelve or thirteen years old, began with simple lessons. They came from the villages, many of them had only three years of elementary education, and the hospital atmosphere was totally new to them. They must first learn basics such as cleaning floors, laundering hospital linens, repairing clothes, serving meals, and so on. Only after that could lessons begin on how to care for the sick. The primary nursing course lasted three years, and after that there were further studies. While aspiring boys were taught to do laboratory work, some of the girls were educated to be midwives, especially for work in the villages, where there was little knowledge of hygiene and modern medicine.

While she taught the Indonesian girls to become good midwives Dr. Dreckmeier also taught them how to talk and pray with the patients. However, there was no time for long bedside discussions and prayers, as the midwives had much to do. Occasionally the missionary noticed a girl taking considerable time with a patient, and if the girl prayed longer than Dr. Dreckmeier thought necessary she interrupted with a loud "Amen!"[11]

Dr. Dreckmeier longed for the day when Indonesian Christian women would be available as evangelists to listen to and talk with the women of the villages and to accompany the medics. This need had been recognized long before Dr. Dreckmeier came to Indonesia. Dr. Flach was very conscious of this when he told the story, a year before Truus was appointed, about a Javanese woman who had become a believer while she was in the hospital. Her relatives tried to talk her out of choosing the Christian life when she came home, and, when she persevered in her new beliefs they threw her out of the family.

Another important part of the hospital ministry was the mingling of the Javanese, Chinese, and Dutch nurses. They heard Christian messages at work, but in the early days most of the nurses were not believers. It seems that there were some conversions and, though that gave joy in the hospital community, it caused pain and broken family relationships in their homes. As yet there were few believers on staff who were ready to show friendship and spiritual care to these fellow workers.

The now elderly women whom I visited on Central Java all spoke highly of Dr. Dreckmeier. Oh yes, she was strict, very strict. She set schedules. When it was time to work everyone should be present and ready, she valued punctuality. But she was also kind and generous. These elderly women talked about her smiles, and her sincere apologies after she had made a mistake.

A retired hospital bookkeeper told the story of an elderly villager who had spent his money to come to the hospital for treatment, and afterwards sat outside the hospital, since he had money for neither medicine nor for transportation back to his village. When Dr. Dreckmeier walked out of the building and asked him why he was sitting there he told her that he had no money for medication or travel and she gave him an allowance for both.[12] There were similar stories from others. People remembered this generosity.

There were few Europeans in Purworejo at that time and Dr. Dreckmeier learned to speak Javanese fluently. Early on she realized that there were two levels of language, one in which a person speaks respectfully as to a higher-placed person and one in which one speaks to a person of a lower rank. Javanese is rich and complex; Dr. Dreckmeier followed the advice to use the language which showed respect,[13] and learned to speak it well.

In 1922 Dr. Flach went on furlough, he was absent for seven months. Dr. Dreckmeier took charge of the hospital during that time. She ably carried on, but seems to have found the work and the pressure a heavy load, though she did receive help from another physician during the last few months.

When the five years of her contract were complete Dr. Dreckmeier traveled to the Netherlands for a furlough. She had requested additional time for specialized studies, and used it to follow a course in gynecology in Paris, financing these studies herself. It must have been disappointing to her that there seemed to be no interest among Christians in the homeland to hear about her missionary work. Apparently she had but one opportunity to speak in a church, but she wrote that frustrations were offset by the encouragement of others.

One highlight of this furlough was the Christian conference in England which she attended. Thousands of people, some retired missionaries, friends of missions, and active missionaries, people of many church backgrounds, attended this annual conference. During one of the sessions all missionaries on furlough were asked to stand. As Dr. Dreckmeier saw the hundreds of individuals who stood she was heartened and motivated to continue her work. In 1927 she returned to the hospital in Purworejo.

Before long Dr. Dreckmeier faced a challenge which became a turnabout in her life. It all started when Dr. Flach was planning another furlough. Dr. Dreckmeier suggested the name of a female acquaintance who had nearly completed her medical studies to be the acting hospital director during Dr. Flach's absence. Her suggestion was disregarded; instead, the mission directors in the Netherlands appointed a retired male, a navy physician who had never set foot in Indonesia. This decision angered the missionary physicians on Java, and, when their appeals were ignored, they refused to perform surgeries in the mission hospital in Purworejo. They went so far as to dismiss the substitute, but mission authorities did not budge, they insisted he stay. It's easy to see that there were ill feelings between Dr. Dreckmeier and the substitute, especially when the workers in the hospital began to take sides.

Dr. Dreckmeier did not even stay in Purworejo until Dr. Flach's return. Conditions at the hospital were such that she could no longer function well. She transferred to a small nearby town where there was a struggling medical work. Here she practiced community health in the clinic until her next furlough.

This was the end of the first period of her work in Indonesia, one which, though started in high spirits, left her dejected and sad. It marked the second time she was passed over because she was a woman.

Truus Dreckmeier was not the only missionary who felt that the church in the home country did not seem to care much about what was happening on the mission field. Another missionary, the Rev. Mr. Aart Merkelijn, sensed when he left the Netherlands for Indonesia in 1912 that there was not much love in the churches yet for mission work.[14] Rev. Merkelijn and his family were assigned to the town of Magelang, on Central Java, to begin a new evangelistic work.

Once Dutch church leaders were persuaded that medical practice was a legitimate means of doing missions they totally changed policy and it became their dream to establish a hospital in each mission post. The Dutch government subsidized such work, a great help to those Dutch Christians who supported these hospitals financially. However, government officials decided not to subsidize medical work in Magelang, because this city had a military hospital where private residents could also be treated. Rev. Merkelijn would soon discover that most Magelang residents had no desire to go to the military hospital, they even refused to enter it.

On the way to Magelang the Merkelijn family visited an older mission post in the area, in Jogjakarta. This was the place of the Reformed mission's first hospital in Central Java, founded in 1900. Rev. Merkelijn observed here how medical help and evangelism worked hand in hand.

Following his language study Rev. Merkelijn began his evangelistic work in Magelang, and for years he dreamed of a possible medical work. When he met Dr. Dreckmeier, he appreciated her efficiency and dedication to missions. He bided his time.

About the time that Dr. Flach of Purworejo went on furlough Rev. Merkelijn asked Dr. Dreckmeier to consider coming to Magelang and to become the director of a future mission hospital. This was just when she faced her second great disappointment, when mission directors in the Netherlands decided to appoint a man as temporary hospital director, rather than the woman she had recommended. We can imagine how she must have been encouraged by Rev. Merkelijn's invitation.

And so, even before she left Purworejo, Dr. Dreckmeier also began to dream, and to plan a layout for a possible hospital. Of course both Rev. Merkelijn and Dr. Dreckmeier knew that there were no funds as yet, that the government would not subsidize a medical facility, and that mission leaders in the Netherlands might not approve their proposal. Dr. Dreckmeier also knew that a position in a new mission hospital would bring up a much smaller salary than that of a government-subsidized hospital, but she did not mind that. All her life she made it a habit to live frugally, and she always seemed to have sufficient to give to others.

Rev. Merkelijn went on furlough and convinced the mission directors in the Netherlands that a small hospital was necessary as part of the project in Magelang. As soon as he received their permission to go ahead he began to raise funds.[15] When he returned to Magelang he was able to purchase a "fine home" from a Chinese military man. It even cost less than the amount which he had raised in the Netherlands!

The house had three detached buildings which had already been put to use by some local doctors in a previous but discontinued clinic. Funds remaining after the purchase were used for reconstruction work. The buildings needed renovation, and together with Rev. Merkelijn, Dr. Dreckmeier busied herself with the work of remodeling, plumbing, electricity, changing of the laundry room and kitchen, and the planning of the large garden.

Dr. Dreckmeier took a brief unpaid furlough; this gave her opportunity to purchase the essentials for a medical practice, and also to look for a qualified nurse. When she was ready to return to Indonesia a commissioning service was held for her in the church, and again she was invited to speak. She was delighted to start this new enterprise, and realized that the challenge was great. She asked the congregation to be faithful in prayer, for her as well as for the new work. This time she must have returned to Indonesia with a spring in her step.

Rev. Merkelijn and Dr. Dreckmeier worked well together in Magelang. He the evangelist and she the physician both needed and appreciated the other. Years later the elderly Dr. Dreckmeier observed that for her, the years of her work in the hospital in Magelang, beginning in 1932 and ending during World War II, had been the most beautiful period of her life.[16]

And no wonder. After her unfortunate experiences in Purworejo not only was she respected now, she also had great freedom. As director of the new hospital she would have opportunity to realize her dreams of medical service, but also to do evangelism, and to develop the education of future Indonesian medical workers.

Although she began work on a rather small scale at first, hundreds of patients had already been treated when the hospital was officially opened two months later.[17] The hospital had sixty beds, of which fifty were intended for anyone in need of medical care. It was planned that the remaining ten beds would be available for patients who could not afford to pay regular fees. Paying patients included Europeans, Javanese and Chinese, and one of the outbuildings was used for these patients.

There was a women's department, and children who had nobody to care for them often ended up at the hospital as well. Though the budget was tight Dr. Dreckmeier believed that these children had to be cared for somehow, or else many of them would die. And so, just as had happened in her former work, before long a children's ward was added to the hospital. She also welcomed prostitutes of the town for, she said, they needed "the Great Healer" and compassionate care as much as anyone else, especially as many of these women had become prostitutes due to poverty. If not at the mission hospital, where else would there be opportunity to tell these women the gospel?[18]

At that time it was common practice for physicians to give half of the money received as professional fees to the hospital and to keep half for themselves to complement their small salary. Dr. Dreckmeier did not consider that the right thing to do for her. She consistently turned over all income from patients to the hospital.

There always seemed to be a need which just had to be met. Everyone knew that Dr. Dreckmeier never turned away impoverished patients. When they came she always treated them, and often gave them a bit of allowance for medicine and immediate needs. Yet she believed that even the poor must pay what they could.

She had a small lock put on a cookie tin, and on the morning of the day the new clinic opened she gave the key to the accountant. She told him that she would ask all patients who came to put something in the tin, even if it was only two pennies. After working three hours on the first day of the clinic she returned to the accountant with the cookie tin, saying, "This is the first income of the new Magelang mission hospital." Eagerly the accountant opened the tin and found 53 cents.[19]

Her compassion was well-known. Once a high official came to Magelang and asked Dr. Dreckmeier to give him a tour of the facilities. While she did this a *dogcar* (rickshaw) unexpectedly pulled up, two women jumped out and deposited — almost dumped — a man on the tiles just outside the operating room. The man was covered with sores. Soon the doctor and her guest came out and saw him. He had yaws, a contagious tropical skin disease, common at that time. The guest pulled back in disgust, and asked, "Doctor, what will you do about this?" The answer was prompt and characteristic, "If I can find even one square centimeter of clear skin this man will return home a healthy man in three months." And that's what happened.[20]

The accountant admired the doctor's efficiency. On her way to the delivery room one evening, Dr. Dreckmeier told him that she wished to talk to him, but she first had to attend to a difficult case of childbirth, and went on her way. Suddenly, while Dr. Dreckmeier was operating, there was a blackout. Seconds later, the accountant saw a white-clad figure dash across the lawn to the nearby garage. Dr. Dreckmeier's car engine roared, and in no time her car came speeding across the lawn and stopped just where the headlines shone right into the operating room. She ran inside and continued delivering the baby.

Everyone who knew her was aware that Dr. Dreckmeier could be abrupt, and stood for no nonsense. If she saw a patient smoking she was not above pulling the cigarette out of his mouth![21] Most of her students were afraid of her.

Her ten years of work in Purworejo had ended sadly, but had given her an invaluable experience in tropical medical care. She had learned much during her first assignment, and seen the overwhelming need for Indonesian health care workers. Therefore, almost immediately, Dr. Dreckmeier began to look for young people whom she might teach to be paramedics. Both girls and boys were offered an education, not only so they might learn useful work, but also that they might do mission work, whether that be medical or evangelistic. This type of education was still groundbreaking work, and was done only in mission hospitals. In addition to helping deliver babies, she wanted young paramedics to be trained for giving expectant mothers prenatal care, and for helping to save lives of both mothers and infants.

From the beginning Dr. Dreckmeier had insisted that she needed women evangelists for the hospital, and also for work in the villages. Whenever a man entered the women's ward in the hospital the women became silent, to be polite. Both women medics and women evangelists were needed, and Dr. Dreckmeier set out to educate them.

One of Dr. Dreckmeier's former students, who was nearly eighty years old, told me how she came to know Dr. Dreckmeier. *Ibu* Urip[22]

Ibu Urip Mirmamigsih, aged eighty in 2002, remembered well that Dr. Dreckmeier helped her to become a midwife, and then a teacher. All her life she recalled that Dr. Dreckmeier used to tell her students, "Be thrifty!" and "Make something from nothing!"

(*Ibu* is a polite way to address a woman) told how, when she was in grade two of elementary school, she had malaria and was brought to the mission hospital. It was the first time she had seen a hospital; she felt lonely, and that evening she cried. While making her rounds, Dr. Dreckmeier noticed the sad little girl. She sat by her bed and told her stories. A few years later she helped the girl to come to the hospital for midwifery training. During that time *Ibu* Urip observed that Dr. Dreckmeier was always busy, that she regularly gave food and clothes to poor mothers at the hospital, and that she left the hospital a few hours several times weekly to teach at a school for girls, the first of its kind in Magelang.

Dr. Dreckmeier had been instrumental in founding a school for young women which offered a home economics course and which also featured religious classes in its curriculum. *Ibu* Urip remarked that Dr. Dreckmeier never thought of herself, always of others. *Ibu* Urip was one of several individuals who said that Dr. Dreckmeier regularly supported young people's studies, and often gave them books. For some time *Ibu* Urip was invited to come to the doctor's house each morning for breakfast which included an egg, a luxury for the girl. *Ibu* Urip maintains that she learned much, and was helped and guided by the doctor in her faith as well as vocation.

When a new Christian kindergarten was going to be established Dr. Dreckmeier again supported *Ibu* Urip, this time to become a teacher. For the next fifty years *Ibu* Urip taught school. Even today she operates a small student dormitory for poor students. She has little money, and considers this her last mission project. After nearly seventy years have passed the elderly lady still recalls two of the doctor's statements: "Make something from nothing," and, "Be thrifty."[23]

Besides her hospital practice Dr. Dreckmeier had private patients among Europeans, and at times she handed out advice instead of medicine. One man, now in his seventies, remembers the time when, as a boy in Magelang, he and his five siblings felt miserable with cold and flu, and his mother, pregnant with number seven, in desperation asked the doctor to come. The children all seemed feverish, and the mother began to fear that something serious was wrong. When the doctor saw the six little children, all hot and miserable and making their mother more miserable, she smilingly suggested that the mother give them less underwear to put on and let them play — they were simply overheated.[24]

Another woman remembers her shy little friend who often stuttered. The girl was ridiculed by her friends at school, and decided one day that she could not face the other children. She knew that her mother would only permit her to stay home if she were sick, so she drank hot water to make her mouth hot, hoping it would make the thermometer show a higher than normal temperature. When the mother called her, Dr. Dreckmeier came to the house. Understanding the little girl's problem, the doctor soon knew what to do. "Just let her play today," she suggested with a wink, "and send her back to school tomorrow. She'll be all right."[25]

Dr. Dreckmeier was not satisfied with training young people merely to be useful in medical care. She well realized that it was often impossible for medical workers to take time to talk with patients about the Christian faith, and saw the need for Javanese female evangelists; Javanese young women must be educated to work among women. And so in 1934 she requested permission at the recently opened Theological School in Jogjakarta (Yogyakarta or simply Yogya)[26] for Sutirah, one of her former students, to enrol in the course for evangelists. *Ibu* Sutirah (1908–1977) was a daughter of the first Javanese evangelist of Central Java,[27] an educated young woman and now a teacher. Still, this request was unheard of! In the past Truus Dreckmeier had been passed over for being a woman, but times were changing, and it was urgent for women to be educated in evangelistic work, so she applied. Once again she pushed for innovation.

The faculty of the school discussed the unusual request, and argued that it would be too lonely for one young woman among the male students. Next they reasoned that the courses would be too difficult. But then missionary pastors sided with Truus Dreckmeier and urged that a simple course of study be provided.[28] After all, how could Javanese women teach the Christian faith to women and girls and become leaders themselves without training? Consequently, a course in evangelism was organized especially for women. Fifteen young Javanese women, aged eighteen to twenty-seven, were enroled that year in a special course of Bible study, Church history, evangelism, and practical skills. Among them were Sutirah and another young woman from Magelang. The girls came from various backgrounds and it was difficult to teach at a level which was meaningful for them all, but it seems that all of them returned to their hometown and worked as evangelists. *Ibu* Sutirah, Dr. Dreckmeier's young friend, became the first female evangelist in the Magelang mission hospital. She became a prominent leader, and twenty years later we find her the principal of a newly-established school for the training of women church workers in Magelang.

While she was the director of the mission hospital Truus Dreckmeier pioneered in several areas. First of all she consulted with patients, did surgeries, and helped improve physical conditions of the sick. During her furloughs she took courses in gynecology, and became an expert. Both rich and poor were among her patients. Numerous couples who feared they were infertile — among them my parents — were treated by her and became parents of healthy babies. Many Javanese and Chinese women preferred to be treated by the female physician, some of them following the doctor from place to place. Those patients who were able to pay helped to maintain the hospital. Dr. Dreckmeier was ahead of her time as she blazed a trail in family planning in Indonesia; in her medical consultations she emphasized responsibility of both husband and wife in the area of parenthood. And she found time to speak to individuals, to comfort and to encourage.

Educating young people to become paramedics who could function in both the hospital and, independently in villages, was one of her attempts to improve general health and hygiene in Javanese society. Teaching Bible studies and health classes for girls and women were important to her. Even though she was very strict and disciplined, Dr. Dreckmeier did enjoy fun times. She laughed with her students, and helped prepare food for Saturday evening fellowship times, as well as parties, especially at Christmastime.

She generously gave of herself in the new home economics school for girls, to help uplift the quality of women's lives as wives and mothers. At the same time she envisioned that some of its graduates would marry medical workers or pastors, and be able to use what they learned in a new setting of Christian leadership.

These were the years when my parents lived in Magelang, and here is where my two older brothers and I were born. My mother used to tell us about life in Magelang, the tropical climate, the trips to the market, the *djongos* (male household help), the *baboe* (nursemaid,) and the way the *kokki* (cook), cooked outside, hunched over a small fire. Mother was one of many missionary wives who taught groups of girls to sew and embroider, and who used this opportunity to teach the Christian faith as well.

We children loved to hear stories about "Pa" ("Dad") Johannes Van der Steur, who became famous for his care of orphans.[29] Van der Steur came to Magelang in 1892 as a young independent missionary, and worked among the soldiers in the military barracks. There were many Dutch citizens in Magelang, the regional capital, and being a military town it had many European residents. His faith in God, love for people and strong desire to serve was soon noticed by the soldiers. One day "a drunken soldier" came to his house and challenged Van der Steur to prove his Christianity by taking care of four orphaned children. Van der Steur took the children into his home and cared for them.

Soon there were more. He took them in as well, and before long his house was filled with orphans. Soldiers often came to the house to assist him with cooking, cleaning and laundry. As the work expanded he received other kinds of help, such as larger housing, food, and labor, but though the physical needs of the children were met Van der Steur felt the need for a mother for the children. He was caring for some three hundred children when he proposed marriage by letter to a young woman in the Netherlands, someone he must have known in his earlier days, in a most unusual way. He wrote simply, "Anna, will you be the mother of my children?"[30] Anna consented, they were married in 1907, and she was a loving and caring mother to thousands of children until she died nearly thirty years later. By the time Rev. Merkelijn arrived in Magelang there were already a few hundred children under Pa Van der Steur's care.

Our family picture albums show pictures of the volcano Merapi, of the *kampungs* (villages), of the *sawahs* (rice fields), and of Pa Van der Steur's orphans, dressed in white, parading through town. There were pictures of swaying palm trees, of school children in classrooms, and schoolchildren lined up in groups in front of the school, of Rev. Merkelijn and other missionaries, and of our family. These were pictures which my parents sent to relatives and friends in the Netherlands. It all looked so idyllic, but also frightening. And when I asked questions and wanted to argue about things I could not understand, my devout mother would simply say, "Child, that's how it was in those days."

The 1930s were a time of change. Discoveries and inventions brought new ways of thinking and living. As early as 1929 telephone communication became available. In 1930 the KLM (Royal Dutch Airlines) began regular commercial flights from Amsterdam to Bandung, Indonesia, and by 1933 an airmail letter from the Netherlands arrived in Indonesia in a mere five days.[31]

These were turbulent years in Indonesia, as they were in the rest of the world. War clouds formed, and when the Germans invaded their country in May 1940 the Netherlands was involved in World War II hostilities. War meant that the Dutch were no longer able to exercise real authority in Indonesia, nor were they able to defend the country when the Japanese military invaded early in 1942. All of life was disturbed in Indonesia, and the Japanese military soon began to round up European, but especially Dutch citizens and to place them in detention camps. Early on men and boys were separated from women and

In 1971 Dr. G. J. Dreckmeier was the first foreign woman to be officially recognized with a medal by the government of Indonesia for her contribution to health and humanitarian efforts. Dr. G. J. Dreckmeier considered that she had only done her duty, but the honor was a significant testimony to the efforts of Christian missions. *Photo courtesy Kerkinactie, The Netherlands, PKN Foto-archive.*

girls and placed elsewhere. As the months and years passed countless people died in various Japanese camps in Indonesia and elsewhere in Southeast Asia; those who survived would be detained, under deteriorating circumstances, until after the war.

Mission hospitals were sequestered, but, as the mission hospital in Magelang received no government subsidy, the Japanese left it alone for nearly a year, and Dr. Dreckmeier was able to continue her medical work. She was pleased to be able to supply people in detention camps with medicines while it was still permitted to do so.

Early in the war her medical expertise had been noted by the Japanese when she expertly aided victims of a train accident, and the local Japanese leader had, on behalf of the Japanese government, publicly thanked her for this. Perhaps this was why she was usually left to go her own way. But of course, Japanese rules had to be observed.[32] As in all public places, the staff was ordered to gather each morning, in front of the hospital, watch the raising of the Japanese flag, and then sing the *Kimigayo*, the Japanese national anthem. Dr. Dreckmeier complied and

221

each morning the assembled workers sang the Japanese words which, translated into English, are,

> May the reign of the Emperor continue for a thousand, nay,
> eight thousand generations and for the eternity that it takes
> for small pebbles to grow into a great rock
> and become covered with moss.

However, Dr. Dreckmeier taught the staff to follow the Japanese national anthem with another song of praise. And so, each morning, immediately following the *Kimigayo*, the entire group sang the words of the old hymn, "Holy God, We Praise Thy Name"

> Holy God, we praise Thy name; Lord of all, we bow before Thee.
> All on earth Thy scepter claim; all in heaven above adore Thee;
> Infinite Thy vast domain, everlasting is Thy reign.

One wonders what the Japanese would have thought of this song which, of course, they could not understand, as it was sung in the Dutch language.

For a year the mission hospital continued as usual, and then Dr. Dreckmeier was also interned. Before she left she was able to appoint a Christian Javanese physician as hospital director; he would do his utmost to continue the Christian medical mission. Together with the two Dutch nurses of the hospital Dr. Dreckmeier was sent to Muntilan, a camp on central Java, and stayed until near the end of the war.[33] This camp had been a Roman Catholic boarding school, designed for three hundred students. Besides an administration building there were classrooms, a music room, an art room, and a swimming pool. All the rooms were changed into barracks, and during much of the wartime there were four thousand two hundred women and girls interned here. The swimming pool was used as a water supply; while it contained water, its water was used for washing, at first some of it was even boiled for drinking and cooking.[34]

Life in the detention camp was difficult. From the beginning there was barely sufficient food, and teen-aged girls were ordered to work in gardens outside the camp to grow vegetables. Food was prepared in a central kitchen, where women were assigned to prepare and distribute the meager meals. As food supplies decreased people became malnourished and ill, and many died. Dr. Dreckmeier was assigned to treat the sick, who were placed in a building towards the back of the compound. There, at first, friends from Magelang brought food and supplies; they handed them through the fence or climbed over it to enter the camp under cover of darkness, but after some time they were found out and the deliveries were no longer possible.[35]

There was always a shortage of medicines, and Dr. Dreckmeier often requested more. When told that she could no longer receive medicines from the mission hospital she said "with a straight face" that the medicines in the hospital were hers, and she often received what she needed.[36] She justified this argument on the ground that she had bought nearly all hospital medicines with her own money. The Japanese tired of her requests, and became angry. She was even severely beaten for repeatedly asking,[37] but she continued. Towards the end of the war, when sick women from other camps were sent to Muntilan they were delighted to find that Dr. Dreckmeier was here. One missionary friend wrote in her journal that, though circumstances were extremely primitive, Dr. Dreckmeier had cared for her "royally."[38] After the war Dr. Dreckmeier gleefully related that she had sufficient anesthesia to extract teeth during the entire wartime.[39]

During this time Dr. Dreckmeier organized a prayer group of five women. They met regularly to pray together and aloud for the physical needs of the large and underfed group of women and children in the camp. They prayed regularly for the men and boys too, expecting that they were also suffering, although they rarely received news about them.

Together with some other women Dr. Dreckmeier gave advice on how the lessening amounts of food given to the camp inmates should be distributed. She had always been interested in planning inexpensive nutrition, and camp life offered real challenges for this. For instance, during the early months there was

> *The Japanese tired of her requests, and became angry. She was even severely beaten for repeatedly asking, but she continued.*

still a milk supply, though it amounted to only about one spoonful per person. Against strict camp rules, the women decided to use the milk only for the sick. Dr. Dreckmeier urged people to eat soybeans, in spite of the fact that these were very difficult to digest, because they had good food value. Then she taught people how to raise and cook snails, as snails contain protein, and are nutritious.

Even after the war ended the Dutch government could not protect their nationals in Indonesia, and Dutch prisoners of war remained in detention camps for some time. It was ironic that during this time the Japanese, who were defeated during the war, were ordered to protect the weakened survivors in the same camps where they themselves had detained them earlier.[40] It was a critical time for the prisoners, now set free; numerous Dutch were attacked and killed outside of camps.[41] As soon as possible, those able to travel were taken from the camps and repatriated directly to the Netherlands.

Once, during those early days after the war, a group of elderly and sick Dutch people had to be brought by train from their detention camp to the city of Semarang, and Dr. Dreckmeier was assigned to accompany them. Along the way the train was stopped by a group of young freedom fighters who demanded that everyone leave the train. Others, in similar circumstances, had been killed. It was a frightening situation. What would happen? Dr. Dreckmeier got off the train, approached the men, and spoke to them in polite Javanese. The men were awed by her ability to speak their language fluently and politely. In turn, they treated her courteously, and bowed to her as they allowed the train to continue on its way.[42] People who heard this story credited her ability to speak the language fluently, but Dr. Dreckmeier probably called it grace.

Dr. Dreckmeier loved Indonesia and her people, but she was among the survivors who were sent to the Netherlands, early after the war, and it then was impossible for her to go back to Java. Instead, she was invited to work in a small hospital and do rural work in Kalimantan (Borneo), and did that for two years. Then, following a furlough, she was able to return to Java; she hoped to go to Magelang, where she

When she was nearly eighty years old Dr. Dreckmeier returned to Indonesia once more. She and a friend were warmly welcomed by former colleagues and acquaintances in Magelang. Expecting that this was their last time together the group posed for a photograph.

loved to work. However, the mission hospital was now a state hospital, there was no room for a missionary doctor, nor for a Javanese evangelist.

It was remarkable that the Indonesian government issued Dr. Dreckmeier a re-entry permit, because it was a time of great tension between Indonesia and the Netherlands. Many Dutch citizens' permits had been canceled, and few missionaries were left in Indonesia. At the same time, the re-entry permit was proof that the government recognized the work of Christian missions, and Dr. Dreckmeier as one who did much to aid Javanese well-being.

She was asked to begin a midwifery training in the city of Semarang, the capital of Central Java, and worked there during the next five years. She organized classes for future midwives, and held maternity clinics where, just like in earlier years, she counseled her patients and taught family planning. The government demanded that workers in a Christian clinic spend one day a week in a government institution and she fulfilled that requirement.

During these years Dr. Dreckmeier became active again in Magelang where Javanese women, supported by Christian women in the Netherlands, were establishing a school, the SPWK[43], for future female evangelists and Christian social workers. The government stipulated that a doctor be on staff in the school, and Dr. Dreckmeier functioned both as board member of and teacher in this school.

In 1959 we see her in the small rural hospital in Parakan, about 30 kilometers from Magelang. The hospital in Parakan had been totally destroyed during the war. An Indonesian paramedic had begun to rebuild the hospital on his own, but needed help. Dr. Dreckmeier had worked in this hospital before, and eagerly devoted herself to what she did well: treating the sick, giving maternity care, teaching future medical workers, and training Christians to do evangelism among patients. People often saw Dr. Dreckmeier driving into the hospital grounds in Parakan, her little car loaded down with boards, nails and other building materials.[44] The small hospital was rebuilt and enlarged to a capacity of fifty beds.

One of her former co-workers in Parakan commented on Dr. Dreckmeier's simple wardrobe. She always looked clean and neat, but usually wore the same outfits, for she owned few dresses. The same person laughingly mentioned that Dr. Dreckmeier knew Javanese better than the Bahasa Indonesia that Indonesians were encouraged to speak after the war. Therefore, when she became upset and had to reprimand a student she had to do it in polite Javanese rather than in the commonly spoken Bahasa Indonesia! But people knew of her love for God and for them, and her personal concern. When a patient in the hospital died Dr. Dreckmeier nearly always attended the funeral.[45]

Dr. Dreckmeier served in Parakan until she was sixty-nine years old. She took her sixth furlough and went to the Netherlands for a short time; then, invited to return to Magelang, she did that. Some Christian Javanese women, midwives and nurses, had established a maternity clinic. They had even shouldered the finances of the clinic by selling or pawning their own jewels.[46] An unused building, left by the former Dutch government, was rented and renovated, and was opened as the Yoga Darma maternity clinic. Government regulations required the presence of a physician in the clinic, and the aging but energetic Dr. Dreckmeier, who was now called "*Tante* Truus" (Auntie Truus) by

"G. J. Dreckmeier, 1895–1992." A simple boulder for a tombstone. Always an example of thrift, she probably chose this stone for her mother and herself.

many, was invited to help. She mostly consulted with expectant mothers, but still had time for other interests.

It was time for another furlough, and she took a lengthy journey to many countries. Though she had retired she was not ready to rest, but was forced to stay in the Netherlands for about a year and a half because of cataract treatments. She planned to return to Magelang as soon as her eyes improved.

The world had taken notice of this gifted woman who had struggled hard to become a missionary physician, who had spent her life helping the sick and the weak, and had tirelessly educated young Javanese. But for Dr. Dreckmeier herself it was a total surprise, early in 1971, when she was informed that she had been chosen to receive the Albert Schweitzer Prize. She even had to postpone her return to Indonesia a few weeks for this event.[47]

This coveted international prize, awarded for achievement in the areas of Christian and humanitarian work in medicine, in cultural philosophy and in art, was presented to the winners in Amsterdam. A close friend[48] tells of the consternation this prize caused Dr. Dreckmeier, for she was not interested in receiving a reward. Formal dress would be required at the ceremony, and the Dutch queen would be present. Dr. Dreckmeier's simple but neat "green silk dress" had to suffice, and her friend lent her dress gloves for the occasion. A few days later she traveled to Indonesia.

In the same year she was honored by the Indonesian government with the *Satyalencana* (Medal of Honor in Social Services),[49] when the head of the Community Health Department of the Province of Central Java pinned the medal to Dr. Dreckmeier's dress. This medal was for health and humanitarian work in Indonesia, and had never before been given to a foreign woman. It was also the only distinction awarded during these years of political unrest. Dr. Dreckmeier cried when she received this medal.[50] She felt that she was no more worthy to receive this honor than were many other Christians. Repeatedly she bent her head towards the floral bouquet someone gave her, to hide her emotions.

She was active in medical missions for another two years, training future medics, and teaching in the school for female evangelists, while she continued to consult with female patients, and again included advice on family planning. She had hoped that she could stay in Indonesia until her death,[51] but her eyesight began to fail, and the hot tropical climate became a problem for her. Then, rather than become a burden to Indonesians, she decided to return to the Netherlands. She was seventy-eight years old when in 1973 she left her beloved Indonesia.

Dr. Dreckmeier was to live for another nineteen years. She sorely missed Indonesia and her friends there. It was difficult to resettle in the Netherlands, but she had no choice. For years she remained busy with correspondence and with receiving mission-related guests. She kept her interest in Indonesia alive, and she read as long as she could. When she could no longer see she listened to friends who came to read to her. She still signed her own name at the bottom of what was probably her last Christmas letter, that of 1990, but the writing is nearly illegible. At the end of her life she was cared for in an institute for the blind, and that is were she died.

The funeral in 1992, in October weather, was a simple ceremony which Dr. Dreckmeier had arranged in advance. She had invited some of her acquaintances, but not the people of the mission office for, in a statement so typical of the woman, she wrote that these people had better things to do than to attend her funeral. She asked that at the cemetery the people would sing the hymn,

> In Christ there is no east or west, in him no south or north;
> But one great fellowship of love throughout the whole wide earth.
>
> Join hands, then, members of the faith, whatever your race may be;
> Who serves my Father as his child is surely kin to me.
>
> In Christ now meet both east and west, in him meet north and south;
> All Christly souls are one in him throughout the whole wide earth.

In order to conserve space and finances, Dutch people sometimes bury the remains of two persons in one plot, one above the other. Truus Dreckmeier's remains were buried in the same plot as those of her mother, who had died thirty-two years earlier. Characteristic of her, the gravestone is a simple boulder, with the names and dates of birth and death of her mother and of herself. Nothing else.

When I was a child I could not have understood this woman. When I looked at the photo of the stern-faced Dr. Dreckmeier I had no concept of the stature of this woman. Now that I am older and have lived to understand more about mission I look at her face, and admire the qualities which she showed in her life.

We may believe that, when Truus Dreckmeier's life on earth ended our Savior said of her, "She has done a beautiful thing for me."

The Chinese can be found almost anywhere in the world. Through the centuries many Chinese have emigrated and settled in other countries, especially in countries of Southeast Asia. They became known for characteristics such as their Confucian values, their diligence, their business acumen, and for the way in which Chinese families continued to educate their children in Chinese schools and to marry other Chinese. In Chinese homes the Chinese language was spoken and Chinese customs were observed.

Some Chinese intermarried with people of the country where they lived, and gradually lost much of their former identity. However, most Chinese and those of Chinese descent have continued to value their heritage. This is why in some countries, even after two or three generations, when Chinese meet they can converse in Mandarin, for centuries the official language of the educated Chinese. It is not unusual at all here to meet people with a Chinese background who are fluent in three languages; first, the language of the country in which they were born, then Mandarin, and even the local dialect of the region from where their ancestors came.

For many Chinese overseas, preserving their cultural values has included maintaining Chinese religions. Traditionally all children, but especially the eldest son in the family, had to be filial. The eldest had to be a dutiful son; his responsibilities included caring for aging parents and ministering to the spirits of the ancestors. It was a lifelong commitment, loyalty and duty to family and clan.

Today many elderly overseas Chinese are concerned that the ancient heritage will not be remembered by the young. As time brings change and people travel throughout the world a weakening of traditions is taking place, they claim. Even fifty years ago, this was not much of an issue, but today change comes rapidly.

The first Protestant missionary to China, an Englishman named Robert Morrison (1782–1834), traveled to China when it was forbidden to teach the Chinese language to foreigners. Yet this brave young man learned the language so well that he translated the entire Bible into Chinese. That was one of the main contributions of his missionary career. When he came to China, government authorities would not allow any Chinese to become Christian, and Robert Morrison baptized very few converts. But the Bible became a precious book to those who were moved by the Holy Spirit to believe its message.

Even today, Chinese loyalty and diligence characterize the Chinese Church, both within China and abroad. Nearly everywhere Chinese Christians have gone we can find churches where members practice their Christian faith in earnest.

Mother of Ten, Woman of Prayer
Tong Tan Tjien Nio[1] (1909–1977)

When Tong Pai Hu saw Tjien Nio he knew that this was the girl he wanted to marry. True, she was only sixteen and he was thirty-six, but it seemed like a suitable match, and she had reached the marriageable age among Chinese. On the same day that Tong Pai Hu visited the modest home of Tjien Nio's parents he had many gifts delivered there, showing his commitment to an engagement and marriage.

Tong Pai Hu was a well-to-do Chinese businessman, working in the city of Semarang on Central Java, Indonesia. He was an intelligent man and well-educated; his father, a doctor and herbalist, had taught him and his brother much about herbal medicine. Because Tong Pai Hu grew up in the city of Fuzhou (Foochow), on the southeast coast of China where Europeans traded, he had opportunities to learn English while he was young. Yet he was born during a humiliating time for China.

Under the 1842 Treaty of Nanking, which settled the first Opium War between China and Great Britain, the Chinese government was forced to allow foreigners to live in five coastal cities, of which Fuzhou was one. From this time there was a British influence in many areas of life there, and some enterprising Chinese learned to use English. It was a distinct advantage for young Chinese to know English, it gave them good opportunities in the business world.

When Pai Hu was a young man, he and his wife, his brother with wife and children, and his parents had all moved south. They had settled some 150 kilometers south of Fuzhou, in Xiamen (formerly called

Tang Tjien Nio in Xiamen, with her first-born, Chung Po (Tonny). Knowing that having a son had made her husband happy, Tjien Nio felt fulfilled. *Photo courtesy Freda Hatfield Tong, daughter-in-law of Tang Tjien Nio.*

Amoy), another one of the five cities opened to foreigners by the Treaty of Nanking, to find employment and Tong Pai Hu and his brother had both landed good jobs. After some time Tong Pai Hu was promoted and offered a managerial position in Hong Kong, and he, his wife and children lived there for six years. Then his employer, Kwee Ho Tong, who had great confidence in Tong Pai Hu, suggested he move to Semarang on Central Java to become manager of a large business branch there. Kwee Ho Tong was a powerful businessman; He controlled seventy-five percent of the world's sugar trade in the region at that time. Tong Pai Hu, as general manager, would receive seven percent of the income of the company branch.[2] Indeed, this was a promising offer.

However, to Tong Pai Hu's wife the six years in Hong Kong had been hard, for she had missed her family. She could not bear the thought of going to Indonesia to live. As it was difficult to take the whole family to Indonesia (there were ten children, several of them of school age), it was decided that his wife would remain in Xiamen, and stay with her parents-in-law for a while. Tong Pai Hu went to Indonesia alone, but finally persuaded his wife to join him. She did make the move, with two of their children, but could not adjust to living in the tropics; after two years she died of heart trouble.

Tong Pai Hu was lonely and when a friend suggested he find another wife in Indonesia he thought about it, agreed, and then made a list of requirements to help the friend find a suitable wife. It went without saying that a possible wife would have to be Chinese, but she should be no more than a second generation Chinese, and she should be familiar with Chinese language and traditions. She should have some education, after all, he himself was an educated man, and finally, he'd prefer a girl from Fujian (Fukien), his home province in China.

After some time the friend, the matchmaker, told Tong Pai Hu that he had found just the right girl. Her parents had emigrated from Fujian Province, China to Indonesia, making the girl a second generation Chinese. She was in the graduating class of a local high school, so she had an education, and she spoke Chinese and Dutch. The matchmaker made an appointment with the parents, and he and Tong Pai Hu traveled to Jogjakarta (Yogyakarta) to speak to the father and to see what the girl looked like. She was only sixteen years old, and he was some twenty years older, but that was unimportant, many Chinese men married young wives. He was pleased, a deal was struck, and Tong Pai Hu returned to Semarang. Now it was time to bring the casket with his first wife's remains to China, and to bring back his two children also, to live with relatives there.

Tong Pu Hai was satisfied; however, the girl was disturbed when she heard the news that she was to be married soon.

Tan Tjien Nio was the youngest daughter in a family of five children, of whom three had died in infancy. She had two older sisters, and a brother who she remembered slightly. When she was five years old her brother, nearly twelve, died in a swimming accident. She remembered her parents' sadness about the death of their son, the only one who could have continued the family name. She vaguely recalled the Buddhist burial ceremonies and the white clothes they wore during the funeral.

Tan Tjien Nio's parents were Chinese nationals but, because of a drought in China several years earlier, had moved to Yogyakarta on Central Java. They lived frugally and saved whatever they could in order to send their only son to school, so that he might have a good education followed by a successful career. After the death of the brother a fortune-teller told Tjien Nio's father that, in order to avoid tragedy, his youngest daughter must marry a widower. Remembering these words and hoping to ensure the chance for a good future for their daughter, her parents had sent Tjien Nio to the Holland-Chinese school, a school with a good reputation.

She was bright and eager to learn, though she found the study of mathematics, Chinese reading and writing, and the Dutch language difficult. All along she knew that, though she was born in Indonesia and spoke Dutch, she was really Chinese by birth and lifestyle. Indonesians would always view her as a foreigner. Of course she would marry a Chinese man.

Her father explained to her that the fortune-teller had said she must marry a widower, and that marriage to Tong Pai Hu was the parents' way of securing good fortune for her, but Tjien Nio had no wish to marry. Why, she was only sixteen years old, and the man was thirty-six! Besides, she was not interested in marrying now, she wanted to complete her high school course, graduation was only seven months away. But no matter how she pleaded or protested, she knew that she'd have to obey her parents.

It was upsetting to think that, when the man she was to marry visited her home, Tjien Nio had not understood the reason for his visit. Her parents reminded her that they hoped she'd escape a life of poverty by marrying Tong Pai Hu, and that they did not dare request that the wedding be delayed until after high school graduation. Eventually, being a dutiful Chinese daughter, she followed her parents' instructions and reluctantly told the school principal that she had to leave school without graduating.

The fortune-teller had said she must marry a widower, and that marriage to Tong Pai Hu was the parents' way of securing good fortune for her, but Tjien Nio had no wish to marry.

Two months after her seventeenth birthday, on 26 April 1926, Tjien Nio and Pai Hu were married. While the groom looked impressive in a fine Chinese gown, Tjien Nio was lovely in a white western bridal gown with a veil. Following the ceremony a Chinese wedding feast was held in Semarang, and Tjien Nio was off to life as wife of a successful businessman. Formally she would now be known as Tong Tan Tjien Nio, but her friends would remember her as Tan, and she would now be known as Tong Tjien Nio.

There were servants who took care of the house in her elegant home in Semarang, she suddenly was a lady of leisure. Tong Pai Hu and Tong Tjien Nio learned to respect and love each other, in spite of their great age difference. Tjien Nio was thankful that her husband treated her kindly and generously, and when she found that she was expecting a child she was a happy young wife.

One day one of her household helpers casually remarked that Tong Pai Hu had a wife in Xiamen. Tjien Nio was shocked, she would not believe it, and could hardly wait for her husband to come home from work so she could ask. But when he came home she learned that it was true. It did not help much to learn that, when her husband was widowed in Indonesia, it was not he but his parents who looked for another wife for him in China, nor that they had found a village woman for him before he returned to Xiamen.[3] When Tong Pai Hu returned to Xiamen with his first wife's remains he had not dared tell them that he had just made arrangements to marry in Indonesia.

It was not unusual for Chinese men to have more than one wife, and, in deference to his parents, he married the wife they chose for him. However, he wanted to return to Indonesia, and did so, two weeks after the wedding. He did not know then that his matchmaker had purposely avoided telling Tjien Nio's father about the wife in China, fearful that the father would not give his daughter in marriage to Tong Pai Hu. Hearing the story, Tong Tjien Nio was heartbroken. She realized that, no matter how things were explained, others would still consider her Tong Pai Hu's third wife.

When her husband's work situation became so tense that he decided to return to Xiamen Tong Tjien Nio was very distressed. Yet she knew that she had no choice. She'd have to do what so many Chinese wives did and that was to move into the home of her parents-in-law.

Her only comfort was that her husband had chosen her, loved her, and that she was carrying their child. She had to resign herself to a situation from which she could not escape, she told herself, as she prepared to leave Indonesia, the country where she was born. At least her husband kindly saw to it that Tjien Nio's mother came to visit for a while before they left.

Tong Tjien Nio's life in the house of her in-laws in Xiamen was very different from married life in Indonesia, with only her husband. She now lived on the third floor of the family house which Tong Pai Hu had bought for his parents. Wife number two, Tong Siem Kin Bau, lived downstairs with several of the children of the first wife, and there was always the mother-in-law, who in many ways ruled the household. Among all these people Tjien Nio immediately felt drawn to her father-in-law, a dignified and gentle man, and learned to love him.

Tong Pai Hu never showed affection for either wife in front of the family, and divided his time between the two wives; some nights he spent with Tjien Nio, others with Kin Bau, who was only a few years older than Tjien Nio. The children of the first marriage were told to call Tjien Nio "Overseas Mother," and Kin Bau "Amoy Mother," so there was no mistaking of identity. Her parents-in-law planned a family gathering, and there they introduced Tjien Nio as the new daughter-in-law of the family, and her Buddhist name tablet was placed with the others' in the family shrine, indicating that she belonged to the family.

Only two weeks after their arrival Tong Pai Hu was sent to Hong Kong by his supervisor, and had to stay there for several months. Tjien Nio felt very lonely in her new home. She had learned the Xiamen dialect from her parents at home, but could not speak the local dialect which she heard around her every day.

Her third floor apartment was her private place, this was her very own area, and this is where she gave birth to her firstborn. She knew that the best way to really become a member of the family was by bringing a male grandchild into the home, so Tjien Nio was overjoyed that her baby was a boy. Many Chinese customs had to be observed for the new mother and baby. Tjien Nio did as she was told, and bravely ate the nourishing foods new mothers were given. Intensely happy with the baby, she still missed Pai Hu. It was difficult to always be respectful to her mother-in-law, and to maintain a civil relation with wife number two, Kin Bau. Yet she took care to be an obedient daughter-in-law, and to observe all Buddhist ceremonies. She regularly went to the temple to worship.

Not long afterwards her father-in-law became very ill and when he was near death Pai Hu was sent a message that, as eldest son, he had to return home before his father died. The day of his return his father died, and so Pai Hu grieved for his father before he could rejoice with Tjien Nio that they had a son. The baby was named Chung Po (Tonny).

After his father's death Tong Pai Hu became the head of the family, and did not return to Hong Kong. Instead, he continued his father's work in Indonesia. His father had taught him much, but he found that he needed additional studies, so Pai Hu followed a course and became a pharmacist.

Over the next several years the family grew, as both Tjien Nio and Kin Bau had several children. Tjien Nio's second and third children were both sons, Chung Ping (Peter) and Chung Bwun; they were followed by daughter Chung Hwa (Mary). While Tjien Nio was pregnant for the fifth time little Chung Bwun died; he was only three years old, and she grieved intensely for him.

The new baby, Chung Ing, was a girl. Tjien Nio's mother-in-law, a traditional Chinese woman, worried when the baby was born, for she believed that if a child died while the mother was pregnant, the new baby would never grow well and be healthy. She demanded that the child be given away. After all, she argued, a girl would leave the family upon marriage anyway, so why even risk problems? Pai Hu, a dutiful son, could not refuse his mother. The baby was given to a childless couple, and lost as a family member.

Tjien Nio had another child, a son, Chung Chu (John). The baby was restless and fretted much. Shortly before his birth thieves had broken in and stolen expensive items from the house, and Pai Hu went to a fortune-teller for advice. Tjien Nio was very upset when she heard that the fortune-teller said that the newest baby was bringing bad luck, and that this child was to be given away too. He was given to Pai Hu's brother and his wife, who were childless. No matter how much Pai Hu explained to Tjien Nio that Chinese tradition required that a childless couple be given one child by siblings who have children, she suffered and became depressed. She had now lost three of her six children.

After this Tjien Nio had two miscarriages, she became weak and ill, and was in bed for nearly a year. When she was near death she had a dream in which she received the message that she would get well, and be able to take care of her children. This dream encouraged her greatly, and she did recover. A year later she bore another child, Chung Ming (Caleb), and she and her husband were thrilled to have another son.

Throughout the 1930s there were fears of worldwide war, and military action did erupt. The Japanese army invaded China, and when they approached Xiamen Tong Pai Hu decided to move his large family to a safer place, Gulangyu (Kulangsu), a small island just across the channel from Xiamen. He expected to stay there only a few months; he was satisfied to rent four small rooms for his family, and opened a tiny drugstore for income. Instead of a few months the family stayed here for several years, and they were difficult years. The family's living space was small, Tjien Nio and Kin Bau quarreled, and their children constantly bickered. While they were on Gulangyu Tjien Nio had three more sons: Chung An (Solomon), Chung Rung (Stephen), and Chung Hway (Joseph). Their family was but one family among thousands of refugees here, many of whom lived under pitiful conditions.

When Tong Pai Hu returned home with his family the Japanese had occupied Xiamen. It was safer now, but there were many difficulties. War news was disturbing, Pai Hu faced business restrictions, money devaluated, food was often hard to get, the children disliked having to study Japanese and to follow new rules at school, and the growing boys frequently found it difficult to stay out of trouble.

Chung An (Solomon) was a little three year-old boy when he became deathly ill. Tjien Nio and Pai Hu cared for him as well as they could, but as the fever crept higher and higher little Solomon became weaker and weaker. Tjien Nio was desperate, she brought her boy to the Buddhist temple and prayed for him, but his condition did not improve.

At home again, Tjien Nio was visited by the mother of Tong Pai Hu's other wife, Kin Bau. This lady told Tjien Nio that she had recently learned about the Christian God who cares about people and who helps and heals. She herself had become a Christian believer, and had learned to pray. She prayed for Solomon, and then told Tjien Nio that, just at that time, a well-known evangelist, John Sung, had arrived in Xiamen for a series of evangelistic meetings. People of the neighborhood were invited to attend the meetings. When she urged her to go there for help, Tjien Nio said, "I have prayed, but it doesn't look good. I have tried Chinese medicine, but it didn't work. If my son can be healed by this man I'll become a good Christian,"[4] and she carried the toddler to where Dr. Sung was.

Many people were present to hear Dr. Sung speak and pray. The man spoke simply, and asked everyone present to pray for Solomon. Tjien Nio had only one sentence, "God, heal my son!" Dr. Sung put his hand on the little boy's forehead, prayed softly and ended with the words, "Praise the Lord."[5]

Tjien Nio returned home and told Pai Hu what had happened, and together they observed the boy anxiously. They were overjoyed when he gradually recovered. From this time on both Tjien Nio and Pai Hu wanted to know more about the God who listens to prayer. They learned about the Christian way, and became believers.

The war situation and the anxieties of earning enough for his family took their toll on Pai Hu. He became ill, had a stroke and died, leaving Tjien Nio a young widow at thirty-two, with seven children. His relatives must have been alarmed that, on the way to the burial place, the funeral

Tjien Nio had only one sentence, "God, heal my son!"

procession stopped at the Christian church for a service before continuing to the cemetery.

Tjien Nio was in an extremely difficult position. Not only did she face the task of bringing up her children, the eldest of whom was only fifteen years old, but from where would she get the finances to do this? In traditional Chinese style, she totally depended on her husband's family, and after all, though she was a legal wife, she was wife number three.

Tjien Nio decided to use her skills to earn some income, and set up a small seamstress business. She worked long hours to earn the income necessary to support her children. Her many hours at work meant that she was often not available for her children, and when they misbehaved she frequently lost her temper. She worked every day so she could earn a basic salary, keeping her small shop open seven days a week, and taking only a few hours on Sunday morning to attend church with her children.

One day an American missionary, Tena Holkeboer,[6] visited her, and chided her for being so stingy with time for Christian fellowship. Tena challenged her to close her shop on Sundays and still expect God's blessing on her efforts to earn a family income. Reluctantly Tjien Nio tried it, only to discover that, even with Sundays for church and family, the Lord provided enough for them all.

Sunday became a special day in the Tong home. In the morning everyone dressed in clean and mended clothes, and appeared at church with combed hair and clean shoes. Tjien Nio had such reverence for the church, God's house, that she sent each of her children to the toilet before going to church, so they'd not need to use church facilities.[7]

The Sunday noon meal was a highlight, and when the whole family crowded around the table, a great deal of jostling and good-natured bantering went on. Always noisy, the children enjoyed the food which Tjien Nio prepared, stretching her meager budget to make the pot of noodles tasty. She herself loved this time with all of her children, clamoring voices and all. Always concerned about her children's spiritual life, Tjien Nio did her best to teach, and let others teach them, about the Christian faith.

Tong Tjien Nio was thirty-two years old when she was widowed, and mother of seven children. Her eldest son Chung Po, in the back row, second from right, was unable to obtain traveling documents to travel with the family when they moved to Indonesia. Tjien Nio is also in the back row, second from left. *Photo courtesy Freda Hatfield Tong.*

When all was settled Tjien Nio received a share of the family capital. She then decided that it was time to return to her native country, Indonesia, at least for a while. Her eldest son Tonny was unable to accompany the family. He could not obtain a visa because he was already employed, and arrangements were made for him to stay behind. Peter, the second son, remained in Xiamen temporarily to complete his high school. And so, some twenty years after she had left her country as a young wife expecting her first child, Tong Tjien Nio returned to Indonesia in 1949 a widow with five young children.

Life in Indonesia was hard. Tjien Nio soon began to sew for other people again. Her widowed mother lived with Tjien Nio for a while and helped with family chores. It was a hand-to-mouth existence for the family with not a coin to spare.

One of Tjien Nio's sons, Chung An (Solomon), remembers the time that Chung Hway (Joseph) came home crying during school hours. He told his mother that he had been sent home because the school fees which were due had not yet been paid, and that at least a partial payment was needed immediately. Tjien Nio had just received a down payment for a sewing order, it was all the money she had. She gave this to Joseph, and sent him back to school. Before long he was home again, and sheepishly told his mother that he had a hole in his pants pocket, and had lost the money. Tjien Nio did not punish him, for she knew that it was really an accident. It was a setback, and she had to borrow some money before she could send Joseph on his way again. We can be sure that the pocket was mended, and that Joseph received strict orders to be careful this time![8]

Tjien Nio did her best to give her seven sons and her daughter a Christian upbringing. Still, her continual concern for the family's needs meant that the young mother had little time for other activities than work. And when, frustrated, she would lose her temper again, she'd feel sorry and inadequate. Yet, she learned much about living a Christian life as she sewed, cooked, cleaned, and found time to help at church. She taught her children about the Christian faith, and was herself a shining example. She became a woman of prayer, and this is what her children especially remember about her.

Chung Ping (Peter) remembers his mother's steadfast faith, and her trust in God no matter what happened. He mentioned her complete confidence that God would always help her with what she needed.[9]

Chung Ming (Caleb) recalled his mother's prayers. When asked what characterized his mother, he unhesitatingly replied, "She was prayerful."[10] Caleb remarked that of the surviving seven sons and one daughter, five sons became pastors and some founded seminaries. He added that his mother had asked God to deduct fifteen years from her own life and give them to her daughter Chung Hwa (Mary) when she was deathly ill. This happened, according to Caleb. Chung Hwa (Mary) lived another fifteen years, while Tjien Nio reached sixty-eight, unlike her own mother, who lived to become eighty-three years old.

Chung An (Solomon) relates that each morning before his brothers rose, his mother went to a "prayer hill" in Xiamen with some of the women of the church. The little family guard dog accompanied them, and waited patiently until the prayers were finished. The dog then trotted home behind Solomon's mother.[11]

"When I was small," Chung Rung (Stephen) relates, "the first words I'd hear in the morning were those of my mother while she prayed. She prayed for each of us children by name, and asked God to guide us." He said that his mother often prayed that she'd be neither so rich that she'd become a thief, nor so poor that she'd be a thief. "When I was eight or nine," he added, "it was arranged that I'd go to a prayer hill some evenings, and I was impressed by that." And, "Each Saturday my mother fasted and prayed for us. Each Sunday she prayed for all the preachers in the world."[12]

It was not only the prayers of Tjien Nio which characterized her, it was also her consistent behavior and her serious approach to life. She loved God and served him as well as she could. Already during the years when the children were young and she had to provide for them she began to visit sick members of the church. Even then she helped to distribute rice, oil and sugar among the poor. The government made these available, and when that stopped the church supplied these foods. And, whenever she could, Tjien Nio gave a little money to people who had less than she had.

One summer, thanks to a missionary who paid the expenses, Chung Ming (Caleb), Chung An (Solomon) and Chung Rung (Stephen) attended a youth conference some 30 kilometers from Surabaya. The featured speaker was Andrew Gih, a gifted and well-known Chinese evangelist who was popular because of his meaningful talks and pleasant way with people. When, a few

"The first words I'd hear in the morning were those of my mother while she prayed. She prayed for each of us children by name, and asked God to guide us."

Tong Tjien Nio was known to be a prayerful woman who delighted in her private time of devotions, and she loved to read her Bible. *Photo courtesy Freda Hatfield Tong.*

weeks later, this man called on her at her home, Tjien Nio was surprised. She was even more surprised when he laid three cards on the table, cards of commitment to serve God, each card signed by one of her sons. Tjien Nio knew that the conference had meant much to the boys, and that Chung Rung (Stephen) had experienced a new sense of being God's child. Solomon was struggling with the choice of how he might best live a Christian life in the world of music. Caleb was interested in becoming a pastor, but had set that dream aside as soon as he was old enough to earn an income to add to that of his mother.

Caleb was excited when Dr. Gih spoke of ways to finance a course of study, and was eager to begin. A generous donor paid school expenses, younger brothers found part-time jobs after school, and Caleb was able to enrol at a nearby Bible College the next term.

This is how all the boys attended school. Help from others, part-time jobs, hard work, and taking turns helping to provide for the family were all viewed as God's gifts. Only Chung Hwa (Mary), a diabetic, could not stand the rigors of a regular job; she stayed at home and helped her mother.

As the children grew older and helped the family, Tjien Nio's load lightened. She could work a bit less and still provide, and had time to help in the church. When the pastor once noted that five Chinese dialects were represented in the congregation and suggested that people begin a visiting program in the various languages Tjien Nio volunteered to visit people who spoke the dialect which she had learned in Xiamen.[13]

After about six years in Surabaya Tjien Nio became a deaconess in the church; in this way she met many people and was active in many church activities.[14] She and other women visited the sick, distributed food to the poor, and prayed with people; they were Christian sisters who took their work of being deaconesses seriously. A former friend, nearly ninety years old in 2002, remembers the visits in homes, the meetings in church, and the prayers of the women.[15]

One after another the boys graduated from high school. Chung An (Solomon) chose to serve God through music. He loved to sing, had a good voice, and learned how to direct choirs. He established a piano business and eventually founded the Surabaya Symphony Orchestra, which he continues to direct. Five of his brothers went to college, and then to seminary, to become pastors. Peter studied in the USA and then became a missionary to Taiwan; John was a pastor in Asia before he moved to the USA and continued there in the pastorate; Caleb became a pastor on West Java and is still there; Stephen has traveled for years and still travels as an evangelist throughout Southeast Asia; and Joseph, a real estate agent for some years, became president of the International Theological Seminary in Los Angeles, California.

Tjien Nio had always told her children that, unlike their mother, they'd be free to choose their own mate, though, as a Chinese parent, she was involved in the process. She did demur when Chung Hwa (Mary) wanted to marry, but when a physician declared Mary physically fit to marry in spite of her diabetes Tjien Nio helped prepare for the wedding. She also accepted a non-Chinese daughter-in-law without great difficulty, when Chung Ping (Peter), who was then studying in the USA, chose to marry an American girl. And when grandchildren were born Tjien Nio delighted in them.

It was a sad day when Chung Hwa (Mary), who had been sick for some time, died. Mrs. Hartono, daughter of one of Tjien Nio's longtime friends, remembers that time, when the usually happy and outgoing Tjien Nio grieved her daughter's death.[16]

When the day came that Tong Tjien Nio became eligible to receive Indonesian citizenship Indonesia was no longer a Dutch colony, and laws had changed. Like other Chinese Indonesians, she had to choose an Indonesian name. She decided to choose the name "Tanjowati" for a family name, and "Dorcas" for a personal name. She must have compared her career as seamstress to that of the biblical Dorcas, who sewed garments for others. Actually, she rarely used the name Dorcas, but it was useful when she applied for a passport.[17]

And she did need a passport. She continued to reside in Surabaya with Chung An (Solomon) and his wife and children, but Tjien Nio traveled far during the last decade of her life. At first her journeys took her to Bandung, Western Java, where Chung Ming (Caleb) and his wife and family lived, for Caleb was pastor of a church there. Later she went to Hong Kong, and visited the family of her eldest, Chung Po (Tonny), who had not been permitted a visa for Indonesia back in 1949, when Tjien Nio returned with her family. He had become a businessman in Hong Kong.

Then she went to Taiwan, to be with the family of Chung Ping (Peter), who was a missionary pastor. While in Taiwan Tjien Nio was reunited with her son Chung Chu (John), the little boy who was raised by his uncle and aunt when a fortune-teller told Tong Pai Hu that the baby was bringing bad luck and should be given to childless relatives. John had also become a Christian and was now a pastor. Eventually Tjien Nio even visited relatives in the USA and experienced culture shock. She was appalled to discover that fish heads, so prized by the Chinese for soup, were thrown away in the USA! She was frugal and could not bear that; she told her son to ask for some, so she could make a delicious soup.[18]

The family tradition of teasing did not stop when Tjien Nio became elderly, and her children loved to bring up happy incidents which they remembered. There was the time when she was out with her children and she left her purse on a lawn chair in a public place. She only noticed her loss when they were already several miles away. Chung

Hway (Joseph) recalled that, all the way back, Tjien Nio sat with her head bowed in the back seat of the car, praying that the purse might still be where she had left it. She did not seem a bit surprised when they actually found it. The children smiled at her childlike faith, but Tjien Nio ably defended herself.[19]

When Tjien Nio acquired Indonesian citizenship she chose "Tanjowati" as her Indonesian family name, and "Dorcas" as a personal name, remembering her many years as a seamstress. Her tombstone displays both Chinese and Indonesian names. *Photo courtesy Freda Hatfield Tong.*

Then there was the matter of the hair dye Tjien Nio had brought to the USA from Surabaya. She had noticed that her hair was greying, and wondered aloud whether it was alright to color her hair. She thought that, as her youngest son was a theological student, he would know the answer. The children asked her why she worried about this, and chuckled when she wondered if Jesus' saying, "You cannot even make one hair white or black," referred to dyeing one's hair! Tjien Nio went ahead and applied the hair color. The allergic reaction which followed was unpleasant, but at least her hair was black again. When, several weeks later, grey was coming through, she again prayed about it, and then applied hair dye again. This time the reaction was so painful that her children had to take her to the doctor for treatment. This settled it for Tjien Nio, she concluded that it was not the Lord's will for her to dye her hair.[20]

The gentle joking of the children, and the love they showed her as she became older, was heartwarming to Tjien Nio. It was her pride and joy to hold her grandchildren on her knee and to play with them. She was happy to be with her family, enjoyed the blessings of life, and had plans to do more traveling and visiting. But that was not to be.

When she was sixty-eight years old Tong Tjien Nio suffered a stroke. In the hospital, she was in a coma for several days and died, without regaining consciousness again. This Christian sister will always be remembered by those who knew her as a woman of prayer.

We may believe that, when Tong Tan Tjien Nio's life on earth ended our Savior said of her, "She has done a beautiful thing for me."

CHAPTER THIRTEEN

Europeans had arrived on a beach in Japan when one of their ships was wrecked in 1542, and Japanese had received them kindly. The Japanese people were fascinated by these Portuguese with their strange speech and appearance, and especially by their guns, even though they called them barbarians. After all, the Europeans ate with their hands, while all self-respecting Japanese ate with chopsticks!

It was only a few years before Portuguese Jesuits came to teach their faith. These Roman Catholic missionaries were as successful as the traders, at first, but when Japanese rulers began to see European foreigners as a political threat they began to prohibit Christianity. They exiled the foreign missionaries and began to cruelly persecute Japanese Christians who persisted in their new faith. Few people outside of Japan know that thousands of Japanese Christians were martyred for their faith, some four hundred years ago. As has often been the case, it was not the Christian religion itself which caused this as much as fear of foreign invasion. To make certain that the threat of foreign religions would not return the Japanese then forbade any foreigner to enter their country, or any of their citizens to leave Japan; if any

Japanese person should leave, he would be sent away if he would try to return.

It was during this time of persecution of Christians that the Filipino mestizo Lorenzo Ruiz arrived in Japan. Together with his companions, Lorenzo Ruiz was tortured then martyred. He was canonized by the Vatican in 1987 as the first Filipino saint.

For over two hundred years Japan's contact with other nations was minimal while inside the country there developed a flourishing culture and a society ruled by the powerful Tokugawa clan. When the Japanese were no longer able to avoid contact with the outside world, in the 1850s, they realized that their country had not kept pace with the rest of the world, and that they must modernize. Within a short time and with great enthusiasm Japanese traveled abroad and studied other cultures, returning with many kinds of knowledge which they absorbed and adapted to their own situation.

As soon as they could get permission to enter, foreign missionaries again came to Japan. It took time for the Japanese mind-set, which had been so set against the Christian faith for long, to come to tolerate and accept this religion. But in time churches were established throughout Japan, many of them Protestant.

Today the Japanese respect the Christian faith and life, but to most Japanese the Christian way does not seem to harmonize with Japanese thought. Biblical teaching appears unsuitable and barriers to faith seem insurmountable. Only about one percent of the Japanese profess to be Christian believers. And there are very few Japanese who can claim to be third, fourth or fifth generation Christians.

"I Am a Fifth-Generation Japanese Christian"

Minato Akiko[1] (1932–   )

Professor Minato looked elegant as she entered the school office. Pearl earrings and a necklace complemented her simple-cut beige suit, the sparkle in her eyes and her warm voice were just as she had been described by others. Her trim figure belied the fact that she was about to turn seventy. This was the first time we had met. We took a good look at each other before we sat, side by side, at the table. Professor Minato had been president of Tokyo Woman's Christian University for only one year, but her history with the school goes back many years, for she graduated from this school when she was a young woman. We drank tea and talked a while, then she started her story.

"I am a fifth-generation Japanese Christian," she began. And with that she looked back to a time nearly one hundred and fifty years ago. At that time Japan was a "closed" country. For more than two centuries Japan did not allow any Japanese nationals to leave, or foreigners to enter the country. It was only after a treaty had been signed by Japan and the USA that businessmen and others were allowed to come.[2] American Christians had been waiting to send Protestant missionaries, and they came immediately when the treaty went into effect.

Foreigners were allowed to stay in the country and practice their own religion, but all laws for the Japanese remained the same. A few hundred years earlier Japanese rulers, fearful that Christian influences in the country would be dangerous, forbade the practice of the Christian faith on pain of death. Now, in the mid 1850s, the pioneer missionaries who came to Japan lived under very difficult circumstances at first, knowing that possible new believers risked their lives if they spoke out. And so at first there were those who, though not baptized perhaps, became secret followers of Christ. Minato Akiko's great-great-grandmother was one of the early Japanese Protestant Christians whose lives were changed by the gospel.

"My great-great-grandmother, Kojima Hiroko of Nagano Prefecture, was widowed when she was thirty-eight years old. She had two sons. One went to Yokohama for business, and there he met James Ballagh, one of the earliest Protestant missionaries. After some time the young man contracted cholera. His mother Hiroko traveled to Yokohama and cared for him, but he died," Professor Minato related.

It was interesting to hear Professor Minato mention James Hamilton Ballagh's name so early in the conversation, and to hear her speak of this remarkable man. James Ballagh was twenty-nine years old when he and his wife Margaret[3] came to Japan as missionaries, and he stayed for fifty-eight years. He was well liked, a dedicated evangelist, a man of prayer, and he always had time for people. Even before Japanese leaders began to tolerate Christianity, a small group of believers began meeting for Christian services in Yokohama, and insisted that they wanted James H. Ballagh to be their pastor.[4] He was reluctant to agree to this because he was not Japanese, but as no Japanese Christian was as yet ready to lead the small group he consented to serve temporarily as their pastor.

He felt compassion for the mother, and spoke with her. Kojima Hiroko was so impressed with what this young blue-eyed foreigner told her, she listened. She stayed to learn more about the Christian faith, became a believer, and was baptized in the church in her home province, Nagano Prefecture, in 1876.

Hiroko then enrolled in the *Kaisei* Bible School in Yokohama.[5] After two years she graduated and was among the earliest to be a "Bible woman," that was something like being a minister. Together with one of her Bible school teachers, Mrs. Louise H. Pierson,

Kojima Hiroko then returned to her home province, Nagano Province, and worked as an evangelist.

Hiroko's daughter Sada married a cousin who was a lawyer, Kojima Tomotaro. This man was a wonderful Christian, and had been baptized in the Ueda church during the same service at which Hiroko herself was baptized. Kojima Tomotaro and his family lived in Matsumoto, in Nagano Prefecture, in a big beautiful home with a pond in the garden. He was wealthy. The couple was very open-minded and modern, and wanted to give both of their two children, a son and a daughter, a good education. This was unusual at a time when few girls received a formal education, yet both of the children traveled to Tokyo to go to school, first by riding a horse from Matsumoto to Ueda, and continuing from there by train.

"The daughter, Shinobu, later became my grandmother. She was really privileged to have such broad-minded parents; they sent her to a famous school for women, the *Joshi Gakuin*, an old school which was known as the best. Here she was well educated. She studied English and even learned to type, and she became a Christian.

"After graduation she returned to Nagano Prefecture, and married a young man who had been a 'disciple' of my great-grandfather. He was also a Christian and a lawyer. This couple had five children, my mother was the only daughter.

"My grandfather had tuberculosis, a common disease in those days. He died when my grandmother was thirty-six, and my mother was only seven months old. My mother never saw her father's face. Grandmother had to take care of the five children by herself; yet all of them grew to adulthood. There were four sons; three of them, all soldiers, were killed in battle during World War II. The fourth died recently.

"My grandmother was a strong Christian, and taught her children the Christian way. She also taught me in my turn. During the war we lived with her in Chiba, because my father, a physician, was sent to war. I remember that I often saw Grandmother praying when I woke at night. She used to say to us, 'Maybe we'll die tomorrow, but today let us pray and read the Bible.'"

"My father was a son of a wealthy family from the south, from Okinawa. He came to Matsumoto, Nagano Prefecture, where we lived, to study. He was a friend of my mother's older brothers, and often came to my grandmother's house, where he enjoyed the openness and warmth of the family."

Together with three high school friends Akiko's father visited the home of a former naval captain, whom they had heard speak about Christianity. The man told the boys of his experiences. He explained that he had been discharged from the navy for his refusal to participate in the required Shinto worship. The former captain opened the New Testament to the book of Acts and told the boys, "The book of Acts is the book of the acts of the Holy Spirit!" and prayed with them. Akiko's father was deeply impressed that a person would willingly endure punishment for his convictions.[6]

"Seeing the example of my grandmother's family, my father wished that he could have a family like that and one day he asked my grandmother if he could marry my mother. My mother was the only daughter, but she was only three years old then! Grandmother told him to wait.

"During the next fourteen years my father completed his studies, became a physician, and then taught at a university in northern Japan. He returned to Matsumoto and approached my grandmother again to ask if he could marry Mother. By then he was thirty-two years old, and Mother was a girl of seventeen.

"Grandmother consented, they married, and Mother was proud of him, because he waited for her so long. Father considered himself a real romantic; Mother, on the other hand, did not feel that way — she felt that he had robbed the cradle!

"My parents had four children, I am number two. The three boys all became physicians later, like my father. During World War II my father was away from home for a long time, and after he returned two more babies were born. This is why my youngest sister and I are seventeen years apart; I was a high school student when she was born.

"Today [2002] my mother is ninety years old, and still lives alone. She still insists on taking care of herself, and regularly shops, goes to church and to the bank, and visits the sick. She is fond of saying 'Please grow up!'"[7]

Akiko learned much at home about the Christian faith, and even when she was young her faith was an inspiration to her. Each morning the fifth grade students in her class at the public school were expected to bow and clap their hands before a small Shinto altar at the front of the classroom and to bow to a picture of the emperor's court but, because she was a Christian, Akiko refused to do that. Her teacher became angry and punished her by making her stand at the back of the classroom the whole day. When she grumbled and cried about this at home her father taught Akiko that "the powerful testimony of an individual touches the souls of others." He reassured her that she had done what was right, and added that, one day, she would understand.[8] It all seemed very confusing, but she decided that, one day, she'd learn more about how government laws and one's faith relate to each other.

Akiko was still in elementary school when her father left for war, and her family moved to her grandmother's house in Chiba. The government would not permit English lessons to be taught at school, thus Akiko learned the basics of English at home from her grandmother. Akiko's grandmother was well educated, had a vibrant faith and a strong personality, and insisted that, when school was interrupted, the children use the time at home to study.

World War II brought problems. One day when Akiko was twelve, an American bomb hit the school. The building collapsed, and a large beam hit her on the head. She and some other children were pinned under debris for quite some time before help came. She was rescued, but had been injured.[9] Her headaches never stopped, and she was often sick because of that blow on her head.

Akiko had always hoped to follow her father's example and

> *Her father taught Akiko that "the powerful testimony of an individual touches the souls of others."*

Professor Minato Akiko, president of Tokyo Woman's Christian University in Tokyo, Japan. She is past retirement age but is energetic, and eager to continue teaching the Bible in her classes of young women. *Photo courtesy Minato Akiko.*

become a physician, but her father advised against it. She was not strong enough, he feared, and would lack the stamina which is required of doctors, but he did urge her to get a good education. When Akiko was a third-year university student she suddenly experienced severe stomachaches and had to be hospitalized. She underwent numerous tests, and the outcome was sad. The gynecologist's report noted that, probably because of Akiko's accident during wartime, her entire body had been affected, and she would be unable to have children. When she heard this news Akiko cried. She cried all night, but by morning she had made up her mind. If she would never have children she would devote herself to getting a good education. Determined to follow this resolution she applied to go overseas to study.

Minato Akiko graduated from Tokyo Woman's Christian University in 1955 with a major in western history, and hoped to do further studies overseas. At that time it was not possible to change yen into dollars, and that made paying fees for studying impossible. Many students therefore applied for a scholarship to study overseas and Akiko did the same. She was one of the twenty thousand applicants for a Fulbright scholarship. Thirty-five of these applicants were accepted, and Akiko was among them, one of only three women in the group. In 1956 she entered the University of Oregon, and transferred a year later to Wheaton College, near Chicago, as a Fulbright graduate scholar. She would graduate three years later with a Master's degree, with a major in New Testament studies.

There was lots of excitement among the young people as they sailed for two weeks on the *Hikawa Maru* on the way to the USA. Akiko became especially friendly with Minato Hiroshi, one of the thirty-two young male Fulbright scholars, a chemistry student. During the leisurely crossing the Pacific Ocean the two young people fell in love and even before they reached America Hiroshi had told Akiko that he'd like to marry her. This was thrilling and romantic; however, the more Akiko thought about it, the more she became convinced that it was only fair to tell him that she'd never be a mother. Rather fearfully, she told him, and was relieved when he said that this did not change things for him; he still wanted to marry her. Once they arrived in the USA their love had to be nurtured by letter-writing, because Hiroshi went to Minnesota to study and Akiko went to Oregon, and later to Illinois.

Although he was raised a Buddhist, Hiroshi was inspired by what his fellow Fulbright scholars told him about the Christian faith, and he became a Christian. From this time on he was an ardent follower of Jesus, and was active in the church.

> For him there was no distinction between simple Biblical faith and brilliant scientific scholarship, for God is a God of truth; and the God of the Christian Bible is sovereign over both the spiritual realm and the realm of physical nature. His worship and his service to God were not limited to a few hours each week but penetrated his whole life and all his activity. He also served God in the laboratory and in the lecture hall, as he labored to bring all of God's creation into perfect order for the glory of God and the service of his fellow human beings.[10]

Hiroshi was an organic chemistry student, but Akiko had no scientific mind at all. Whereas Hiroshi needed data to reach a conclusion, Akiko would begin with a conclusion, and from there figure things out. Playfully, Akiko compared their relationship to a scientific symbol and reasoned that, as he was a scientist, his reasoning was governed by the symbol ∴, meaning, therefore. She, on the other hand, as a historian, considered herself more of a romantic.

Her thinking was more like the symbol ∵, meaning because, just upside down from his!

Living in America was an eye-opening experience for the young Japanese. In Japanese society there is a strong sense of unity, of being part of a group, and Akiko learned many lessons about living in a society made up of individualists, of people of different backgrounds. One experience which still embarrasses her so many years later is the memory of the time she was teaching a fellow student some Japanese words. Judy, one of Akiko's new friends, was a black girl. Judy would pick up a crayon from its box, hold it up, and ask what the color of that crayon was called in Japanese. "Red is *aka*, white is *shiro*," Akiko told her. When Judy held up the light beige crayon, Akiko unthinkingly said, "*hadairo*," which means "skin color." Judy looked at Akiko, looked at the crayon, and asked, "skin color"?[11]

After some time Akiko again worried that it might not be fair to marry Hiroshi if they could never have children. After all, wouldn't any man hope for a child, a son? After much prayer and soul-searching she wrote him a letter that they'd better not marry, and that from now on she would devote herself to studying. How difficult it was to wait for his reply!

Hiroshi wasted no time. Immediately, via special delivery, Akiko received a letter. In it Hiroshi had written the chemical formula

$$NaOH + HCl = NaCl + H^2O$$

This means that, sodium hydroxide ($NaOH$), added to hydrogen chloride (HCl), results in table salt ($NaCl$) and water (H^2O). He explained that the first atom in each chemical element is positive and the second one negative; the positive and the negative attract each other and form table salt and water, stable and useful elements.

In the same way, he wrote, he represented the positive formula, because he loved her dearly, and she was like the negative, because she had told him they should not marry. If their feelings for each other, just as in the formula, the positive and the negative, could only be combined, then they would become intertwined, and, just like salt and water are useful and stable, theirs would be a practical and stable harmony.

Akiko was profoundly impressed with this declaration of Hiroshi's love and needed very little time to respond, positively this time. She had no further misgivings about not becoming a mother, there was now a mutual and loving understanding. The calculating trait of the scientist and the romantic side of the historian would, from now on, form a stable relationship.

Akiko and Hiroshi were married in 1959 at Wheaton College, with the school president officiating. Akiko wore the traditional Japanese kimono at the wedding ceremony, but also a white, western-style veil. She chose to combine her Japanese background with the symbolism of the white veil. Though no family members could be present, some one hundred and fifty guests of the university community attended and celebrated this happy day.

Together they moved to Harvard University, where Hiroshi continued his studies in organic chemistry, while Akiko enrolled in courses in Church history, this time as a special student at the Divinity School. She remembered her experiences as a fifth grader, and was still interested in the relationship between government and religion. She wondered about the persecuted Christians during the early centuries of the Roman Empire, and wanted to learn more about the Christian witness of the Early Church and the frequent church–state struggles throughout the centuries.

She had completed all her courses, and began to write a book, *The State and Church*, when, to her great but unexpected delight, she discovered that she was pregnant. This seemed unbelievable, but it was true! In time a healthy son was born. This ended Akiko's formal education, she now concentrated on being the mother she had thought she'd never be. She completed her writing, and the book was published in Japan in 1961. Later Akiko and Hiroshi had two more children, another son and a daughter.

After Hiroshi's graduation the Minatos returned to Japan. Dr. Minato busied himself with his work and writing and became a distinguished senior professor at the Tokyo International University, later at the Tokyo Metropolitan University, and was "held in high honor in Japan, in Europe, and in America as a lecturer and trusted authority

Four generations. From left to right, Minato Akiko, her grandmother, daughter and mother. *Photo courtesy Minato Akiko.*

in his chosen field of organic chemistry."[12] He was an elder in his church (Morning Glory Church of Tokyo), always participating in the evangelistic program of their congregation, and was active in Christian organizations. Furthermore, he also traveled widely for scientific conferences. Mrs. Minato was a busy housewife and mother of small children, yet she always made time for study. She planned short study sessions during the day, often only fifteen minutes at a time, but she made certain to study and write daily. As soon as the children's ages allowed it she went to school to teach, and she has continued that nearly without interruption until now.

In October 1977 Dr. Minato returned home fatigued from a two-week trip to France, Germany and Hawaii, where he had attended conferences. The next day was Sunday, and the family spent most of it in church, there was little time for relaxation. Early Sunday evening the ten-year old daughter, who was so happy to have Daddy home again, wanted to play ping-pong with him. Dr. Minato did not want to refuse, and together they went to the garden. They both enjoyed the game, and the ball shot back and forth. Suddenly a sharp hit sent the ping-pong ball up high, and it landed in the grapevine. Dr. Minato reached as high as he could for the ball and, as he did so, he had a stroke. He lost his balance, falling heavily, and cracking his skull. Unconscious, he was brought to the hospital, where he lay in a coma for five days. There he died, without regaining consciousness. An overflow crowd attended his funeral.[13]

Mrs. Minato was left with three children, sixteen-, fourteen-, and ten-years-old. She mourned for her husband, and asked why God had to take him when he was only forty-four years old. The words of friends who tried to comfort her seemed hollow, her grief was so deep. But she must continue, and her children looked to her for loving guidance.

In an interview with *Leadership* magazine, Professor Minato related: "There were many opportunities to remarry after his passing. I did not consider proposals of marriage, because many children have only a physical father but no spiritual or mental father. I set before my children a strong image of their father as head of our family. They had a sense of his example and spiritual guidance, even in his absence. He even supported them after his death with the royalties from his books, thus enabling all three of them to complete their education."[14]

To help the children remember their father, Mrs. Minato prepared a "Papa Corner." She placed a bookcase in a conspicuous place in the house; on the shelves she set a copy of each of the twenty-three books her husband had written as well as a bound copy of his one hundred and twenty-five published papers. On the top shelf she placed a Bible, opened at Psalm 34, the passage which the family had read during their devotions on their last day together. Whenever one of the children came home with a certificate, an award, or anything special, she placed that beside the Bible. In this way Mrs. Minato hoped to keep the memory of her husband alive in her children's minds. Also, this was her way of demonstrating that her husband, their father, would always be the head of their family.

A generation later — Minato Akiko's mother on page 262 picture is now the grandmother on the left here, while the baby of the first photo has become a mother. Minato Akiko's daughter is the sixth-generation Christian in this family. She holds her own daughter. *Photo courtesy Minato Akiko.*

Looking back Professor Minato remembers years of

busy, difficult, yet blessed experiences. Being the only parent and teaching full time took all her energy, but she trusted her heavenly Father to provide everything necessary. She reflects that not having a husband any longer made her more independent, and it motivated her to become more involved in the role of women at home, in church and in society. This, added to her earlier interest in the role of Christians during persecution, made for much reading and writing to be done.

As she pondered on the role of women in Japan Professor Minato concluded that Japanese women, kept back in most of society and even in the church, are different from women in the early church. She wrote about women such as Priscilla (Romans 16:3), Euodia (Philippians 4:2–3) and others, who were called co-workers in the New Testament. How were they different from contemporary Japanese women? She examined the position of women in feudal and in today's Japan, and wondered why the place of women in Japanese society today differs so vastly from the place of women in the West. She looked at the Japanese term *jiritsu*, which is made up of two Chinese characters. The first character means "self" while the second one means "stand." When put together they form the word *jiritsu*, which is translated as "independence." Professor Minato questioned what independence really means for contemporary Japanese women. How can there be an acceptable bridge between the discrimination of bygone days and the often strident feminism of today?

She has attempted to explain her belief that, though women interrelate with each other, and though the husband should be the head of the home, a woman needs a personal independence which will influence her to "stand by herself" in matters concerning the heart. This type of independence, according to Professor Minato, will motivate her to exercise her conscience, to stand up for her faith. Akiko had finally learned to understand what her father meant when he

Minato questioned what independence really means for contemporary Japanese women. How can there be an acceptable bridge between the discrimination of bygone days and the often strident feminism of today?

encouraged her not to clap before the Shinto altar when she was in the fifth grade, even though she was punished by having to stand at the back of the classroom all day. Now she knew what he meant when he said that, even if persons are ridiculed by others, their strong convictions will touch others' souls.

It is Minato Akiko's conviction that the Japanese woman must analyze such independence, and then apply it to today's Christian living. Women must be willing to speak out, to serve as leaders, and to help strengthen the Church. How can they be shown the way?

About a century and a half ago American pioneer Protestant missionaries came to Japan. They came to preach the gospel, but one cannot be separated from one's culture, and thus they inadvertently taught their own culture as well. Some Japanese rejected this, others listened and absorbed foreign and new ideas into their minds. One of those who became captivated by American thought was Nitobe Inazo, the founder of Tokyo Woman's Christian College (University today). Professor Minato Akiko was intrigued by this Christian man who had promoted education for women long ago, and she made a study of Nitobe Inazo's life as well as that of his American wife, a Quaker.

Nitobe Inazo[15] became a Christian while he was a student in Sapporo, in northern Japan. When he was applying for university and was asked why he wished to continue his earlier English language studies he said, "I wish to be a bridge across the Pacific Ocean . . ."[16] a dream that has defined his life. He found opportunities to build relations with other nations, and was the first Japanese exchange professor to lecture in the USA. Nitobe became a Quaker while in the USA, something which might seem puzzling until one realizes that there was a long Quaker influence among the elite in Japan, even among royalty.[17]

A distinguished scholar, Nitobe served his country courageously, and he did his utmost to explain Christian thought and ideals to the Japanese people. While he was in Philadelphia he met and married a woman of a well-known Quaker family;[18] she was as eager as he was to spread Christian teachings. She moved to Japan with him, and was his faithful companion for the rest of his life.

Professor Minato was impressed with Nitobe's thinking, it matched hers precisely. Nitobe's biblically based teaching was that men and women are equal before God, both created in his image (Genesis 2:18). He said that women, like men, are redeemed in Christ, and are co-heirs to the riches of the Kingdom of God, and that this has implications for society. He believed that because women are equally important to God, they must develop their own Christian personality. Nitobe taught this theory of personality and identity in Japan, where it was considered radical thinking. Because he really wanted to teach these ideas to Japanese women, he founded the Tokyo Woman's Christian College (now University), of which Minato Akiko is president today.[19] She became an active member of the Christian women's movement in Japan, and helped create and then chaired the Women's Commission of the Japan Evangelical Association, a movement which today has some one hundred fifty thousand members.

Minato Akiko's teaching reflects her desire to help Japanese women to be Christians who are conscious of their identity as God's children. Though tradition and society may either push women into the background or elevate them at a worldly level, Minato insists that Christian women must base their identity on their relationship with God. She has written extensively both in English and in Japanese in her efforts to circulate her research and knowledge about home, church and society, and of the role of Christian women.

"During many years I worked hard to take care of my children. They grew and became an accountant, a lawyer, and a distinguished organist. They all married, and one day I realized that eighteen years had passed since my beloved husband died.

"My eldest son married a girl with the same name as mine, Akiko, I knew the parents. Some time after the wedding my daughter-in-law's mother died of cancer and her father lived alone. I felt sorry for the man. He was wealthy, but so lonely. He struggled with breathing problems, I pitied him. He became a Christian and was baptized in my church, I often saw him there.

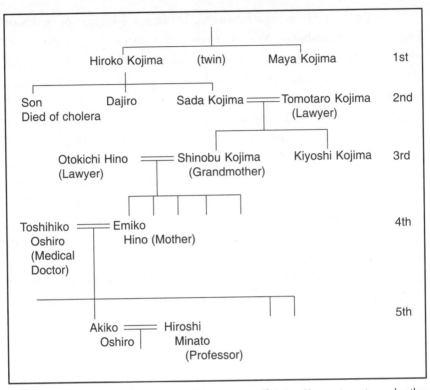

Her family tree shows Minato Akiko to be a fifth-generation Christian. Her great-great-grandmother Kojima Hiroko was baptized in 1876. *Diagram courtesy of Minato Akiko.*

"One day he shocked me when he asked me to marry him. This was not what I had expected! As I looked at him I realized that in all his life he had not experienced real love until he fell in love with me. We were married in our church. I decided not to leave my work but, since I was of retirement age, to continue working part-time. This way we had time together. I wished that he could see some of the places where I had been when I was young, and we visited the USA for two glorious weeks. For three and a half years he was such a happy man. Then he died, and I was alone again.

"Now I am aging, but I still have challenges. I am President of the university, and hope to do more writing. There is more I would like to do to help Japanese Christian women find fulfillment in their lives. I thank the Lord for the many opportunities He gives me each day."

Twice, at a gathering of women, Professor Minato spoke about losing a loving husband. As they listened the women wept with her as they heard her share her sorrow.[20] But Akiko is not one to sit down and give up; she asserted that, each time, God has given her a new challenge. Her latest challenge, that of being a university president, gives her more opportunities to teach the Bible and to make it real to her students. She views this as an opportunity to evangelize in a way she's not had before.[21]

When Professor Minato's first name, Akiko, is written in Japanese, its character is made up of a combination of three suns. Her father explained to her once that she was given this name because the three suns designate her role as wife, as mother, and as an individual in society. She herself professes that she has tried to achieve this meaning in her life as wife, mother, and educator.[22]

We may believe that one day, when Minato Akiko's life on earth ends our Savior will say of her, "She has done a beautiful thing for me."

From the beginning of the twentieth century Filipino Protestants were missionaries to their own people. At first many Filipinos opposed American Protestantism when it arrived, partly for political and partly for religious reasons. When Protestant missionaries spoke about the Bible they were bringing new ideas to Filipinos who had long been forbidden to study the Bible. But those who listened to biblical teaching and were given faith could not keep their joy to themselves — they wanted to spread it.

It is said that a Protestant Filipino went from house to house, selling Bibles. When the priest of the town told his parishioners to destroy the Bibles they had bought, one owner of a small business tore pages from his Bible and used them to wrap merchandise. Noticing that her purchase had been packaged in Bible pages, a devout and elderly customer grumbled, "Those Protestants are utterly godless, otherwise they would not use the Gospel of John to wrap foodstuff." She then read the pages, and the words of John 3:16. Reading that text was the beginning of a turnabout in her life. Before long she had shared her happiness with others in the town and became, in this way, a missionary.

In a village along the east coast an elderly man who was a new Christian had memorized several Bible texts. He bought a Bible, and as he was unable to read he asked someone to find and mark those verses which he had memorized, and place a string at each page which had one of those verses. The man knotted the strings, one had one knot, another two, and yet another three, so that he himself would know where to find each particular verse. Then, excitedly, he went into the village and invited others to read a verse he had chosen. When he asked them if they knew what it meant and they could not tell him, he invited them to come to church the next Sunday, promising that someone there could give an explanation. In this way he helped to let people know who the Savior is, and was a missionary to his own people.

Later in the 1900s the Bible became a more familiar book. It was translated into a number of Filipino languages, and gradually became more easily available to Filipinos. Though the numbers of Protestant Christians remained small, they too talked about their faith. Among them was the woman who graduated from a Bible school in Mindanao, and worked in churches for forty years, many of those years as *pastora* (female pastor). Then there was the woman whose background was one of spirit worship, but who became a lay church worker in Northern Luzon. They were both missionaries to their own people.

Towards the end of the century there were Filipino Christian teachers, pastors, nurses, social workers and evangelists, all missionaries to their own people. Some of the stories of the lives of these people are remembered, but the stories of many others have gone undocumented only to be forgotten.

This chapter tells the story of one Filipina who dedicated her nursing skills to God as she served together with her husband in the work of evangelism. It is recorded here so that we may remember.

A Missionary to Her Own People

Lucy del Carmen Apostol (1937–   )

It was not very cold, but Lucy del Carmen shivered as she looked at the welcoming crowd standing on the dock in San Francisco. Among these people there should be a man and a woman who had come to meet her. Lucy's father had sent them a photograph showing Lucy wearing a pink dress, decorated with a black flower on the bodice, and she was wearing the dress now, so that she might be recognized. Standing on the deck of the ocean liner, Lucy shivered, as it slowly approached the dock, and she wondered if the people were really there and if they would be able to recognize her among all the travelers standing at the railing of the ship.

She felt uncomfortable and awkward as she looked over the heads of people. Would she be able to understand these people she had never seen before? Lucy had done her best to learn to speak English fluently, but she was a young Filipina, and the people she had to meet were Americans, and much older. What would they look like? Lucy's eyes scanned the crowd down below. Yes, she could see a man and a woman looking in her direction and pointing at her. Quickly she stepped as close to the railing as she could and opened her coat wide. The man smiled and the woman waved. At once Lucy felt relieved, yet felt her stomach tighten as she remembered that she had come from a faraway village in the Philippines, and was about to begin the next chapter of a big adventure.

No longer a teenager, Lucy is now a grandmother. She smiles as she remembers being that excited yet fearful young woman, standing on the deck of the ocean liner as it entered the harbor. She tells her story.

"I was born in Banate, 50 kilometers north of Iloilo City, in 1937. I was the older of two girls in a family of seven children, and became my father's favorite. Even while I was in Banate Elementary School I had my ambitions. My parents took me to the town hospital when they visited the sick, and there I saw nurses in white uniforms and caps. They seemed so efficient, and able to help the patients. I wanted to be like that. My mother had made me a rag doll and I often dressed my doll in white, so that it could personify my dream. I wanted to help the sick.

"When I was about five years old my dad became a pastor. Around the same time World War II broke out and the political situation in our country became tense. Numerous people of our town evacuated to the mountains; my family also went. There, away from town and school, our missionary life began. My parents involved the whole family in the work of helping others. Thus, in the most natural way, we children became missionaries. Much later, my husband and I would teach our own children to visit the sick, to run errands for the elderly and to be useful to others. My parents' love for the people in the mountains, and also in the lowlands, became part of us.

"My desire to become a nurse became more intense after the war when I attended high school. I prayed for the opportunity to go to nursing school, but it seemed an impossible dream. My father's salary was barely sufficient to provide for our family of nine. I remember that, at that time, the Sunday offering was given to my parents for our food; sometimes there was a total of five pesos. Right after the service my mother would go to the market and she always returned home with what seemed to be enough food. But there was no money for further education.

"I never gave up hope that my dream would come true. Still, when I graduated from high school in March 1954 I had no idea how my dream might become reality.

"During my last year in high school my father became acquainted with an American lady who lived in Grand Rapids, Michigan, USA. This lady, Jane Roodvoets, belonged to the Nederduitse Church, a community which then did not encourage overseas missions. However, Jane's ideas were different, and she began to collect items for shipments to foreign countries. Other women in her church wanted to help, and so the Friendship Missionary Society was born in the basement of Jane's house. There the women packed boxes with clothing and food, and then sent them to missionaries around the world. The first missionary box sent to the Philippines was sent in care of my father, who was glad to distribute the contents.

"As their correspondence continued Dad wrote Jane about our family and my ambition to become a nurse. Promptly Jane replied, 'If Lucy wants to come to the USA we'll help her,' and added that she and her husband were excited about the idea of sponsoring me. I was excited too, but also fearful. I was only a country girl, living in a remote village of the Philippines. How could I ever travel to the USA, far, far away from home, and become a nurse? We always spoke Hiligaynon in our village, and, though I had studied both English and our national language in school, I'd have to learn much more English than the little I knew. At the same time I believed that this offer was an answer to my prayers. I readily agreed to the idea, and told my parents how eager I was to go. When it was time to leave I knew that my father was anxious about my safety, yet I resolutely packed my few belongings and bade my parents farewell.

"I was barely seventeen when I traveled all alone to Manila. There I stayed with an aunt who was a dentist. For six months I visited the American Embassy daily to ask if my documents were

> *"I never gave up hope that my dream would come true."*

ready, walking the two miles each way. During that time I steadily practiced my patience, and learned much English and Tagalog. Finally, in November, my frustration ended. The necessary documents, including a plane ticket, arrived! I believed it to be God's will for me that I go to the USA and study nursing. I was so excited!

"My aunt saw me off when the *President Wilson* of the American President Lines left the Manila harbor. What an exhilarating experience that was! But my exhilaration left me less than twenty-four hours later when I became violently seasick. Suddenly I felt very small and lonely. Gone was my bravery. Fortunately I was billeted in a cabin with eight bunks, and my roommates were all Filipinas. I was able to communicate with them in Tagalog, and also in English.

"The ship docked in Hong Kong, Kobe, Yokohama and Honolulu on its twenty-one-day journey. One of my roommates was an older lady, a Filipina who lived in California, she was returning there from a visit with her family in the Philippines. She was concerned about me and warned me to be careful, very careful, when dealing with strangers.

"As the days passed my concerns grew more disturbing. Was this ship really headed for the USA? If not, how would I know? And would someone really be there to meet me? I knew that America was a big country with many people, and perhaps they had forgotten about me. But then I reminded myself that Jane and her husband had a married son in California whose parents-in-law had offered to meet me.

"On the day of arrival I wore the pink dress with the black flower on the bodice. It was cool on deck, but my shivers were from fear as much as cold, I think. When I saw an older couple looking at a piece of paper and then scanning the passengers on the ship, I opened my coat wide, so they could recognize me. My heart thumped as I waved at them and pointed at the flower. Needless to say, I was overjoyed to see the woman wave her paper (my photograph) and, when I disembarked, to meet the couple. They were Dutch Americans, just like Jane Roodvoets and her husband. As I looked around on the dock I saw big people all around me and felt overwhelmed. I had seen American missionaries in the Philippines, but these people all looked so tall!

"My hosts were wonderful. They showed me around the town, then took me home. I answered their questions shyly, but was mostly silent. They gave me warmer clothes, even a pair of nylons. Now I can laugh about it, but that evening I didn't know that I should take off my nylons, so I kept them on in bed.

"The next day my hosts gave me a plane ticket for the last leg of the trip and brought me to the airport. They gave me a ticket to travel to Grand

Lucy Apostol as a new nursing graduate. *Photo courtesy Lucy Apostol.*

Rapids, Michigan. By then I was numb with fear. There were no jets yet then, and the roar of the airplane engines was loud and frightening. The instructions I received seemed too vague to follow. The flight attendant had been asked to help me during my transfer in Chicago, but I was very nervous as I boarded the plane.

"When I arrived in Chicago a tall American approached me. He must have been an airline employee, I was too afraid to notice. 'Are you Lucy del Carmen?' he asked, and when I nodded in agreement he bent over and asked, 'Can I take your bag for you?' Remembering what the lady on the ship had said about being careful I almost snarled as I tightened the grip on my bag and gave him a terse 'No!' I was so tense that I really wasn't aware of what was going on. The man brought me to a waiting room, and after a while a female flight attendant guided me to my seat on the plane to Grand Rapids.

"It was evening when I arrived in Grand Rapids, and Jane Roodvoets and her husband met me at the airport. When we came outside I saw my first snow. Of course I'd heard about snow, but this was real. I bent over to take some in my hand. Brrr! It was cold! Jane and her husband laughed as I quickly dropped it."

Lucy was enroled at the Reformed Bible Institute (now Reformed Bible College) for the remainder of the school year, so she might become accustomed to life in America and practice English conversation. She had been insecure about her ability to communicate in English, but soon found that she was more able than some of the other Asian students, especially the Chinese. Mr. and Mrs. Roodvoets soon became "Uncle Jack" and "Aunt Jane" to Lucy. Aunt Jane and Lucy often talked about their faith. Lucy discovered that Aunt Jane's faith was not as optimistic as her own; to Lucy's singing "Now I belong to Jesus," Aunt Jane once asked her, "But Lucy, how do you know that for certain?" It was customary in their church to be so concerned with one's own sinfulness that people frequently absented themselves from Communion services. This astonished Lucy, who had no doubts about being a forgiven sinner.

Lucy experienced further consternation. When she was asked to attend catechism class, a class where biblical teaching and church doctrine were studied, she dutifully walked to the parsonage. Entering the house she was shocked to notice a heavy smell of cigar smoke there. She was unaware of Dutch culture and the customs of Dutch Christians. Smoke? And in the pastor's house at that! After the lesson she rushed home and told Aunt Jane that she would never go back. "I think it's a sin to smoke. I have my convictions!" she exclaimed. The Roodvoets understood and did not ask her to attend catechism again.

In September 1955 Lucy began her studies at the Roseland Community School of Nursing in Chicago. During her three years there she returned to Grand Rapids for weekends whenever this was possible. Lucy was grateful to her sponsors, and wanted to show that. The Roodvoets owned a grocery store, and many a Saturday Lucy worked there, side by side with Aunt Jane. Aunt Jane loved missions, and frequently reminded Lucy to listen to God's voice.

As time went by Lucy's wish to be a missionary nurse grew. While she washed windows, shoveled snow, or helped in the store, she knew that she was learning more than nursing and English, that she was gaining valuable life experience. Aunt Jane encouraged her to join Sunday evening visits in their home, when friends came after the worship service, and discussed many topics. But Lucy was usually too shy to join the circle, and would sit on the stairs, listening to the conversation and learning. The people of that church loved their young Filipino friend, and were kind to her, they spoke kindly to her and often gave her small presents. It probably felt strange to always be called "Lucy," rather than the familiar "Neneng," her nickname at home.

After her graduation as registered nurse in 1958 Lucy returned to Grand Rapids and to the Reformed Bible Institute, to prepare for missionary service. She was happy to find part-time work at the hospital where she had been trained, and to be able to support her studies in this way. She had no way of expecting the big change which would soon come into her life.

"I noticed Vince very soon after I went back to Grand Rapids. Vince Apostol (his name is actually Vicente, but in America everyone called him Vince) was a young Filipino who had arrived at the Reformed Bible Institute the previous year. We were totally astonished when we saw each other and recognized that we were both Filipinos. He was shy, and mostly silent, at first. Gradually we began to talk, and were delighted to discover that both of us were born on Negros Island. Naturally, we then lapsed into Hiligaynon, the language spoken in both our hometowns! I had not spoken my language for more than three years, and could hardly imagine that here, in America, I was using it. We then realized that Vince's home church in Iloilo City, the Doane Baptist Church, was the church where my father had been pastor several years earlier. But Vince seldom spoke to me, though he probably noticed that I was fast becoming interested in talking with him more. Sometimes we met on campus and, while walking together, told each other about our past. We were intrigued to know that both of us were preparing ourselves for missionary work in the Philippines. Our conversations were friendly, but not really personal.

"Unknown to us, some of our American friends were thinking ahead. When one of my friends requested me to babysit one evening, I readily agreed. Little did I know that her husband had asked Vince to do the same thing. We were surprised to meet each other at the friends' home, but did not react, even when the couple left. After the couple's children were put to bed, Vince and I found ourselves alone in the living room. Silently we sipped tea, feeling awkward. I then told Vince that, after graduation, I hoped to return to the Philippines. 'I am going home,' I said. 'My father can use my help, and I want to follow God's guidance as a missionary nurse.'

"Softly, Vince's words came. 'We can go home together, if you wish.'

"That was the beginning of our romance."

Lucy del Carmen and Vince Apostol were married in September 1958, and returned to the Philippines after their graduation from the Reformed Bible Institute in 1961. Lucy had been away for seven years, and had to learn many things. Not only had the situation in her country changed during those years, Lucy herself had also changed. She had left home as a teenager, unfamiliar with anything outside her small hometown, and she returned as a twenty-four-year old, a registered nurse, wife, mother of John Mark, and pregnant again. Vince had also changed. He'd been a fairly new Christian when he left the Philippines, and now he was a Bible School graduate, trained to be an evangelist.

After the first glow of meeting their families had subsided somewhat, Lucy talked with her father for hours. Lucy and Vince were glad to receive Pastor del Carmen's advice, for they keenly felt themselves novices. He gave them pointers on how to talk to people, how to use pictures in teaching and gave them other helpful advice for evangelists. Lucy felt very much that she was learning to live in two cultures. Of course, as a Filipina, she knew Philippine thought and life well, but having lived in America for long, she had also acquired some of the

American ways of life. For instance, she could be more direct now with people than she used to, and had learned to speak up. She understood non-Filipinos better, something which became valuable later, when she worked with foreigners. And she had learned much about American cuisine. Others loved her cooking and baking, which tasted

Lucy del Carmen Apostol with husband Vicente, late 2002. Lucy has used her nursing skills together with her gift of evangelism and is still involved in both areas. *Photo courtesy of the author.*

so different from the food to which Filipinos were accustomed.

They were advised to move to Bacolod City to begin work, but had no acquaintances there. Housing was hard to find, and the apartment which they rented was filthy. Here, they scrubbed and scrubbed to make the place livable. Reminiscing, Lucy believes that this was a positive experience, for it not only taught them patience, it also was good for their attitude. Perhaps they had been somewhat proud, being new graduates and having come from the USA so recently.

Lucy and Vince Apostol planned to work as a team, and they did this for many years. Their first missionary experience unexpectedly quickly turned sour. A group of people who had left their own church in Bacolod City over disagreements invited the Apostols to lead Bible studies in members' homes, and the young couple eagerly put their best foot forward. But before long the people of the church became displeased, accusing the Apostols of interfering in local matters, and working "in an area which had already been ploughed." Lucy and Vince quickly left that work, feeling that they had learned a valuable lesson.

Lucy and Vince next ventured to Pulupandan, 30 kilometers southwest of Bacolod City. Lucy was very hesitant to move to a town where they had many relatives and friends. In her own words, "I wondered if the people there would look at me as a dollar."[1] But since they were encouraged to go, they went, and stayed for ten years. Here two more children were born: Faith Joy and Nathaniel. In addition to caring for her growing family Lucy was busy helping Vince in ministry, and was glad that now they had household help, giving her time for church activities.

Lucy and Vince were invited to lead Bible studies, and later, church services, in a home in Pulupandan. They started very carefully, remembering their previous experience. Eventually the family members of this home became Christians, and those first home meetings resulted in the establishment of a congregation. Vince had various relatives and friends in the town and had opportunity to exercise his gift of speaking with community folk. The Apostols always included children in their evangelistic efforts. They held Sunday school classes, told neighborhood children about the gospel, and advised urged the children to lead Christian lives. In addition to Bible studies, children and neighborhood evangelism, the Apostols distributed goods sent by Jane Roodvoets through the Friendship Missionary Society. Bales of clothing, sacks of powdered milk and medical supplies began to arrive regularly; once there was even a carton of shoes.

While Vince spoke with townfolk Lucy practiced community health. She volunteered with the health department, using the medical supplies sent by Christians in the USA. She was thrilled to be a trained nurse, and made herself available any time to give treatments and medications to anyone in need. Whenever she treated patients she'd tell them that medicine alone — without God's power — cannot heal. When she added that Jesus Christ is the only Healer, no patient ever disagreed! People were glad with Lucy's care, and most responded positively to her. Many came to her not only with their medical problems, but also with personal challenges, and marriage difficulties. Lucy began to feel burdened. She always prayed for strength before she met patients, but, like many pastors' wives, she sometimes wondered to whom she herself could turn if she'd have a problem.

Though often exhausted, Lucy felt fulfilled. Hers was a life of prayer and action, and she relished her role as wife, mother, youth counselor, choir director, and Bible teacher. Often she provided people with rice, money, or clothing. One day when a boy had no shirt she gave him her son's favorite shirt. When her son discovered what his mother had done he was angry with her. Only then did Lucy remember that one the day, long ago, when her own mother had given away Lucy's favorite dress, a dress which had been a gift in a missionary parcel, to a mountain woman. Lucy had been so upset with her mother that she had cried herself to sleep that night.

Lucy estimates that, during the first few years in Pulupandan, she used about ten percent of her nursing skills, while she and Vince worked hard to develop their ministry skills. Two nursing experiences of that time stand out in Lucy's mind.

Remembering that their family lived upstairs in the first chapel, and that neighbors often came to ask for necessary items or advice, Lucy recalls:

"One morning, while I was baking, a woman came running to the chapel where we lived in some rooms upstairs, and shouted, 'Please come quickly!' It shocked me and, with flour still on my hands, I rushed downstairs. A lady neighbor was having a baby, while her husband was still in the town, fetching the midwife. Another neighbor was with the mother, holding the baby's head, which was dark purple. I had to coax the mother to relax while I helped the baby to be born. I then held the baby by her feet, slapped her twice and, as she began to breathe, the ugly purple changed into a healthy pink. Not only was the mother deeply thankful, so was I! The parents of this baby were devout Roman Catholics. They honored me by asking me to name the baby, and soon began to send their older children to our Sunday school. This was an unexpected development. There were others.

"One night a neighbor woke us up. He told us that his wife had been in labor for three days, and

Hers was a life of prayer and action, and she relished her role as wife, mother, youth counselor, choir director, and Bible teacher.

Lucy Apostol at work in a feeding program for poor children. Many of the children need medical attention, and they also need attention at lunchtime! *Photo courtesy Lucy Apostol.*

had greatly weakened. She badly needed immediate help. Vince and I took her to the hospital, but on the way the baby was born. It was already dead. In such cases my nursing skills were so helpful, because you always have to be ready, to know what to do. You have to answer for what you do, you know."

In the 1960s an American missionary couple joined Lucy and Vince in their work. While they were struggling to learn Hiligaynon they were chagrined to find that their three boys learned to speak it more quickly than they themselves. For some time they took their children everywhere they went in town, to encourage friendly conversation. The young couple's gifts matched those of Lucy and Vince well, and they enjoyed good cooperation. Lucy and the missionary wife both enjoyed music; they often taught songs to the people in the church, Lucy directing and the missionary wife playing the small portable organ. Together they organized several church choirs which performed at various occasions.

As the years passed Lucy and Vince's own family also grew. After John Mark, Faith Joy and Nathaniel, a fourth child was born, Lori. But before that, one baby was stillborn, and another lived only a few weeks. The last baby spent more time in the hospital than at home, and Lucy was there most of the time. One night, while Lucy and Vince were getting some much needed sleep at home, their missionary friends received a call from the hospital that the Apostols' baby had died and that the body had to be claimed. The Apostols had no telephone then, so the missionaries picked up the baby's corpse at the hospital and brought it to Lucy and Vince's home.[2]

Those were the days when they were distributing three parcels of food, clothing and medical supplies monthly, and many of the people whom they had helped attended the funeral. There were some one hundred and fifty people at the cemetery. People in town wondered why so many joined the funeral procession to the cemetery for an infant's burial. They were even more surprised to see all the town's policemen at the cemetery. They would not have been so surprised had they known that each of the policemen was wearing shoes from that missionary parcel filled with men's Hush Puppy shoes!

When later missionaries of the Christian Reformed Church joined them, Lucy and Vince always did the orientation. Lucy sometimes felt as if she were a big sister, and, being loving and generous, never had a problem with missionary wives. But it wasn't always a simple task because Lucy had to be the bridge between her own culture and that of the Americans. Thanks to her seven years in the USA Lucy understood the American way of life, and was able to initiate the newcomers, together with Vince. Still, mistakes were made.

When Lucy and Vince looked for a home for their first new family, they found a house outside of town which they thought was suitable for Americans who had just left their own country and must learn new ways. They cleaned the house thoroughly, and remodeled and painted the kitchen.[3] In their desire to give the missionaries the privacy which Americans cherish, Lucy and Vince had not reckoned with the possibility that this particular couple might be eager to live near others, and prefer to live in town rather than in a home further away which had appeared so suitable to Lucy and Vince. It seemed reasonable to these Americans to rent an apartment in town and to move there, but they had no idea what this meant to the Apostols in terms of "losing face."

There were times when it seemed impossible to both satisfy the foreigners and cover up for their mistakes in the Filipino community. Many years later a colleague remarked that Lucy's "roundabout ways" of dealing with situations helped when new American recruits had as yet little sensitivity to Filipino values.[4] Lucy once wrote, "sometimes we feel 'sandwiched' between our missionaries (expatriates) and the national workers, but it's OK!"[5]

Soon there were four couples, Lucy and Vince and three American missionary couples. Their children grew up together, and the work of evangelism expanded grew. As more people joined the three churches which had been organized, it was decided to establish a Bible school in order to educate young Filipino Christians as pastors. Classes would be held in the home of one of the missionary families. While trying to decide on a name for their Bible school, someone suggested calling it "Reformed Institute Of Theology," but the others soon noticed that the school would then be a RIOT! After a good laugh, it came to be called RIT, which still stood for "Reformed Institute of Theology." Much later the school became the Christian Reformed Bible College. All four men, and most of the wives, taught here with Lucy involving herself with teaching health and hygiene, and even some basic nursing skills.

While Lucy and Vince's own children were growing and requiring more of their parents' time the church work also increased. Lucy was always on the run at home, at church, or with her community health care. She was also now using more of her nursing skills as she gave treatments and consultations.

In 1973 an American missionary and his wife, having just arrived, were being welcomed by the other missionaries. But the man did not feel comfortable. It seemed as if he and his wife were being interrogated, rather than welcomed. Then, as he looked around the room he noticed Lucy — "She appeared approximately thirty to thirty-five years old, almond-shaped eyes, perfectly smooth, olive-hued skin and a few tiny 'smile wrinkles' near the corner of her eyes. She had high cheekbones . . . and carried herself with grace when she walked in and as she sat in her chair. She had an easy, soft laugh; I heard it when she and her husband arrived earlier. . . ."[6] When snacks were served, "Lucy walked up to us, shook our hands and said with a smile, 'Hi, welcome to the Philippines and welcome to Bacolod.' She told us she would pray for us and hoped we would be happy in Manila. She told us where she and Vince lived and invited us to their place any time."[7]

In 1976 three churches in the area officially became independent congregations. This, Lucy says, marked the end of an era. Lucy and Vince were now ready to begin new work, and they moved to Iloilo City, leaving the other missionaries in the area of Bacolod City.

Lucy and Vince were hoping to establish a city church, but beginning evangelistic work in the urban setting of Iloilo City was very different from doing the same in the rural area of Bacolod. Whereas Vince had been able to approach people he knew in the Bacolod City region, both Lucy and Vince were total strangers in Iloilo City. Even finding a home seemed impossible. When a friend of Vince's brother was willing to rent his small house in a nearby town, Pavia, Lucy and Vince quickly took the opportunity and moved in. But how to go about evangelism in a place where they knew no one?

Lucy began by taking care of the family, and making their home a place where they could invite visitors, while Vince used his gift of talking with strangers. Each morning he went to town and visited the market, where there were always people ready to chat.

It was during one of these early days that he sat in the barber shop, striking up conversations. That morning the barber talked about his baby daughter, who had a skin disease. Since she was four months old she had been covered from head to toe with sores which frequently became infected. The barber and his wife had gone to the town doctor and to the *albularyo* (the folk healer) but for four months nothing had helped. Vince mentioned that his wife was a nurse, and offered Lucy's help.

That afternoon Lucy and Vince went to the house of the barber. Lucy was amazed that neither the doctor nor the *albularyo* had seen any success after treating the baby. She told them, "I don't know if I can help, but let's trust that God will bless my medicine." She proposed to treat the baby in her own home. The parents resisted that idea, but they were desperate, and brought the eight month-old baby that same afternoon.

When Lucy was still a girl, her mother had taught her how to mix several ointments for skin treatments. Lucy had often made this medicine, and the homemade ointment was so successful that people had dubbed it "Mrs. Apostol's Miracle Medicine." That is what Lucy prepared for this baby.

The infant was filthy. The mother never washed her, because it was so painful for the child. Very carefully Lucy bathed the baby with warm water and soap, applied the ointment to her whole body, and the baby girl was ready to be taken home. That night was the first night of her life that she slept the whole night through.

For a week the parents brought the baby daily, and every day Lucy bathed her gently and applied "Mrs. Apostol's Miracle Medicine." With the passing days the lesions healed and the skin dried, and Lucy was quick to point out to the parents that it was God's blessing on the medication that had healed their baby. They were ready to hear more about God, and eventually became the first members of a new church established in Pavia. When neighbors heard how the baby's sores had been healed they also came, asking help for their problems.

This was the beginning of the Apostols' ministry in Pavia. Through medical help the door was opened, after which Vince took over by visiting people and leading Bible studies. Lucy also conducted Bible studies with women and held discussions with them on various topics.

When a group of believers had formed in the town of Pavia Lucy and Vince started work in a nearby hamlet, Buyo. Again, there was ample opportunity for Lucy to practice her nursing skills. She always spoke about God's love to her patients, and reminded them that it was God who healed, not Lucy.

One day a woman in Buyo was hit by a tree branch which fell on her, cracking her skull. The wound bled and the injury was obviously serious, but the woman was adamant, she dared not go to the hospital. Lucy and Vince then took her home, Lucy praying all the way. Lucy washed the wound, covered it with ointment, bandaged the woman's head and gave her an antibiotic. She then stayed up with her all night to observe her. For a week she repeated the medical process daily. Much to everyone's delight the injury healed without any infection. Later the woman had only the scar as a reminder of the time she could easily have died; frequently she showed it to others, when she told how this experience had led her to the Christian faith.

Then there was the teenaged girl who had heard the Christian message at a students' Bible study, and who had become a Christian. Her parents were strongly opposed to her new faith, and ordered her to leave the church, or they would disown her. Not knowing how to face her father and still be faithful to her newfound faith, the girl ran away from home. For two months she lived with a church member's family. She maintained that, though it would be harsh if her parents disowned her, it would be worse to be disowned by Christ. After two months her parents relented and took her back. They were still opposed to her belonging to the church, but became more lenient with their daughter.

Besides her nursing, Lucy continued to work in the church. There were wonderful occasions when people became believers, but there were also sad stories.

Once a lady who had become a Christian asked Lucy to advise her with a problem to which she knew no solution. Her husband was very much against his wife's new convictions and did all he could to discourage her. Lucy often talked and prayed with the woman, and encouraged her in her Christian walk. The woman seemed to love Jesus deeply. Though the husband demanded that his wife stop attending church, she insisted on going. He then threatened to leave her. This was more than she could bear, and after some time she left the church, and perhaps the faith.

During Lucy and Vince's years in Buyo a Christian medical society, the Luke Society of the USA, began medical missions in the Philippines. The Luke Society and Lucy needed each other in order to be effective, and Lucy volunteered her services for twelve years. Usually they conducted day-clinics three times monthly, mostly in villages in the same region. Equipped with doctors and medicine, most of the clinics were held in rural areas.

Many of the patients who came to the clinic suffered from tuberculosis, due to crowded living conditions and inadequate hygiene. One of these patients was another Buyo woman. *Nang* Puring had an advanced case of tuberculosis, her lungs had collapsed, and the medical missionaries feared that she would not live. Her only hope lay in receiving long-term care, a difficult thing for a woman living in poverty. Lucy took it upon herself to treat *Nang* Puring regularly, and God blessed Lucy's work. He also worked in the woman's heart; after a year of regular care *Nang* Puring had not only fully recovered physically, she had also become a believer. She became a faithful Christian member in the Buyo church.

Once more Lucy and Vince moved to a new place to start a church community. Again Lucy found medical needs where she could help. During this time their children grew up, studied, and married. She and Vince also received a fifth child, a daughter, whom they adopted. A poor woman who was about to die and was fearful that her baby would be neglected, asked Lucy to take that baby into her own home and bring her up as her own child. This Lucy and Vince did, and as the little girl grew up she gave her new parents much joy.

Life was busy but not easy. Soon after they moved to Barotac, in 1992, Lucy wrote,

> The first two nights we slept in our new home, stones were thrown over [sic] our roof at night. We just prayed for strength.... After a month we got to know people. They are suspicious and afraid of us. They think that we are bringing an evil design or teaching in their midst. These people are squatters, and their lifestyle is below poverty-line. Vices are rampant.[8]

When asked if anything stands out in Lucy's mind about her life and work, she answered simply:

"I think that, most of the time, my work was the same. I was missionary wife, mother and nurse. Vince and I always worked as a team, though I worked mostly with women, young people and children. One thing which has kept me busy at home is company. Extended families are important in the Philippines, and I cannot remember a time when we did not have people in the house — Vince's family, my family, church members or others who needed help. And one thing which I have stressed with young people is that they must be educated. We can't help others unless we ourselves learn something."

After nearly thirty-five years of mission work Lucy and Vince officially retired from the Christian Reformed World Missions in 1996. Looking back on a life of Christian service, Lucy says:

"Even when I haven't been active in nursing care for a while it always comes back. My desire to do the work is still there. I still love to do it.

"I have never regretted doing the ministry we had. Even in our last assignment I was still excited about the work and helping Vince, and to help equip the people to be mature in their Christian lives. At one point we wished for a time of rest, a breather. We did not realize how difficult it would be once we retired.

"We love the church, we love the people, and we miss the work. At times it is lonely, and we like to be ministered too, also. But younger people do not see that we have that need, they don't understand that. We're glad to still be a part of the church and to help with some things."

When Lucy and Vince retired from their missionary work and were honored at a retirement dinner each of them offered some advice for a new generation. Lucy had three things to say. First, she said, "Love people." Next, she urged the believers to spend much time and prayer with and for people. And lastly, "Teach your own children to be concerned for others and help them." Unobtrusive and modest, she has always focused on others, never taking a prominent position for herself.

An American missionary wife, also a nurse, who worked with Lucy in the rural clinics, expressed her gratitude for having observed

Lucy at work, and for noting Lucy's example. The same woman adds her admiration for the way Lucy was able to work in two cultures, without being negative about either.[9]

A Filipina, another co-worker, also expressed her praise for Lucy's love, her unselfishness and hard work. She noted Lucy's positive outlook, her reliability, and her custom of always having enough food on the table for the unexpected guest.[10] Indeed, numerous persons remarked on Lucy's readiness to share time and food with others. It's no exaggeration to say that people who have benefited from Lucy's nursing care and appreciated it, are legion.

Today Lucy and Vince live in retirement. Whenever she sees a need, or is called upon, Lucy is ready to go to work, and she hopes to continue that as long as she is able. As a retired person she does not sit still. Together with Vince, she reaches out to others and always has the door open.

We may believe that one day, when Lucy del Carmen Apostol's life on earth ends, our Savior will say of her, "She has done a beautiful thing for me."

"Honor your father and your mother." When God gave the Ten Commandments to his people in Old Testament times he directed them to honor their parents. It was a commandment, but in a loving family relationship it has always been natural for children to honor their parents. How they do this may be expressed in different ways, depending on their culture, personalities and environment.

In Asia the elderly have traditionally been honored for their position in the family. Among the teachings of Confucius, the famous Chinese philosopher-teacher who lived five hundred years before Jesus, is that of honoring old age. His ideas spread to most Asian countries. It is said that he himself mourned the death of his mother for three years, in order to show his respect for her. Through the centuries much of Confucian thought has been passed from generation to generation in Asian society, and those people who became Christians maintained Confucian customs which harmonized with Christian teachings.

Asian society has a long history. After a life of hard work the elderly usually live with their children and are cared for by them. In North America, where history is short, and the early settlers developed more individualistic traditions, most seniors prefer to remain active and independent as long as they are able.

In rural China children used to grow up on a family compound. Since the eldest son would be the next head of the family, he and his wife continued to live with the parents. As long as the parents lived they were honored and obeyed, and after death they were remembered. In Japan I had a friend who, with her husband, purchased a house with an extra room where the mother of the husband, an eldest son, would live when she retired.

Dr. Melba Padilla Maggay, whom we meet in this chapter, cherished her mother, and expressed love for her mother when she took the elderly lady into her home. She honored her mother in respectful ways and showed her affection as long as her mother lived. This is what she had seen her mother do when Melba was a young girl and her grandmother lived with the family.

In other parts of the world honor and respect are shown in different ways. My mother, when she was widowed, treasured her independence. She told us that she knew we loved her and that she appreciated her visits with the family but, on a permanent basis she preferred to live by herself. She visited us all in turn, staying six weeks at a time, and at the end she insisted that she was glad to return to her own environment, with her church activities, friends and relatives. Only the last few weeks of her life did we care for her physically, and she died in a pleasant room, with some family members nearby as well as bouquets of yellow flowers which she had always enjoyed.

How do we honor our parents, and particularly our mothers who carried us, cared for us and concerned themselves about us? Many grandmothers and grandfathers pray for children and grandchildren by name each day. What a privilege, to be prayed for daily. How fitting then, in turn to honor our grandparents and fathers and mothers as long as they live.

Thinker, Writer, Christian Activist

Melba Padilla Maggay (1950–   )

They were of the old gentry, the Padilla family. According to family lore an ancestor, a Spanish soldier, had been granted a vast tract of land which he worked, and which eventually became a successful plantation. By the second part of the nineteenth century the family had become part of the gentry of Palawan Island, and Melba Maggay's mother Carmen was born into a leisurely existence among people endowed with old country education, as well as a close acquaintance with the land. Her life was permeated with a mixture of Spanish and Filipino customs and with the unhurried affairs of mestizo life on the hacienda.

Melba remembers bygone days, when families lived communally, several generations under one roof. Among her earliest recollections is the great-grandaunt who lived until her mid-nineties, who was mostly silent, and who liked to swig *cerveza negra* (dark beer) in the late afternoon. Then there was her mother's mother who lived with the family for some time. This grandmother's ancestry was never clear, but her stories, especially those of Muslim pirates and their much-feared incursions along the coast, kept the family absorbed.

But the grandparent who really made an impression on Melba's young mind was her father's mother. Her father was of Cavite origin and, according to family narratives, was a member of the *Katipunan*. The *Katipunan* was the revolutionary movement founded in 1892 whose goal it was to gain Philippine independence from Spain. He was said to have been banished to Palawan for being part of the disturbances attending the Cavite Mutiny of 1872. Melba's paternal grandmother was of a fairly political and musical family. A mother of sixteen children, she was, when younger, a politician and a writer of *zarzuelas*.[1] Her stories captivated the mind of the young girl during evenings when Melba was assigned to put up her grandmother's mosquito net, and to sit beside the bed while Grandmother recited her rosary. At times, when Grandmother's prayers were lengthy and Melba fell asleep Grandmother would promptly elbow her into waking, to make sure Melba would attend to her duties. The reward for these tasks was one of Grandmother's stories, a prize which made the task of assisting Grandmother at her prayers meaningful. For Grandmother's stories were from an age gone by, an age when Grandmother herself was a young girl. That was around the turn of the century, during the time of the Philippine Revolution, when *bolos* (Philippine machetes) and guns clashed, the air crackled with fiery rhetoric, and people were filled with passion. While Melba listened to Grandmother, the world of reality seemed to blend with that of fanciful spirits who might be prowling in the dark shadows of the room, and of enchanted creatures who could fly and existed in mysterious ways. These were the stories, this was the world, in which Melba's imagination leaped and whirled, far away from everyday reality.

Melba's parents moved to Muntinlupa, Rizal, before she was born. Her father was an accountant in the prison compound, where the family was part of a community of government employees and their families. As Melba grew in age the family grew in size. There would to be twelve children, of whom she was number nine. In this rural and pleasant prison community were some convicts, soon to be released, who were permitted to work as household helpers within the compound. The Maggay family's helpers were mostly young and sometimes included hardened men waiting to be paroled. And so, Melba chuckles, "I was raised in a secure environment, and partly raised by criminals." Although there were tough convicts in the prison, there were also those who had been less seriously amiss and who did their best to redeem themselves. There was the young man, for instance, who had stolen a typewriter, and who, after his release, went on to become a scoutmaster.

There were always guests in the house besides the family of fourteen, and the house was constantly filled. Melba's parents were both the eldest in their families, which meant that they had responsibilities for younger siblings. Invariably there seemed to be uncles and aunts who lived with the family while they attended school. Rice was cooked in an enormous cooking pot, one which could hold about eight *gantas* of rice; a *ganta* holds about two kilos. Life was brimming with people and the realities of life, some harsh, others merely colorful, were part of every day. Mother had no concept of status and class, to her each human being was a creature to be respected. She cheerfully fed whoever came, including "riffraff and drunks." Later, when she had returned to Palawan, she would write Melba and tell about her parrot, her dog, and people, all in the same sentence.

Melba's mother, though always busy with her family, was perhaps the most important person in shaping young Melba's mind. Mother's stories, many of them set in the years of the Japanese Occupation during World War II, some fifty years after the stories of Grandmother, were equally absorbing, and allowed Melba's mind to wander from the commonplace to an unknown world.

"Before you were born there were already eight children in the family," her mother told Melba. "When I was expecting you I knew that something was wrong. When we went to the doctor he did some tests and then told us that I should have an abortion."

The doctor went on to explain that he could detect some tissue in the womb, and was uncertain whether Melba's mother, who was then having severe thyroid problems, could safely carry her baby to full term. Other physicians examined Melba's mother, and confirmed the worry that the pregnancy would be life-threatening to her and might not result in the birth of a healthy baby.

> Her mother told Melba:
> "When I was expecting you
> I knew that something was wrong.
> When we went to the doctor
> he did some tests and then told us that
> I should have an abortion."

The fetus, they feared, might be malformed. Melba's mother was advised to take an abortion-inducing medicine.

"But I already loved you then," Melba's mother, who was usually not quick to speak such words, told her daughter. "Your father and I thought about it, prayed about it, and decided *bahala na ang Diyos*, [We would leave the matter to God]."

For years Melba would have fearful thoughts at night, waiting for sleep to come. Was she, after all, just a piece of tissue? This fear would combine with other fears of the unknown, fears of capricious spirits flying at night, and fears that people may not be all that kind. She lacked a certain confidence in the world, always in dread of some threat, some danger of being pushed out of the way. She doubted that there was goodness at the heart of existence. These phobias haunted her even though she knew that she was loved, that she belonged to a caring and warm family.

According to her mother, Melba was an easy child but also a strange one. Until she was two years old she neither walked nor talked, and as she grew she often sat quietly in a corner, watching people and the action around her. "Definitely an introvert," Melba smiles.

One of her older sisters was a teacher who, when Melba was five, persuaded her parents to enrol Melba in grade one. This proved to be a disaster. As the children were learning to read and write numbers the teacher sometimes asked several children to come to the blackboard and write the numbers one to ten. Those children who did not write them correctly had their ears pulled. Melba disliked the teacher, and had not yet learned to write. One day, when the teacher told her to go to the front and write the numbers Melba could not manage the numbers seven and eight. She heard footsteps approaching and knew whose they were. Before the teacher could pull her ears Melba turned, bit the teacher's hand hard, ran out of the classroom and headed home. She told her mother that she wouldn't go back. That evening she overheard her mother saying that Melba was perhaps too young emotionally to attend school.

This was the end of that episode, but it gave her a lasting dislike for "school," or at least the formal and structured aspects of the system.

Throughout these years deep-seated fears were part of Melba's life. As she looked out of her window at night she feared the odd shadows of tree branches waving in the wind. She often agonized over the fact that a human being could be, in scientific eyes, a mere tissue. And she would feel eerily haunted by the sound of the *balut* vendor's voice as he walked through the neighborhood in the evening, shouting to attract buyers for his delicacy, the boiled partly-developed duck eggs. During the day, when it was playtime, Melba often climbed the tamarind tree on the outer edge of their garden. She would sit there for hours, watching roofs, shadows and people, living in her own little imaginary world. She would brood about her family's history during a time before she was born.

During World War II, before Melba was born, life had changed drastically for her family. The Japanese military had swarmed across the Philippines, including Palawan Island, and the family's relaxed lifestyle of the hacienda was changed forever. One night there was a knock on the door. Three American soldiers fleeing from the Japanese military pleaded for protection. Melba's father considered it his Christian duty to help them, so he hid them and took care of them for a few weeks, and then helped them to escape. He led them through the thick Palawan forest and, when they reached water, guided them to a boat. Unfortunately someone saw him help the men into the boat, and reported him. Melba's father was imprisoned.

Her mother was afraid that the Japanese would come for her and her children as well, but carried on with the farm and the house. Once she was able to bribe the Japanese sentry of the prison grounds with some fresh eggs, and was allowed to meet her husband briefly. And on Christmas Day she brought her four daughters to sing for the Japanese soldiers. The Japanese commander was so pleased with the performance of the youngest that he sat her on his lap and spontaneously said that he'd give her whatever she'd like. But when the girl quickly replied, "Release my father," the commander stiffened and turned away.[2] Melba heard all these stories as she grew up and they helped shape her world of thought, in which she tried to understand how the brave and generous and the crooked and degenerate live in our world side by side.

The many stories she had heard became part of Melba. She began to realize that she had stories to tell too, and often wrote them down for the pleasure of it. Stories assigned for school and for contests usually won prizes, but Melba thought nothing of it. To her it was just part of living, like talking and walking and working, of growing up. But then she began to notice that others liked her stories. Once a teacher reviewed her story, looked at her sharply, and commented that Melba's imagination had a "peculiar turn." That bewildered Melba, for it seemed as if the teacher had looked inside her mind, and seen her thoughts. And she desperately wanted to keep her secrets inside, they were hers to cherish. It began to seem as if life had two spheres, that of everyday reality with its activities and concerns, and then that part which dealt with dreams, fears and the supernatural.

Melba's parents were devout Roman Catholics. Her father always led the family in *novenas*, daily *oracion*, prayer at 6:00 p.m., and the *rosario*, the prayer of the rosary, for thirty minutes. When relatives died they had evening prayers to help the dead pass from purgatory to heaven. During Holy Week the family was not permitted to be boisterous or to do regular work, and her father read the Gospel to the family. To Melba this was the most boring time of the year. Only many years later did she understand that her father's faith was genuine, as was that of her mother. She then realized that her parents had enveloped the family in observing ritual which they themselves found meaningful.

Her childhood stories of creatures who fly by night, of heroes who became martyrs for the fatherland, and even the family ritual of prayers seemed to lose their luster as she, along with fellow students, faced a new world at the University of the Philippines, the state university. In her home surroundings she had faced difficult realities, but in the university environment life itself seemed marred and fractured. Sure, her mother's tales had included evil beings, yet, somehow problems in those stories generally seemed to be resolved and grief tempered.

Society in the city and the nation seemed so different, so full of injustice and problems which could not be solved. Marxist doctrines about revolution and class struggles, which abounded in university circles, seemed so attractive. Within herself Melba felt empty. She felt a pain almost physical as she wanted to write, yet seemed to have nothing to write about; within her there was a large dark hole she could not fill. The world of her youth had vanished, and what was there to take its place? She was part of the student activism of the time, in which there was an earnest search for peace order and justice. They talked about helping the poor, about love, about social justice. It was an exciting time but also confusing, and Melba became embroiled in activities of social idealism and revolutionary politics.

One of her friends, who knew Melba to prize intellectual honesty, challenged her to discover an alternative vision of social transformation and invited her to attend a noon lecture by an Englishman, Dick Dowsett. He was a missionary who, at that time, was assigned to the InterVarsity Christian Fellowship (IVCF). She accepted the invitation but as she listened to the Caucasian speaker Melba thought to herself, "Oh oh, here we go again — we are being colonized all over again." And when he spoke about Jesus' resurrection Melba responded by asking sarcastically, "So what?" She fired questions directly at the speaker, but remained aloof and kept her distance from others who were there.

After the lecture a student approached Melba and invited her to talk. All afternoon they talked, she and the student both skipping their classes. Melba had no idea that this girl, together with other IVCF members, would pray for her earnestly during the summer break.

When it was time to register for the new school year this girl, a bright and vivacious student named Kalayaan Perez, volunteered to take Melba's place in line. Registration was a tedious, lengthy procedure, and Melba gladly let her new friend do it for her. What she did not realize was that the friend managed

When he spoke about Jesus' resurrection Melba responded by asking sarcastically, "So what?"

to register for most of the same classes Melba was going to take, and would accompany her in her journey to faith.

This was a time of much evangelistic fervor on campus, and many students became believers. The IVCF group had daily prayer times and met at noon behind the university library. Melba had no idea that they also prayed for her and that they did so for the whole semester.

Gradually Melba became impressed by this group of students, particularly her new friend. Melba felt rather proud that she was quite sophisticated intellectually, and was already into reading much existential literature. She was puzzled that her friend had read nothing of the sort, though she was intelligent and would later graduate at the top of her class. Instead, the friend always wanted to talk about Jesus and, one step at a time, Melba became intrigued. She was struck by the sense of commitment and purpose of these people, knowing full well that she herself had none. Melba also realized that she could not go through life flitting here and there like a butterfly as she changed interests and priorities.

"One day I prayed to God, about whom I had heard during all of my earlier life, and told him, 'I have no way of knowing if you are real or not. If you are, you'll have to show me.' And then one morning I woke up and felt a joy welling up within me. It was a lightness, a brightness about things. I knew I had changed. I just could not understand it, I hadn't even prayed or made a conscious decision. Somehow, the world no longer appeared the same."

This was the beginning of the change for which her friends had been praying. Melba joined a Bible study led by one of the group and became a member of the IVCF.

"As students, we had space to think. We learned from Scripture, and then had opportunity to do what we thought was right. Our Bible studies gave us confidence in our ability to handle Scripture. The IVCF gave me that foundation, as well as the confidence in ministry that I acquired. Thus I felt no need to take up theological studies, as I had enough biblical grounding to move on from there.

"Besides the IVCF group there were two missionaries who helped form my new identity as a believer. God taught me much through these two, one American — Miriam Adeney, and one British — Rosemary Dowsett, wife of the speaker at that first IVCF noon meeting I attended. I was anti-American because of our historical experience, and was at first cold towards Miriam's overtures of friendship. But I eventually turned up at her dinners. Gradually I began to see these people as individual persons rather than as foreigners, or members of a hated, imperialistic nation. I learned to appreciate them, even if later I became more and more critical of western missionaries.

"I even joined a month-long camp, a *Kawayan* camp on Negros Occidental, in a location so remote we crossed seven rivers and climbed mountains to reach the place. It was a camp for IVCF student leaders, and my American friend was on staff. She sort of took me by the hand. There, with that group of Christians, I began to understand what my faith meant and what the Body of Christ is all about."

But when Melba attended a worship service in a Bible church in Manila she felt disillusioned. During her growing years there had been a richness of religious ritual — the colorful liturgy, the imposing statues and inspiring architecture. She saw none of that during that first time she attended a Protestant worship service, and it would be a long time before she returned. Another shock was incurred when she was told that women were to take a back seat in the church community. "In our culture we weren't raised this way, we had no clue that we'd be treated as only second fiddle to men," she sighed.

It was a gratifying experience for Melba, after graduating in 1972 with a degree in Mass Communications, to start work as a journalist for the *Manila Chronicle*, one of the major daily newspapers of the day. However, even before she even received her first salary, a sudden darkness fell on the nation. On the morning of 21 September 1972 then President Ferdinand Marcos declared Martial Law, and all newspapers and radio stations were shut down. Transportation came to an abrupt halt. "It was a good thing that I had already been a Christian for some three years, so I was no longer on the membership rolls of the activist organization to which I had earlier belonged," Melba comments. "Many of my activist friends had to go underground."

Personally, this was a traumatic experience for Melba. Her employment had evaporated, but worse, her opportunity to be a journalist had disappeared. She then worked for the government for a few years, writing speeches. But as she began to work with influential people in the bureaucracy she learned what went on in government circles. This was distressing, she said, especially as she saw that corruption of the powerful remained well-hidden and the poor in society were made to suffer.

Melba began to pray for guidance, and to ask that she might know what she should do. She wanted desperately to help, but didn't know where to turn. She felt disillusioned by the evangelical community, and felt that they were unwilling to stake themselves out for justice. Their views seemed ultraconservative. She felt that Filipino Christians needed theological reflection to see the political realities in the country, and then apply Christian principles in seeking a way to counter wrong. She discussed this once with a Canadian woman writer who then lived in Los Baños, near Manila. Mrs. Betty Mae Dyck promptly encouraged her to air her ideas and to elaborate on them in writing. Now Melba had something to write about again. She saw an urgent need, and began to explain it in writing. Years later she observed, "The sense that this 'I' was a writer only began much later, coinciding with my newfound awareness of the God who had been present all along in my life."[3]

Something was brewing among those who were genuinely moved and concerned about the Filipino people. Melba worked part-time for IVCF for some years, and had much contact with students. They were getting restive, wanting solutions to the increasingly difficult situation. They did not miss noticing that numbers of even the socially committed "went to the hills," or left for the USA in fear and disgust. Melba and her like-minded friends did not wish to lose these people. She found that, among the professionals connected with the IVCF, there was a band of friends who were prepared to dedicate themselves to bringing change. This was the vision Melba wanted to follow, this was what guided her speech and action in the succeeding years. Later she would write that, for people of all cultures, today's primary question about the gospel must be not "what are the facts?" but "so what?"[4]

The members of the closely-knit group of young Christians clung to each other. Melba left full-time government employment and shifted to being a technical consultant while still working part-time with the IVCF. Her income as consultant tided her over since employment with IVCF gave her but a very small and uncertain salary. In later years she would feel humbled and warmed by the generosity of her friends, as when one would notice the "faded glory" of her clothes and now and again would take her to the store and buy her new jeans and shoes.

On a rainy evening early in 1978 Melba was interviewed during a live program of DZAS, the local Christian radio station. When she was asked her ideas on what was happening to the country she openly expressed her unhappiness with Martial Law, and also with the quiescence of the Church. She voiced her frustrations and communicated her idea that Christians must do something.

While she spoke on the air Mac Bradshaw, then working with Partnership in Missions, was listening absentmindedly as he drove down the street. As he heard Melba speak he became interested and listened more attentively. He was surprised and concerned when he heard her say that, while all the national problems were boiling over, she herself had been reduced to merely writing speeches, and had even ended up supplying rhetoric for the likes of Mrs. Imelda Marcos who was then head of the Human Settlements Ministry to which Melba's office was attached. Mac was electrified at what Melba said about prophetic voices being silenced.

Mac Bradshaw was one of a group of missionaries who went to other countries with the goal of helping nationals to pursue their own vision of what the Kingdom of God should be in their countries. They would listen to local people who believed they had a challenge to meet, then got alongside them and assisted where they could.

Mac recalls, "I was stunned with a sense that God was saying, 'You do something about this!' I had to pull the car over and get myself composed before I could move on."[5] The next morning he called two friends, Alex Chua and William Dyrness, and they agreed to get in touch with Melba and hear more about her dreams. They and their

The young Melba Padilla Maggay interviewing Adrian Cristobal (far right), former presidential assistant during Martial Law, for the "Philippine Realities" issue of *Patmos* in 1979. With Melba is Dr. William Dyrness, one of the founders of ISACC, and another ISACC writer. *Photo courtesy the Institute for Studies in Asian Church and Culture (ISACC)*

wives, together with some IVCF friends, met with Melba. They talked, prayed, and began to formulate their newly-received vision.

In July 1978 Melba left her position in order to establish a new work, which would be called the Institute for Studies in Asian Church and Culture (ISACC). Its goal was clearly stated to be one of integrating Christian principles with the professions, the academic world and with politics and the arts. Initially Melba, Mac Bradshaw, Cora Vasquez and Ruth Castillo, who served as administrator and secretary of the new organization, held office in a basement room of the Bradshaw home in Manila. It was a step of faith. Melba had no idea what the future would hold, she certainly did not know if she could even earn a living in this venture, but she felt in the depths of her heart that God was calling her to help Christians think through the implications of what it meant to be a Christian in a country where there was a dictator, much corruption, injustice and exploitation of the poor.

"We viewed ourselves as some sort of daughter organization of the IVCF. I was grateful for the IVCF as a foundation for the faith and solidarity we enjoyed. Our members needed each other, especially when we discovered that the evangelical community was even more conservative than we knew.

"I was delighted to be writing again, but during the early years of ISACC the evangelical community, mostly the leaders, were disturbed by my writing. They viewed ISACC with suspicion; consequently we had to find support elsewhere, and turned to tentmaking.[6] We survived by working at various research and media jobs, holding seminars, and so on. We found it not only difficult but painful to experience rejection corporately.

"Personally, I found it difficult to realize that I was still viewed as a Marxist. Some church leaders complained to Bill [William] Dyrness, 'What right does this girl have to talk about contextual theology and write about all these issues? She is not even theologically educated!' At first I was so disturbed by such criticisms I was ready to go back to my old job, but I was given the strength to hold on. I felt that the Lord was telling us we must carry on in order to help all those people who were counting on us and quietly cheering from the sidelines."

Melba found that it was difficult for a woman to lead the process of "doing theology." Evangelicals seemed to expect that women would teach Sunday school, serve meals and such, but not lead meetings or theologize. Besides, Melba was only twenty-seven going on twenty-eight years old. In Philippine society, where age matters, it seemed odd that a woman so young was spearheading an organization of Christian leaders in the professions, in the academe, in the arts and in politics.

Some women helped, such as Grace Dyrness (wife of William Dyrness), who started to put together orientation seminars for new missionaries, but the missionaries did not always agree with Melba's thinking. William Dyrness, who strengthened ISACC's theological moorings in the early years, thought that, as Melba was better educated in Philippine social realities, and a better writer than most, she had much to teach and ISACC should continue. It was also difficult to attract conservative evangelical Filipinos to the new

305

organization, and Melba and her friends felt this rejection keenly. Yet, ISACC had much to offer.

There were so many social needs crying to be heard, and Melba desperately wished for quiet and time, in order to write. But harsh reality called for action, the poor constantly faced immense struggles and, while political uncertainty threatened regularly, there was no time for much personal reflection and subsequent writing. This bothered her so much that she once traveled to Scotland to visit the couple who had mentored her in the early years of her spiritual life. "I was, at the time, in one of my crises over the conflict between an activist life and my inner need for creative space and quiet. Rosemary [Dowsett] was crisp and to the point: 'What is it you really want to do?'

"The question was like a sword thrust at the tangled web of feelings surrounding me then, trapped in what I felt was my own deep sense of social commitment and an equally compelling sense that I was withering away and wasting my once considerable gifts. Like the sound of rain in a dry well, I heard myself saying, 'I want to write poetry.'

"She looked me in the eye and in her usual fierce lucidity asked, 'What does poetry have to do with where your country is at the moment?' I almost cried. I knew the answer to that one. I knew there was no other way but to be where I was, alongside my people and in the thick of the struggle against a power that had gone haywire.'" [7]

Numerous issues were troublesome, and Melba felt it acutely that she had no spouse with whom she could discuss personal matters. There were family concerns, her father died, and people kept teasing her and asking when she was planning to marry. Even her mother was beginning to get worried about Melba's marital prospects.[8] Melba usually just smiled, shrugged her shoulders and answered that she was too busy with her work at ISACC to consider marriage. She often felt unable to explain that she believed called by God to her work, that this was her main concern, because others didn't seem to understand her.

Because of the churches' gender conservatism she would invite men to be up front when ISACC held large religious meetings, but she herself would speak to the larger world and had no trouble gaining respect in academic and other secular circles. It took time before she felt old enough, when she turned forty, to speak in pastors' conferences and at other meetings of the clergy.

The work continued and grew steadily. Most of the people who took part were lay Christians, though ISACC did have some clergy as members. The staff gathered information, trained people in seminars, conferences were held, and fresh theological views were presented to Filipino Christians. By the use of various

Driven by her convictions, and the needs she observed around her, Dr. Melba Padilla Maggay continues to lead ISAAC. *Photo courtesy the Institute for Studies in Asian Church and Culture (ISACC).*

media they were challenged to reflect on what they could do for their nation and people. Melba herself continued her studies in anthropology and in intercultural communication, and earned a Ph.D. degree in Philippine Studies at the University of the Philippines. She lectured to numerous audiences, consulted on a host of issues related to the Christian faith, society and culture, and traveled a great deal. And though she had to struggle to set aside time for it, she always wrote.

Dr. Maggay's writing of the time shows her personal struggle with determining the best way to serve both her Lord and the suppressed people around her. As she reflected on this she observed that Jesus became *like us*, so that we may become more truly *ourselves*, human beings made in his image and called to the love of God and neighbor.[9] She reminded her readers repeatedly that Christians need to be humble, obedient unto death, and have confidence in the risen and exalted Christ as they seek to help the poor and face political pressures.[10]

In time Dr. Maggay became convinced that she should move outside the more sophisticated circles of politics, the academe, the professions and the arts. She believed it to be her responsibility to reach out to the poor for whom she had been so concerned for years, but whose world she did not really share. This is why she left the church community where she had felt she belonged, and began worshiping in a small fellowship group in the depressed area near her home.

The experience was an eye-opener for her. To sit on the sidelines rather than playing an active role, to move from the English-speaking society within which she had always mingled to the Tagalog-speaking squatters was oh so difficult, at first. And then she began to see Christian faith in action here also. It was a new awareness of God's spirit moving among the poor when she heard one of the members of this church in the slums speak up during the time when people offered their praise for blessings they had received.

> "Nagpapasalamat ako sa Panginoon na pinagaling niya ang aking alagang baboy .... [I thank the Lord because he has healed the pig I am raising]." Apparently, the pig, which she had been fattening all these months as a potential source of income, had fallen ill. It was about to die when, in desperation, she laid her hands on the pig and prayed over it. The sweating pig then sprang on its hoofs and shook off the heat of the fever. Unable to contain her joy, she went about spreading the news among her neighbors, this woman with an invalid for a husband and numerous children to feed. That morning she talked with great feeling of this God who hears the cry of his people, even for a pig.[11]

This incident strengthened Dr. Maggay's conviction that, though the Kingdom of God may seem weak to the outsider who looks at the destitute in their particular setting, that outsider may fail to notice that here too, the Kingdom can be strong.[12] It confirmed in her the idea that community development only truly happens when people are wakened to the power of God, as well as to the demands of community in the process of development.[13] It also fueled her growing belief that

It confirmed in her the idea that community development only truly happens when people are wakened to the power of God.

globalization is hurtful to individual cultures, as it forces what she called a "flattening of cultures" in which everyone is expected to follow the example of leading cultures. Instead, from her position as a social anthropologist, Dr. Maggay would encourage people to retain their cultural characteristics and weave the Christian message and lifestyle together seamlessly with earlier traditions, where this is possible. Diversity, not homogeneity, she would insist, is God's design for the world.[14]

Her brothers and sisters had grown up and Dr. Maggay's family circumstances changed as siblings moved, some to the USA. Her mother continued to have special memories of those Americans who had been kind to her and her husband during the war years and she had a long-standing wish to go to America. She emigrated and lived there with her children. However, these were not good years for her; she never felt at home. Becoming an American citizen was a disturbing experience for her and she always yearned to return to her homeland.[15] When she was older she did indeed return and was able to spend the remaining years with her daughter Melba. Dr. Maggay saw her mother widowed, then becoming aged. This seemed contradictory to the way she always remembered Mother, for in her mind she envisioned a striking woman, an authoritative figure directing an extensive household, telling captivating stories to the children as they sat around the table at mealtime, and having a wondrous imagination.

"Somehow I had always known that my mother loved me, though it was more by instinct than what was apparent by sight. As a child I only knew her as Mother, a big, bustling woman busily feeding a large household of a dozen children and assorted relatives that more or less stayed as permanent transients. She had little time to sit by me. I would play on my own in a corner and at most get a pat from her or a touch on the cheek now and again. Yet I knew that there was between us a bond deeper than either of us fully understood." [16]

As the elderly lady lost contact with the world through sickness and eventually death, Dr. Maggay lost an intimate relationship which could never be replaced, and the memory of this loss still aches.

Some of her deepest emotions found creative expression when she wrote about her mother.

As she recalls her mother's death she describes that, after her mother's body had been removed from the hospital bed, it was brought to the morgue. Not wishing to leave, Dr. Maggay followed the hospital worker to a back hall of the building. The door to the morgue was locked and while the hospital worker went to get the key, Dr. Maggay was left with the corpse on a boxlike container while the worker went to get a key. It was early in the day, and near the door were several yellow plastic bags with garbage, waiting to be picked up.

> In the dark, cavernous hall, a shaft of light began to filter in. *This is not judgment day,* I said, turning my face full into the flood of morning light. My eyes were stunned by the fistful of light but I did not turn away. Instead I felt my eyes burn with anguish and anger that the body that I used to call Mother and the big yellow trash bags should be lying here as if they had always gone together.[17]

Dr. Maggay's family experiences and relationships often figure prominently in her writing. Thanks to her perceptive way of writing, family relationships become three-dimensional. At one time her older brother, who had suffered damage to his mental health during a swimming accident, was hospitalized because of violent fits. When he returned home his former exuberance had disappeared entirely. Hauntingly the author reveals a personal moment.

> For a while, the stranger that had come to us lived a vegetable life, eating and sleeping and sitting immobile near the window. The thing that had come out of the valley of dry bones soon gained a mass of flesh. Yet he remained lifeless and without spirit. Then one day, watching from my play corner, I saw his feet tap to the music on the radio. I rose and stood where he sat and looked squarely into his eyes. He looked down at me and for a while didn't seem to know what to make of the little girl who stared up at him, unblinkingly curious. A flicker of recognition glimmered in his eyes. Then, faintly, the hint of a smile played at the corners of his lips. He was home.[18]

Dr. Maggay is a prize-winning writer of prose, and her sensitively written narratives draw her readers along. In a story titled *"Mang* Ambo Burns His Last Urn of Ashes" she vividly describes an elderly man who pines over a childhood friend and a lost relationship. The girl was of a family of much higher social status than he, and he has secretly loved her all his life. While she was young she was taken away from home unwillingly, and she returned only after she had grown up. When the man saw his beloved, the sight

> [. . .] stopped him short when the woman he dimly remembered as a little girl returned like a porcelain goddess, enthroned atop a mountain of luggage, finished and polished by the city. He had trembled at sight of her coming out into the fields, fair and bright in the morning gold of sunshine. Her white, wide skirts rustled in the grass and startled the frogs and dragonflies out of the way.
>
> It was the ache in her, the helpless pain of her eyes as she looked at him drawing away, that had clutched at his heart. You are someone else, he wanted to say, a voiceless conversation he rehearsed faintly and fitfully somewhere in the labyrinth of his mind where it echoed soundlessly. But he was too shy and could not bear to even look at her, a blur of soft white light under the shade of the mango tree. She had gone there and waited, as in the days when they were small and she would climb up and sit on a branch and hide behind the tangle of leaves and throw little twigs at him. She stood there and waited, as secretly he watched her from a distance, not daring to come near.[19]

Her interest in social, political and national affairs have frequently become topics for Dr. Maggay's pen. When Flor Contemplacion, the Filipina domestic helper working in Singapore to earn an income for her family, was accused of murder, imprisoned and executed in 1995, Filipinos were outraged. Many Filipinos believe that she was innocent and had not had the full assistance of the Philippine government. There was a public display of grief and protest. Dr. Maggay joined in,

> Rizal shot at the Luneta betrayed the skittishness of a nervous colonial government and marked the impending end of the Spanish era. Aquino's killing unmasked the cold, criminal nature of a despotic power whose long subterfuge was a carefully cultivated air of culture and benevolent

paternalism. Contemplacion's futile hope for a reprieve surfaced the sad social cost of earning a few dollars more and the gross indifference of a government anxious not to offend and keep those fabled investments coming.[20]

Dr. Maggay often writes about the Christian faith and lifestyle. Activist on many occasions, convinced that people need to be aroused and live what they profess to believe, she walks with her Lord, and pursues the calm which comes when one has time to think, dream and meditate. Responding to the story of Mary and Martha she muses,

> In Mary, Jesus tells us that the main task of life is not really doing, but being: Listening to the hymn of the underground, the whistle in the dark, the strong and silent rhythm of the life that is hid in Christ. We are to let him touch us in the morning so that we may walk as in a dream, our hearts full and our arms wide open, sufficiently impressed to keep the joy and wonder as we perform the daily and difficult "sacrament of the brother." We are to recover the rhyme, the tattered bits of the song that have been muffled inside us by the humless machine in which most of us are forced to live.
>
> The substance of the Christian life is worship rather than service; Mary on her knees takes priority over Martha on her toes. Martha and her hard-driving passion for activity is essential to the routine gestures of survival. Mary and her supple faculty for communion with the Almighty is what lends romance to the otherwise dreary business of survival. Her feel for the Presence, her graceful entrances and exits while all the while absorbed in the quiet duties of the moment, elevates the humdrum prose and beggary of our lives to the status of poetry.[21]

And so the little introverted girl grew into a social activist, a sincere believer, an administrator of a think tank and an oft-invited speaker. Over the years ISACC has expanded, and it now involves many people. Yet Dr. Maggay remains at the head, involved in the many aspects of the organization. She says, "Years ago it was OK to carry the load of ISACC. It was smaller. Now it has become too much. The problems are too many and too big. I worked at building the organization because I believe that the Lord called me to do it. But I am not an administrator by inclination nor by gifting. It is difficult for me to spend my working days in fundraising and in management, yet I spend about 70 percent of my time doing just that. I've decided to start pulling back. We must search for someone who has the vision and who can lead."[22]

Inside Dr. Maggay, there is always the urge to take the time to meditate and to create with words. She verbalized her deepest desire when she wrote: "As a Christian writer I have grown to the high ambition of simply living my life as God has called me to live it."[23] One of her friends succinctly expressed her opinion, and others are bound to agree, when she defined Melba's writing as "a winsome, articulate expression of the Christian worldview in the Philippine setting."[24]

We may believe that one day, when Melba Padilla Maggay's life on earth ends our Savior will say of her, "She has done a beautiful thing for me."

DOING A BEAUTIFUL THING

Which appeals more to you — to look forward to tomorrow or to look back at the yesterdays of your life? Your answer will probably depend somewhat on your age; while youth has only a brief past to remember and tends to look forward, seniors have limited tomorrows in this world to look forward to, and often recall past experiences. When people reflect on their past they are often amazed that life has unfolded so differently from what they had expected or could ever have imagined.

One ancient writing, composed in AD 196, speaks of Christian "sisters" who lived a thousand and more kilometers away from the center of Christianity.[1] Who were these women? Could they perhaps have been prisoners of war? They probably met great unexpected changes in their lives, whether they heard the gospel in their home town or whether they were prisoners and carried their faith in their hearts while going into exile.

Sorkaktani, mother of four Mongol rulers, could never have dreamt, when she was a Christian Kerait princess in her father's tent, that she would one day have a son whose name and whose empire would be remembered almost two thousand years later. She surely cannot have surmised that her Christian influence would be far-reaching in history.

While Ramabai Dongre was a pilgrim and used Hindu holy scriptures to earn a living she cannot have envisioned herself at the head of a Christian home for Indian widows and orphans. Yet today she is remembered for becoming exactly that, and for being an inspiration to the widows in the home she founded.

Tong Tan Tjien Nio, the girl who was not able to graduate from high school because she was to be married, had no idea that she would become a young widow, and then a Christian, and live a prayerful life. Her children still honor and respect her and remember her prayers.

And the woman who anointed Jesus? Her sins were forgiven, and she was so overwhelmed with gratitude that she did the socially unacceptable when she gave a gift worth at least a year's worth of salary. The disciples called it extravagant, they seem to not have understood her way of expressing heartfelt thanks, but Jesus blessed her.

When did I feel so grateful to God for his love that I wanted to give him my best?

A.C.K.
Lent 2005

Doing a Beautiful Thing
Questions and Reflections for Today

Chapter 1
Introduction

1 How does the "beautiful thing" done by Mary compare to something we might do today?

2 Does it happen today that friends criticize a Christian for spending too much for Jesus?

3 How, do you suppose, did the women martyrs in Iran like Candida and Martha receive Christian encouragement for their perseverance? What about today's Christian workers like Helen Madrid in the Philippines? How can we be partners with other Christian women?

Chapter 2
Women in Mission

1 Imagine yourself in Dorothy Carey's situation, the wife of a poor laborer, and pregnant with your fourth child. Then your husband tells you that he feels called to take the gospel to a place about which you know little. Would you call his sense of prompting one of faithfulness or one of foolishness? Would you be prepared to go with him, or would you refuse?

2 Remembering those women who, two hundred years ago, felt called to mission service, but were unable to go alone, how do you think you would feel if this was your experience? Would you be willing to marry someone you hardly knew just to be able fulfill your dream to become a missionary?

3 If a woman becomes involved in Christian service locally because she was unable for some reason to fulfill her hope of being a cross-cultural missionary overseas, should she feel that this is second best? What does God ask of each of His children?

Chapter 3
Mother of Four Rulers
Sorkaktani (d. 1252)
1 Considering that Sorkaktani was unable to read and her Bible knowledge was probably very little, do you think that she was a true Christian?
2 Sorkaktani distributed favors among Buddhists and Muslims as well as among Christians. What did that mean, and what would be the results?
3 How could the Mongol khans be so cruel if Sorkaktani's Christian faith really influenced them, and why was Sorkaktani's Christian faith so important for Asia's future?

Chapter 4
A Teenaged Pioneer Missionary
Harriet A. Newell (1793–1812)
1 Do you think that Harriet's commitment was to God and missions, or to Samuel Newell?
2 Imagine yourself in Harriet's mother's place. Remembering her place in time and culture, would you have let Harriet leave for a far-away country about which you knew very little?
3 What do you think about the marriage arrangements of some of the pioneer missionaries?

Chapter 5
Letters Home from Japan
Margaret T. K. Ballagh (1840–1909)
1 How would you feel if you were a young missionary in a foreign country and you and your husband had a baby? Remember your faith, family, culture, health, education, and other personal circumstances.

2 The early missionaries in Japan faced the fact that, should Japanese become Christians, the new believers faced the death penalty. Was this a moral question for the Japanese and/or for the missionaries? Did it have implications for the work of evangelism?

3 Many who were missionary children have returned as missionaries to the countries in which they grew up. Please cite several possible reasons for this, and comment on those missionary families who have had of two, three, or even four generations in the same country.

Chapter 6
The Law of Service
Isabella Thoburn (1840–1901)

1 What do you think of Isabella Thoburn's idea of the law of service?

2 Do you think that, after many years in India, Isabella still felt at home in her own country?

3 How important is it, in your opinion, for a single missionary to have a close relative or friend living nearby, the way Isabella and James (sister and brother) were near each other geographically and enjoyed a close relationship?

Chapter 7
A Woman's Voice in India
Pandita Ramabai Dongre (1858–1922)

1 Why, do you think, did Pandita Ramabai want to cooperate with the Hindus when she started her *Sarada Sadan*, "Home of Wisdom"?

2 What do you think of the concept of "faith missions" such as the Mukti Mission? Does God always provide when we ask?

3 Do you think that Pandita Ramabai was a fulfilled woman? Or a lonely one?

Chapter 8
Physician to the Korean Queen
Lillias H. Underwood (1851–1921)

1 Do you feel a kindred spirit with Lillias? Why?

2 Do you think it is better for a missionary to be married or single? Why? What do you think of women who work "in a man's world,"

and who have to fight prejudice? Think of the military, certain science projects, etc. Is there prejudice against women in your country today?

3 Is it better for missionaries' names to be forgotten or should they be remembered with plaques, names on buildings and such?

Chapter 9
Healing Among the Poor in Manila
S. Rebecca Parrish (1869–1958)

1 It has been said that missionaries always seem to come on the coattails of traders and the military, and that has often been true. Why was this so?

2 Becoming a missionary in a country which is influenced by one's home country offers certain benefits. What could they be? Are these a help or a hindrance to one's work?

3 Some missionaries have been loved in spite of their faults, because people have seen Jesus' love in the missionaries. That applies to us in our home country as well. How does that make you feel?

Chapter 10
"She Became the Tiger of the School!"
Tena Holkeboer (1895–1965)

1 Do missionary adventures appeal to you? Would you want to tell others about them or do you think it better to be silent about them?

2 Have you ever been afraid of a missionary or of facing evaluating the work she does/did?

3 Do you think that Tena Holkeboer respected Chinese culture as she should have? How far should missionaries and local Christians go in adapting to other people's customs (e.g., dress, food, marriage, work methods) or in criticizing the customs of other cultures?

Chapter 11
"Do it! Do it! Do it!"
Geertruida J. Dreckmeier (1895–1992)
1 Is it always right to go ahead when we think we ought to do something, even if others advise us against it?
2 What do you think of Truus's practice of singing a Christian song after the Japanese national anthem? What do you think would have happened if the Japanese knew what the hymn meant?
3 What do you think Truus would have appreciated when she was old and blind, and living in a home for the blind?

Chapter 12
Mother of Ten, Woman of Prayer
Tong Tan Tjien Nio (1909–1977)
1 How would you have felt if, at a young age, you had to marry a much older man?
2 Do you think that it was right for Tong Pai Hu to bring Tjian Nio to his parents' house? Remember Chinese customs as well as Tjian Nio's feelings.
3 How do you see Tjian Nio as a person who did a beautiful thing for Jesus?

Chapter 13
"I Am a Fifth-Generation Japanese Christian"
Minato Akiko (1932–   )
1 Do you think that Akiko did the right thing when she told Hiroshi that she could not marry him?
2 How do you feel about the "Papa Corner" Professor Minato put up in memory of her late husband?
3 When you are convinced that something which goes against your culture is right, should you accept things the way they are or should you try to bring change? What about when it seems impossible? Or are there other ways to handle this?

Chapter 14
A Missionary to Her Own People
Lucy del Carmen Apostol (1937–   )

1 Imagine yourself going to a foreign country to study, as Lucy did. How would you feel, and would you want to do it?
2 Do you, like Lucy, have a skill which you can use in serving the Lord? Can the skills of people in your group be combined for some work or project?
3 In her retirement Lucy still looks for ways to serve her community. What do you think of this?

Chapter 15
Thinker, Writer, Christian Activist
Melba Padilla Maggay (1950–   )

1 Until she was a young adult Melba did not realize that she was a creative writer. Should we tell young people what their gifts are, or should we let them find out for themselves?
2 Why was it difficult for Melba to leave the church where she felt at home and to become part of a fellowship group among the poor?
3 What do you think of Melba's relationship with her mother?

Questions for further discussion and thought:
1 Which of the women in the book have impressed you most? Why?
2 Do you feel critical of any of the women in this book? Why?
3 How, in your opinion, can the life stories in this book be of help to Christians today?

Notes

Acknowlegment
1   Samuel M. Zwemer, *Raymond Lull, First Missionary to the Muslims.* Internet. Written in Bahrain, Arabia, March 1902.

CHAPTER 1
Introduction
1   Matthew 26:6–13; Mark 14:3–9. Matthew seems to have based his writing on that of Mark. Some scholars believe that Luke (7:36–50) and John (12:1–8) describe the same event, but it is generally agreed that these passages probably point to one or two separate occasions; see, e.g., the notes in the NIV Bible text.
2   The Bible, *Contemporary English Version.* The *New International Version* has "to me."
3   Romans 16.
4   Quoted in Samuel H. Moffett, *A History of Christianity in Asia,* vol. 1, *Beginnings to 1500* (San Francisco: HarperCollins Publishers, 1992), 207.
5   Moffett, 97.
6   Quoted in John C. England, *The Hidden History of Christianity in Asia: The Churches of the East Before 1500* (Delhi: ISPCK and Hong Kong: CCA, 1998), 21.
7   Sebastian P. Brock and Susan A. Harvey, transl., updated version, *Holy Women of the Syrian Orient* (Berkeley: University of California Press, 1987), 26.
8   Ibid., 64.
9   Ibid., 67–73.
10   England, 28.
11   Ibid., 46–48.

CHAPTER 2
Women in Mission

1 Pierce R. Beaver, *All Loves Excelling: American Protestant Women in World Mission* (Grand Rapids: Wm. B. Eerdmans, 1968), 14; Alice L. Hageman, "Women and Missions: The Cost of Liberation," in *Sexist Religion and Women in the Church*, edited by Alice L. Hageman (New York: Association Press, 1974), 173.

2 Beaver, 13.

3 Jane Hunter, *The Gospel of Gentility: American Women Missionaries in Turn-of-the-Century China* (New Haven: Yale University Press, 1984), 42.

4 Dana L. Robert, *American Women in Mission: A Social History of their Thought and Practice, The Modern Mission Era, 1792–1992, an Appraisal.* Series editor Wilbert R. Shenk (Macon, GA: Mercer Univ. Press, 1996), 22.

5 Stuart Piggin and John Roxborogh, *The St. Andrews Seven: The Finest Flowering of Missionary Zeal in Scottish History* (Edinburgh: The Banner of Truth Trust, 1985), 104.

6 Richard Lovett, *James Gilmour of Mongolia: His Diaries, Letters and Reports* (New York: Fleming H. Revell Co., n.d. [±1920], 243.

7 Lovett, 242.

8 Quoted by Martha Huntley, "Presbyterian Women's Work and Rights in the Korea Mission," *American Presbyterian* 65 (Spring 1987), 37.

9 Quoted in Mary S. Donovan, "Women as Foreign Missionaries in the Episcopal Church, 1830-1920," *Anglican and Episcopal History* 61 (1961): 17.

10 Quoted in Donovan, 34.

11 Huntley, 48n. 19.

12 Ibid., 41.

13 James M. Thoburn, *Life of Isabella Thoburn* (Cincinnati, OH: Jennings & Pye, 1903), 315–317.

14 Frederick B. Hoyt, "When a Field was Found Too Difficult for a Man, a Woman Should Be Sent: Adele M. Fielde in Asia, 1865–1890," *Historian* 44 (May 1982): 334.

15 Thomas Russell, "Can the Story Be Told Without Them? The Role of Women in the Student Volunteer Movement," *Missiology: An International Review* 17. (April 1989): 160–161.

16 Beaver, 54.

17 Ralph R. Covell, W. A. P. Martin: *Pioneer of Progress in China* (Washington: Christian University Press, 1978), 53n. 38.

18   Quoted in Anne C. Kwantes, *Presbyterian Missionaries in the Philippines: Conduits of Social Change* (1899–1910). (Quezon City: New Day Publishers, 1989), 164.

19   John G. Fagg, *Forty Years in South China: The Life of Rev. John Van Nest Talmage, D.D.* (New York: Anson D. F. Randolph & Company Inc., 1894), 95.

20   Maina Chawla Sing, *Gender, Religion, and "Heathen Lands": American Missionary Women in South Asia (1860s–1940s)* (New York: Garland Publishing, Inc., 2000), 87.

21   Ibid.

22   Arabella [W.] Stuart, *The Lives of the Three Mrs. Judsons*, comp. by Gary W. Long, Missionary Series, first pub. in 1851 (Springfield, MS: Particular Baptist Press, 1999), 206–207.

23   Dorothy C. Wilson, *Dr. Ida: The Story of Dr. Ida Scudder of Vellore* (New York: McGraw-Hill Book Company, Inc., 1959), 5.

24   Ibid., 3.

25   Martha Huntley, *To Start A Work: The Foundations of Protestant Mission in Korea (1884-1919)* (Seoul: The Presbyterian Church in Korea, 1987), 579n. 81.

26   Ruth Tucker, *From Jerusalem to Irian Jaya: A Biographical History of Christian Missions, Academie* Books (Grand Rapids, MI: Zondervan Publishing House, 1983), 202.

27   Quoted in Kwantes, *Presbyterian Missionaries in the Philippines: Conduits of Social Change (1899-1910)*, 162.

28   Ibid., 100.

29   Julia H. Johnston, *Fifty Missionary Heroes Every Boy and Girl Should Know* (New York: Fleming H. Revell Co., 1913), 184.

30   Ibid., 118.

31   Carla Gay Agus Romarate, "The First Ordained Baptist Pastora," in *Chapters in Philippine Church History* edited by Anne C. Kwantes. (Manila: OMF Literature Inc., 2001), 390–399.

32   Helen Madrid, e-mails to author, 1 May 2004, 6 May 2004.

CHAPTER 3
Mother of Four Rulers—Sorkaktani

1   Leo de Hartog, Genghis Khan: *Conqueror of the World* (New York: Barnes & Noble, 1989), 7.

2   Sorkaktani, often spelled Sorghaghtani. See Samuel H. Moffett, *A History of Christianity in Asia, Vol. 1, Beginnings to 1500* (New York:

HarperSanFrancisco, a division of HarperCollins Publishers, 1992), 416, n. 14; Harold Lamb, *The March of the Barbarians* (New York, NY: The Literary Guild of America, 1940), 79.

3   Morris Rossabi, *Khubilai Khan: His Life and Times* (Berkeley: University of California Press, 1988), 3.

4   The Bible tells about New Testament Christians traveling west, but there were also those who went east. They organized churches which, together, were simply called the Church of the East. In the 400s a major theological disagreement erupted. Bishop Nestorius (d. 451) was at its center, and his followers came to be called Nestorians. They were the people of the Persian Empire, and they sent out missionaries who traveled the Old Silk Roads to Central Asia and China. For the sake of convenience, the name "Nestorian Church" is still used for early Christians of Central and South Asia, China, and the nomadic tribes of the north. Sorkaktani and her family, along with all others in her environment who professed the Christian faith, are usually called Nestorian Christians.

5   Moffett, 400.

6   Toghrul Wang Khan died in 1203. See Jeremiah Curtin, *The Mongols* (Boston, MA: Little Brown & Co., 1908; Cambridge, MA: Da Capo Press, 2003), 60; Leo De Hartog, *Genghis Khan: Conqueror of the World* (Barnes & Noble, Inc. ed., 1989; paperback, London: I.B. Taurus & Col., Ltd., 1999), 27.

7   The eldest sister was Ibaka Beki, and the sister who became the wife of Temujin's eldest son Jochi was Bektutmish. See Harold Lamb, *Genghis Khan: Emperor of All Men* (New York: 1963), 34 Robert M. McBride & Co. ed., 1927; Bantam Pathfinder ed., 1963), 34.

8   Harold Lamb, *Genghis Khan: The Conqueror, Emperor of All Men*. Bantam Pathfinder (New York Doubleday & Co., Inc., 1963; New York: Bantam Books, 1963), 56. This title is sometimes translated as "World-Ruler," or "Great Khan of the Mongols"; see also Moffett, *A History*, 402.

9   Leo de Hartog, 31. Meetings of Mongol clan leaders, when new leaders were elected, were called *quriltai* (also *kuriltai*) and the new Mongol kingdom was named Mongol ulus.

10   http://Internet, accessed 3 March 2003.

11   Ibid.

12   R. P. Lister, *Genghis Khan* (New York: Dorset Press, 1969), 159.

13   Ibid., 56, 191–192.

14   Leo de Hartog, 6.

15 The Uighurs had a writing system because Nestorian missionaries from West Asia, wanting to provide Scripture for them, had devised a script for the people. This was a simplified version of Syriac, actually Aramaic, the language of the first translation of the Greek New Testament.

16 Lamb, *Genghis Khan: Emperor of All Men*, 189; Moffett, 401.

17 Moffett. 401.

18 Lamb, *Genghis Khan: Emperor of All Men*, 189; Moffett. 401.

19 John Young, *By Foot to China: Mission of the Church of the East, to 1400* (Tokyo: Radiopress, 1984), 27–28.

20 Lamb, *Genghis Khan: Emperor of All Men*, 86; Lamb, *The March of the Barbarians* (New York: The Literary Guild of America, 1940), 93.

21 "Women," internet, accessed 3 March 2003.

22 Lamb, *March of the Barbarians*, 83.

23 Leo De Hartog, *Genghis Khan: Conqueror of the World*, 159.

24 Young, 30.

25 Http://www.ucalgary.ca/applied_history/tutor/islam/ilkhanate.html, internet, accessed 15 January 2004.

26 "Sorghaghtani Beki, Mother of Great Khans," *Female Heroes of the Regions of the World*, Internet, accessed 11 January 2003.

27 A. C. Moule, *Christians in China Before the Year 1550* (London: SPCK, 1930), 13, 15.

28 Moffett, 443.

29 Jeremiah Curtin, 322; Lamb, March, 200.

30 Lamb, *March of the Barbarians*, 81; Morris Rossabi, 48.

31 Rossabi, 1.

CHAPTER 4
A Teenaged Pioneer Missionary—Harriet Atwood Newell

1 Sarah D. Locke Stowe, *History of Mount Holyoke Seminary During its First Half Century* (1837–1887), (Springfield, MA: Mount Holyoke Seminary, 1887), 7.

2 Quoted in Dana L. Robert, *American Women in Mission: A Social History of their Thought and Practice, The Modern Mission Era, 1792–1992: An Appraisal*, Series editor Wilbert R. Shenk (Macon, GA: Mercer University Press, 1997), 15.

3 H. W. Pierson, ed., *American Missionary Memorial, Including Biographical and Historical Sketches* (New York: Harper & Brothers, Publishers, 1853), 77.

4   Eddy, Daniel C., *Heroines of the Missionary Enterprise, or Sketches of Prominent Female Missionaries*, ed. John Cumming, 3rd edition (London: Arthur Hall, Virtue, and Co., n.d.), 11, 12.

5   Pierson, 78, 79.

6   Robert, 11–12.

7   _____ [Samuel Newell], *The Life and Writings of Mrs. Harriet Newell*, revised by the Committee of Publication of the Philadelphia American SSU. (Philadelphia. Philadelphia American Sunday-School Union,1831,) 72.

8   Ibid.

9   Ibid., 74.

10   Ibid., 75.

11   Ibid., 96.

12   Ibid., 97.

13   Ibid., 101.

14   Ibid., 108.

15   Eddy, 16.

16   Ann White, "Counting the Cost of Faith: America's Early Female Missionaries," *Church History* 57 (March 1988): 20.

17   Eddy, 5.

18   Quoted in Robert, 2.

19   Sharon James, *My Heart is in His Hands—Ann Judson of Burma: A Life, with Selections from Her Memoirs and Letters* (Durham, England: Evangelical Press, 1998), 59.

20   Newell, Writings, 258.

21   Robert, 41.

CHAPTER 5
Letters Home from Japan—Margaret Tate Kinnear Ballagh

1   Ribi, Kurt, "The Age of Christian Martyrs in Japan," Arthur Reynolds, ed. *Japan in Review: Japan Harvest Anthology, 1955–1970*, Vol. I (Tokyo: Japan Evangelical Missionary Association, 1970), 9.

2   Ibid.

3   Quoted by Winburn T. Thomas, *Protestant Beginnings in Japan: The First Three Decades, 1859–1889* (Tokyo: Charles E. Tuttle Company, 1959), 91.

4   Margaret Tate Kinnear Ballagh, *Glimpses of Old Japan: 1861-1866* (Tokyo: Methodist Pub. House, 1908; Avon, NY: The Abcedarian Press, 1993). This is the first of many quotes from this book, and for many of them page numbers are not recorded.

5   James B. Moore, great-grandson of Margaret and James H. Ballagh, telephone interview by author, 4 February 2004.

6   "James H. Ballagh Correspondence," W94–1186.5–Ballagh, James H. History Research Center, The Joint Archives of Holland, typewritten document.

7   *Glimpses*, I.

8   Lorenzo Ruiz, a Chinese mestizo from the Philippines, was one of a group of missionaries who, in defiance of the ban, traveled from Manila to Japan in 1537. The group was captured and martyred. Ruiz was beatified in 1981 by Pope John Paul II and was canonized in 1987, the first Filipino Roman Catholic saint.

9   D. B. Simmins, M.D. and his wife were among these pioneers, but they left the mission after a short time.

10 J. M. T. Winther, "The Big Four," in *Japan in Review*, A. Reynolds, ed. (Tokyo: Japan Evangelical Missionary Association, 1970), 41.

11 James B. Moore, telephone interview by author, 4 February 2004.

12 Ibid.

13 Mizugaki, Kiyoshi, transl. J. A. McAlpine, "One Hundred Years of Evangelism in Japan: A Memorial to the Missionary Labors of Three Generations," typed document, in W92–1049–James Ballagh, The Joint Archives of Holland, 21.

14 Quoted in Kiyoshi Mizugaki, ibid., 26.

15 Mizugaki, ibid., 13.

16 Ferris Seminary began with classes for children which were started by a woman who boarded with the Brown family, next to the Buddhist temple in Kanagawa. The first class was held in 1870 in Yokohama. It focused on girls in its second year, and became Ferris Seminary, a boarding school for girls in 1875. See also *Fifty Years in Foreign Fields*, 30–31 .

17 Mizugaki, 17–19.

18 "The Seventy-Eighth Annual Report of the Board of Foreign Missions of the Reformed Church in America and the Fifty-third Year of Separate Action," *The Acts and Proceedings of the One Hundred and Fourth Regular Session of the General Synod of the Reformed Church in America* (New York: Board of Publications of the Reformed Church in America, 1910), 96.

CHAPTER 6
The Law of Service—Isabella Thoburn

1   James M. Thoburn, *Life of Isabella Thoburn* (Cincinnati, OH: Jennings and Pye; New York, NY: Eaton and Mains, 1903), 368.

2   James Mills Thoburn (1836–1922) later became the Methodist Bishop of India and Malaysia.

3   This family information was given by Crawford Thoburn, great-grandnephew of James M. Thoburn, letter to author, 6 March 2004. I thank him for providing it.

4   Earl K. Brown, "Isabella Thoburn," Methodist History 22 (July 1984): 210.

5   William Oldham, a contemporary who knew Isabella Thoburn, wrote in the early 1900s (William Oldham, "Isabella Thoburn, Christian–Teacher–Missionary, 1840–1901," photocopied document, n.p., 3–4; originally this was probably a pamphlet published by Jennings and Pye, in the opinion of Crawford Thoburn, Isabella 's great-grandnephew), and had a slightly different perspective than Earl K. Brown (Brown, ibid., 211–212), who wrote some eighty years later.

6   Oldham, 4.

7   R. Pierce Beaver, *All Loves Excelling: American Protestant Women in World Mission* (Grand Rapids: Wm. B. Eerdmans, 1968), 121.

8   James M. Thoburn, 78.

9   Brown, 213.

10 Maina C. Singh, "Gender, Mission, and Higher Education in Cross-Cultural Context: Isabella Thoburn in India," *International Bulletin of Missionary Research* 25 (October 2001): 166.

11 James M. Thoburn, 98.

12 Ibid., 146.

13 Ibid., 115.

14 Ibid., 139.

15 Ibid., 187.

16 Lilavati Singh, in James M. Thoburn, 363.

17 Oldham, 10.

18 James M. Thoburn, 188.

19 Ibid., 181.

20 This was given at the Ecumenical Missionary Conference in New York in April, 1900.

21 James M. Thoburn, 325.

22 Ibid., 330–331.

23   Isabella's death was one of three in Bishop James M. Thoburn's family in a short time. His eldest son, the son by his first wife, had died two years earlier, in 1899; Isabella succumbed to cholera in 1901; and his second wife, Anna, died the following year, 1902. Letter of Crawford R. Thoburn, great-grandson of Bishop James M. Thoburn, to author, 6 March 2004.

24   James M. Thoburn, 361.

CHAPTER 7
A Woman's Voice In India—Pandita Ramabai Dongre

1   Edith Deen, *Great Women of the Christian Faith* (New York: Harper & Brothers Publishers, 1959), 280.

2   Ibid.

3   Pandita Ramabai, *A Testimony*, 9th ed. (Kedgaon, India: Ramabai Mukti Mission, 1968), 15.

4   Nancy A. Hardesty, *Great Women of the Christian Faith* (New York: Harper & Brothers Publishers, 1959), 126.

5   Ramabai, 15.

6   Ibid., 17.

7   Anandibai Joshi, Ramabai's relative, became the first Indian woman to graduate from the Women's Medical College in Philadelphia in 1888. When she returned to India she was appointed as hospital physician but unfortunately, she died of tuberculosis after only a year.

8   Paul Hiebert, "Mission to Hindu Women: Pandita Ramabai, 1858–1922," in John D. Woodbridge, ed. *Ambassadors for Christ* (Chicago: Moody Press, 1994), 170.

9   Ibid.

10 Ramabai, 18.

11 Ibid., 20.

12 Ibid.

13 Deen, 281.

14 Hiebert, 161.

15 Ramabai, 21–22.

16 Ibid., 27.

17 Ibid., 30.

18 Ibid., 33.

19 Dana L. Robert, *American Women in Mission: A Social History of Their Thought and Practice. The Modern Mission Era, 1742–1992: An Appraisal.* Series editor Wilbert R. Shenk (Macon, GA: Mercer University Press, 1997), 245.

20 Deen, 285.

21 Ibid.
22 Ramabai Mukti Mission, e-mail to author, 22 March 2004.
23 Wright, 45.
24 Gary B. McGee, "Baptism of the Holy Ghost and Fire! The Revival Legacy of Minnie F. Abrams of India" Enrichment (Summer 1998), www.agts.edu/faculty/faculty_publications/articles/ mcgee_abrams.pdf. Internet, accessed 14 February 2004.
25 Dana, ibid.
26 Stanley M. Burgess, "Pentecostalism in India: An Overview," *Asian Journal of Pentecostal Studies* 4 (2001): 88.

CHAPTER 8

Physician to the Korean Queen—Lillias S. Horton Underwood

1 Leonora Horton Egan, "Lillie in Korea and Contributing Circumstances," ed. Nancy K. Underwood, a booklet bound with the 1977 reprint edition of *Lillias H. Underwood, Fifteen Years Among the Topknots* (Seoul: Royal Asiatic Society-Korea Branch, 1977), 372.
2 Ibid., 370.
3 J. Busteed, quoted in Martha Huntley, *To Start A Work: The Foundations of Protestant Mission in Korea (1884–1919),* (Seoul: The Presbyterian Church of Korea, 1987), 335. Yet, there was great interest in the medical practices of the foreigners, for the two Presbyterian physicians, Horace Allen and John Heron, "treated 265 inpatients, 10,460 outpatients, and performed 394 minor operations and 150 operations requiring anesthesia during 1885, the first year of work in the small and simple hospital," quoted in Huntley, 335.
4 Huntley, 323.
5 Winifred Mathews, "Lillias Underwood, She Followed 'A Red-maned Star, '" in Winifred Mathews, *Dauntless Women: Stories of Pioneer Wives, Biography Index Reprint Series* (Freeport, NY: Books for Libraries Press, 1947), 147.
6 James Smylie, "Women in Mission," *American Presbyterians* 65 (Spring 1987), 41.
7 Ibid., 238.
8 Egan, 387.
9 Ibid., 388
10 Ibid., 149.
11 Lillias Horton Underwood, in an undated clipping of an article of *Women's News.*

12 His father sold a variety of paper and ink, and all the sons helped in the business, at times. This was the beginning of the Underwood company, and later son John Thomas became famous for the Underwood typewriters his company produced. Grace Underwood Harkness, granddaughter of Lillias H. and Horace G. Underwood, telephone conversation with author, 30 April 2004.

13 Huntley, 133.

14 Egan, 388–90.

15 Mathews, 145.

16 Ibid., 153.

17 Ibid., 156–57.

18 Huntley, 442.

19 Ibid., 167.

20 Jean Welch Underwood, wife of John Thomas Underwood, one of Lillias's and Horace's grandsons, e-mail letter to author, 24 April, 2004.

21 One of these men was among the first Korean Presbyterian ministers to be ordained.

22 Huntley, 361.

23 Arthur J. Brown, "No. 594 – To the Chosen Mission," letter Arthur J. Brown, Mission Secretary, to Presbyterian missionaries in Korea, 7 November 1921.

24 Huntley, 326.

25 Mathews, 159.

26 Brown, ibid.

27 Huntley, 435.

28 Internet, accessed 16 April 2004.

29 Horton Horace Underwood was a missionary in Korea from 1912 to his death in 1951. He married Ethel Van Wagoner, and together they had six children. Since the days of Lillias and Horace G. Underwood there have been Underwoods in the Korean mission. Today's generation of missionaries by the name Underwood are the fourth generation. Grace Underwood Harkness, granddaughter of Lillias, e-mail to author, 8 March 2004.

30 Jean Welch Underwood, wife of a grandson of Lillias and Horace G., unpublished paper, n.d.; Grace Underwood Harkness, telephone conversations, 30 April 2004, 10 February 2005.

31 Grace Underwood Harkness, e-mail to author, 13 May 2004.

CHAPTER 9

Healing Among the Poor in Manila—S. Rebecca Parrish

1   Rebecca Parrish, *Cabin In Th' Clearin,'* n.p.
2   Mary L. Devolder, *Rebecca Parrish: A Medical Missionary in Manila* (Cincinnati, OH: Woman's Division of Christian Service, Board of Missions, The Methodist Church, 1956), 3.
3   Ibid., 4.
4   Leon Woods, "Rebecca Parrish, Who Went to the Philippines," in *The One Who Went and The One She Found* ([New York]: Woman's Foreign Missionary Society, 1929), 224–225.
5   Devolder, 6.
6   Zenaida Lumba, "Harris Memorial College: The Spiritual Journey of a Faith Community," *Phronêsis: A Journal of the Asian Theological Seminary* 8 (2001): 32. Dr. Lumba was president of Harris Memorial College for nineteen years.
7   Ricardo Fernandez, interview by author, Manila, 18 February 2001. Dr. Fernandez, a Filipino physician, remembers Dr. Parrish and her dedicated work.
8   Woods, 226.
9   Woods, 227.
10 "History is Recounted," *The Manila Times*, 26 August 1952.
11 Ibid.
12 Ibid., 232.
13 "The Mary Johnston Hospital Story," Internet, accessed 29 October 2000.
14 Devolder, 9.
15 Woods, 233.
16 "The Mary Johnston Hospital Story." In 2004 there were one hundred forty-three beds in the hospital, and the OB-Gyn department is still known as the Rebecca Parrish Pavilion, Myrna P. Velasquez, M.D., e-mail to author, 28 April 2004.

CHAPTER 10

"She Became the Tiger of the School!" —Tena Holkeboer

1   Early Portuguese traders were able to secure Macau for their own use in 1557, and from there traded with Chinese in the city of Guangzhou (called Canton by foreigners).
2   The five cities were Xiamen (Amoy), Guangzhou (Canton), Ningbo (Ningpo), Fuzhou (Foochow) and Shanghai.

3   The information about Abeel's arrival in Xiamen comes from "The first letter written (from China) by the Rev. David Abeel, and sent from Xiamen. I March 1842." Hong Kong Baptist University archives, special collection.

4   Lim Jin-gi, "The History of the First Protestant Church in China, After One Hundred Years," JAH, W88–0055, "Holkeboer, Tena–articles–1920–1950," typed document

5   Walter de Velder, "Across Three Continents," Joint Archives of Holland, W88-0033 "De Velder, Walter, (1907–), typed document, 9.

6   Stephen (Chung Rung) Tong, Chinese-Indonesian evangelist, interview by author, Kowloon, 23 July 2003.

7   Nelle Vander Ark, cousin of Dr. T. Holkeboer, interview by author, Grand Rapids, Michigan, 14 May 2000.

8   Chris Holkeboer Homkes, younger sister of Dr. Tena Holkeboer, interview by author, Lowell, Michigan, 21 June 2001. Chris was nine years younger than Tena. This interview took place when Chris was ninety-three years old. She died several months later.

9   Tena Holkeboer, "Urging a Decision," Church Herald, 21 May 1942.

10   Board of Foreign Missions, Reformed Church in America, *Tena Holkeboer.* Brochure. April 1948. The Joint Archives of Holland, History Research Center, Hope College, Holland, Michigan, W88-0055. "Tena Holkeboer (1895–1965)," I.

11   Chris Holkeboer Homkes, ibid.

12   Ibid.

13   Ibid.

14   Jean Nienhuis (1887–1975) was one of Tena's best friends in Gulangyu for many years.

15   Tena Holkeboer, letter to family, 27 September 1920.

16   Tena Holkeboer, letter to family, 22 October 1920.

17   Cecilia A. Holkeboer Mereness, daughter of a brother of Tena Holkeboer, interview by author, Lowell, Michigan, 19 November 2003.

18   Edward A. Van Baak, interview by author, Grand Rapids, Michigan, 10 May 2000. He did become a missionary, served in Asia for more than two decades, and remained involved with missions until his retirement.

19   Agnes J. B. Angus, "Pieces of China," typed document dated 8 September 1970, in "Wm. R. Angus," The Joint Archives of Holland, 1–9, passim.

20 Tena Holkeboer, letter to friends, 10 November 1936.

21 Sarella Te Winkel, "The Amoy Mission, China," The Sixth Decade of the Woman's Board of Foreign Missions, Reformed Church in America, *1926–1935: A Sequel to Mrs. W. I. Chamberlain's* 'Fifty Years in Foreign Fields' (New York: The Woman's Board of Foreign Missions of the Reformed Church in America, n.d.), 27.

22 Tena Holkeboer, letter to friends, 14 November 1935.

23 Tena Holkeboer, 10 July 1936.

24 Wesley K. Shao, former student of Dr. T. Holkeboer, interview by author, Manila, 27 October, 2000.

25 Ibid.

26 Tena Holkeboer, letter to friends, 10 November 1936.

27 Te Winkel, "The Amoy Mission, China."

28 William. R. Angus, Jr., "RCA China Mission Reports–194–1946," n.d. Joint Archives, H00–1381, I.

29 Tena Holkeboer, *God's Bridge, or the Story of Jin-gi*, 2nd ed. (Grand Rapids, MI: Wm. B. Eerdmans, 1945).

30 Lin, Jiu-gi [Lim, Jin-gi], "The History of the First Protestant Church in China, After One Hundred Years," Joint Archives of Holland, W88-055, "Holkeboer, Tena–articles–1920–1950," typewritten document, 25.

31 Tena Holkeboer, letter to friends, 23 March 1944.

32 Tena Holkeboer, 4 December 1945.

33 Ibid.

34 Tena Holkeboer, 29 December 1945.

35 Tena Holkeboer, letter to friends, 21 January 1946.

36 Ibid.

37 "About World Vision," Internet accessed 10 January 2004.

38 Chris Holkeboer Homkes, ibid.

39 Tena Holkeboer, "Latest News from China," The Church Herald, 11 November 1949, JAH, W088–55, "Holkeboer, Tena–articles–1920–1950."

40 Wesley Shao, ibid.

41 Christina Wang never married. She remained principal of Hope Christian School until she died in 1966, and was buried in the Manila Memorial Park. E-mail message Rosa Ching Shao to author, 5 November 2000.

42 Jean Homkes Rockett, daughter of Chris Holkeboer Homkes, and Cecilia A. Holkeboer Mereness, daughter of Tena's brother Oscar Holkeboer, ibid.

43 Interviews with Chris Holkeboer Homkes (21 June 2001), Jean Homkes Rockett, and Cecilia A. Holkeboer Mereness (19 November 2003).

44 Tena Holkeboer, letter to friends, 7 April 1960.

CHAPTER 11
"Do it! Do it! Do it!"—Geertruida Johanna Dreckmeier

1 My parents were in Indonesia from 1931–37. My father taught in a mission school in Magelang, Central Java.

2 Truus Dreckmeier was born on 22 December 1895 and died on 24 October 1992.

3 M. C. Jongeling, letter to author, 22 March 2003; see also Rienke Dekker, "Dokter Geertruida Johanna Dreckmeier (1895–1992): Een Kerk-historisch Onderzoek naar haar Bijdrage aan de Zending, in het Bijzonder aan de Emancipatie van de Vrouw," ["Doctor Geertruida Johanna Dreckmeier (1895–1992): A Church History Research of Her Contribution to Missions, Particularly the Emancipation of Women" (Doctoral dissertation in Church history, Theologische Universiteit, Kampen, the Netherlands, 1998), 17. I don't know if this is a Ph.D. diss., it just says in Dutch: "doctoral diss in church history."

4 Dreckmeier, Geertruida J., "Opvallende Toespraak" ["A Striking Speech"] Zendingsblad, May 1971, 113.

5 J. van der Linden, "Herinnering aan Truus Dreckmeier" ["Memories of Truus Dreckmeier"] Centraal Weekblad, 6 November 1992, 7.

6 Marja Van der Veen-Schenkeveld, *Stuur Haar Maar: Drie Markante Vrouwen in Gereformeerde Zendingsdienst* [*Just Send Her: Three Remarkable Women in Gereformeerde Mission Service*] (Leusden: Kerkinactie, 1995), 28.

7 Ibid.

8 The actual words, in Dutch, were "Ja, stuur haar maar." Van der Veen-Schenkeveld, ibid., 29.

9 Dekker, 39.

10 G. J. Dreckmeier, in a speech delivered during the celebration of her fifty years as physician, 30 November 1970, in A. A. van der Woerdt, "Voor het Zendingswerk Kan de Arbeid van een Vrouw van Evenveel Betekenis Zijn als Die van een Man," ["The Labors of a Woman Can be as Meaningful to Mission as those of a Man"], issue title: "Vrouwen in de Zending: Een Stukje Geschiedenis," ["Women in Missions: A Historical Vignette"], *Allerwegen 2 (1985)*, 56.

11   Bunjamin, S., and J. Van Vliet, "Heel de Mens" ["The Whole Human Being"] Vandaar (January 1993): 18, quoted in Dekker, ibid., 39.

12   Herry Sutjipto, interview by author, Parakan, 30 March 2002.

13   A. Merkelijn, 26 Jaren op het Zendingsveld: Herinneringen van een Missionair Predikant [26 Years on the Mission Field: Memoirs of a Missionary Pastor] ('s Gravenhage: D. A. Daamen's Uitgeversmaatschappij, N.V., 1941), 85. Rev. Merkelijn wrote that he was taught that there were two levels of speech: ngoko, the speech used by superiors to inferiors, and krama, which was spoken by inferiors to superiors. His teacher advised him to use krama.

14   A. Merkelijn, 15.

15   Rev. Merkelijn anticipated that he would need 45,000 guilders to begin, but decided that it would be possible to start with the 35,000 guilders he was able to raise. He was able to purchase a building for 32,000 guilders. Merkelijn, 212. See also Dekker, 35.

16   Van der Veen-Schenkeveld, 36.

17   While one hundred and sixty-four patients and four hundred and ninety-six consultations were recorded for March 1932, this had grown to two hundred and fifty-six patients with eight hundred sixty consultations by the opening day, 16 May 1932.

18   Dekker, 37.

19   Van der Veen-Schenkeveld, 38.

20   Ibid., 38–39.

21   Mirmamigsh Urip, interview by author in Magelang, Java, 30 March 2002.

22   Ibid.

23   "Maak iets van niets," and "Wees zuinig."

24   Edward Brouwer, letter to author, 24 April 2001. Edward is the son of (Clarence) Klaas Brouwer, one of the children. Clarence was born to missionary parents in Magelang in 1931.

25   Juul van der Leuv, letter to author, 18 September 2003.

26   A. A. van der Woerdt, De Zending van de Gereformeerde Kerken in Nederland en de Vrouw op Midden-Java: Een Historische Studie over de Jaren 1896 tot 1945 [Missions of the Gereformeerde Churches in the Netherlands and the Woman on Central Java: A Historical Study of the Years 1896 to 1945], unpublished document (Veenendaal: Kerkinactie, 1985), 29–31.

27   Rineke Van der Woerdt, Werken Zolang het Dag is: Jacqueline Cornélie van Andel-Rutgers (1874–1951), Gereformeerd Zendelinge in Midden-Java [Working as Long as it is Day: Jacqueline Cornélie van Andel-Rutgers (1874–1951),

Gereformeerd Missionary in Central Java] (Kampen, Netherlands: Kok, 2004), 168.

28   Ibid.

29   Internet, accessed 1 February 2005 (This page is written in English. A similar one, in Dutch, differs slightly in content). Van der Steur's work grew rapidly, as more and more needy children were brought to him, most of them the offspring of Dutch soldiers and Indonesian women. Pa van der Steur continued his work with orphans as long as he lived, and literally cared for thousands of them. He died in Indonesia at the age of eighty.

30   Internet, accessed 1 February 2005.

31   Geert Mak, *De Eeuw van mijn Vader* [*The Century of My Father*] (Amsterdam: Uitgeverij Atlas, 1999), 137–38.

32   Dekker, 44.

33   Truus Dreckmeier was sent to Muntilan in December 1943, and stayed there until August 1945. As member of a large group she was then transferred to the Ambarawa 6 camp for some time. She became ill and was hospitalized for a while. Then, together with other women and children, she returned to the Netherlands, where she finally arrived in May 1946.

34   Juul van der Leuv, letter to author, 1 September 2003.

35   Hidajat, P. Laksana, and Moeljono, interviews by author, Magelang, 29 March 2002.

36   Dekker, 45.

37   "Mej. Dr. Dreckmeier Ontving Hoge Onderscheiding" ["Dr. Dreckmeier Receives a High Distinction"], *Centraal Weekblad*, 6 February 1971, 2.

38   Van de Woerdt, 89.

39   Dekker, 45.

40   Juul Van der Leuv, and Anneke Oldhoff, interviews by author, 29 August 2003.

41   Mak, 337.

42   Bunjamin and Van Vliet, ibid., 18.

43   The school's name was Sekolah Wanita Kristen or School voor Vrouwwelijke in Dutch [School for Female Evangelists] *Ibu* Sutirah, its first principal, was the first female student to enrol at the Theological School in Yogya in 1934. She was taught by Dr. Dreckmeier who helped her to complete a graduate education, and became Dr. Dreckmeier's respected colleague and personal friend.

44 "Mej. Dr. Dreckmeier Ontving Hoge Onderscheiding" ["Dr. Dreckmeier Receives a High Distinction), ibid., 2.

45 *Ibu* Nastitik, interview by author, 30 March 2002.

46 G. J. Dreckmeier, from a letter (in the Indonesian language) which was included in a book which was published for Yoga Darma's fifteenth anniversary in 1979. I received only the translation in a letter from Mrs. L. Hidayat, 9 May 2002.

47 "Mej. Dr. Dreckmeier Ontving Hoge Onderscheiding," ibid.

48 This friend wishes to remain anonymous. She is a nurse who was chosen by Dr. Dreckmeier to work with her in Magelang, was interned with her in wartime detention camps and became a lifelong friend.

49 "Dapat Satyalencana Social" ["Celebration of the Medal of Honor in Social Services"], Semarang newspaper,19 April 1971.

50 P. Laksana Hidajat, interview by author in Magelang, 29 March 2002.

51 Ibid.

CHAPTER 12
Mother of Ten, Woman of Prayer—Tong Tan Njien Nio

1 Chinese names show the family name first, thus Tong is the family name of the husband, Tan the woman's maiden name, while Tjien is her personal name and Nio means that she is female. Much of this chapter is based on the book written by Tong Tjien Nio's daughter-in-law Freda Hatfield Tong, *Sons for the Master* (Singapore: Pathseekers, Ltd., 2001).

2 Solomon (Chung An) Tong, sixth son of Tong Tjien Nio, interview by author, Surabaya, 3 April 2002.

3 Ibid.

4 Ibid.

5 Ibid.

6 See Chapter 10, "She Became the Tiger of the School!"

7 Stephen (Chung Rung) Tong, seventh son of Tong Tan Tjien Nio, interview with author, Hong Kong, 23 July 2003.

8 Freda M. Tong, 238–39; Solomon (Chung An) Tong, ibid.

9 Peter (Chung Ping) Tong, e-mail to author, 13 January 2004.

10 Caleb (Chung Ming) Tong, interview by author, Manila, 2 December 2000.

11 Solomon (Chung An) Tong, ibid.

12 Stephen (Chung Rung) Tong, ibid.; Freda Hatfield Tong has a slightly different version of Tjien Nio's prayer, she quotes Proverbs 30: 7–9,

"Two things I ask of you, O Lord; do not refuse me before I die: Keep falsehood and lies far from me; give me neither poverty nor riches, but give me only my daily bread. Otherwise, I may have too much and disown you and say, 'Who is the Lord?'" in *Sons for the Master*, 213.

13   Freda Hatfield Tong, 311.

14   Solomon (Chung An) Tong, ibid.

15   Mrs. Ang Se Niu, interview with author, Surabaya, 4 April 2002.

16   Mrs. Hartono, interview with author, Surabaya, 4 April, 2002.

17   Solomon (Chung An) Tong, ibid.

18   Freda Hatfield Tong, 348.

19   Ibid., 350–351.

20   Ibid., 349–351.

CHAPTER 13
"I Am a Fifth-Generation Japanese Christian"—Minato Akiko

1   Following Japanese custom, the family name comes first. Thus Minato is the family name, and Akiko the personal name.

2   Several treaties were signed beginning in 1854, the earliest ones were very limited. From 1859 outsiders were permitted to enter and reside in Japan, and missionaries were here that same year. At first foreigners were restricted to two towns, one in the north and one in the south. Little by little Japan opened its doors to the outside world.

3   See chapter 5, "Letters Home From Japan."

4   This small group consisted of eleven believers, nine of whom were baptized at that first meeting in Yokohama in 1872. This became the Kaigan church of the Nihon Kirisuto Kookai (Japan Christian Public Church).

5   The school was called the Kaisei Bible School for Women and was founded by Louise Henrietta Pierson (1832–1899).

6   Minato Akiko, "Expectations Concerning the Laity in Contemporary Japan," *The Japan Christian Review* 64 (1998): 68.

7   "Otona ni nari nasai!"

8   Minato, "Expectations," ibid.; Minato Akiko, "The Japanese Church's Most Critical Issue," *Christianity Today*, 8 April 1991, 30.

9   Sandi Wisley, "Spotlight on Akiko," *Japan Harvest* 43 (Spring 1994): 8.

10   K. S. Kantzer, "Christian Scientist Dr. H. Minato," photocopied page dated March, 1978.

11   Minato Akiko, "Expectations Concerning the Laity in Contemporary Japan," *The Japan Review* 64 (1998): 70.

12 Kantzer.

13 Siegfried Buss, e-mail letter to author, 2 October 2003.

14 Sandi Wisley, "Interview with Professor Akiko Minato," *Leadership* (Spring-Summer 1993): 3.

15 Nitobe Inazo (1862–1933) was born into a samurai family in Morioka, northern Japan, and died in Victoria, British Columbia, Canada. His teacher, William S. Clark, president of the Massachusetts Agricultural College, was invited to found an agricultural school on the island of Hokkaido, in northern Japan, and to train people who could help the development of Hokkaido. Clark spent only eight months in Japan in 1876, but had such Christian influence that all of the fifteen students in his class became Christians. Nitobe was one of these, converting during his second year at college. He is so well-known in Japan that, since 1984, his photograph has been shown on all five-thousand-yen currency bills (as of 2004 new bills no longer depict him).

16 from Kodansha's *Encyclopedia of Japan*, Internet, accessed 2 February 2005. Minato places this phrase at a later time, quoting Nitobe Inazo, "The Japanese Nation," Nitobe zensho [*The Complete Works of Nitobe Inazo*], vol. 13 (Tokyo: Kyo Bun Kwan, 1969): 9.

17 Sterling Seagrave and Peggy Seagrave repeatedly speak of the Quaker influence in Japan in *The Yamato Dynasty: the Secret History of Japan's Imperial Family* (London: Bantam Press, 1999; Corgi Books, 2000). There were many influential Japanese Quaker women in the late nineteenth century, they claim (p. 101). They describe the life of Empress Haruko, mother of Emperor Hirohito, and tell of her upbringing among Quakers. Empress Haruko is described as "unquestionably a lifelong Christian" (p. 359).

18 He married Mary Elkinton (born in 1857), the daughter of a prominent Quaker family in Philadelphia.

19 Minato, Akiko, "Women's Jiritsu and Christian Feminism in Japan," Japan Christian Review 59 (1993) : 12.

20 JoAnn Wright, Baptist General Conference missionary, e-mail letter to author, 6 November 2003.

21 Ibid.

22 Wisley, "Faculty Profile," 3.

CHAPTER 14
A Missionary to Her Own People—Lucy del Carmen Apostol

1   Lucy and Vince Apostol, in a farewell speech during the last mission business meeting before their retirement, Christian Reformed World Mission meeting, Manila, 13 February 1996.
2   Clarice Blankers, e-mail to author, 4 February 2001.
3   Ibid.
4   Judy and Henry De Vries, e-mail to author, 21 January 2001.
5   Lucy Apostol, Reports to the board of World Missions of the Christian Reformed Church, CRWM files, "Apostol, Vince and Lucy."
6   Ivan De Kam, e-mail to author, 17 October 2002.
7   Ibid.
8   Lucy Apostol, 10 July 1992, letters to friends,1986–1995. Christian Reformed World Missions, file "Apostol, Vince and Lucy."
9   Patty Hogan, interview by author, Manila, 15 March 2000.
10   Nita De la Peña, letter to author, 4 December 2000.

CHAPTER 15
Thinker, Writer, Christian Activist—Melba Padilla Maggay

1   A *zarzuela* is a theatrical piece, both story and music, with a Spanish background. Around the turn of the twentieth century many *zarzuelas* were written in the Philippines and were a major form of entertainment.
2   See Luningning S. Tala [Melba P. Maggay], "Mother of Stories," 1997 Don Carlos Palanca Memorial Award for Literature, Second Prize, Essay in English category, photocopied document, 5.
3   Melba P. Maggay, "Time Must Have a Stop," *An Asian Palette: Personal Journeys of Christian Writers*, ed. Bernice Cheng (Singapore: Armour Publishing Pte., Ltd., 1998), 58.
4   Maggay, "Our Text in Context: Shaping a Life-giving Word for Today," *Patmos* 13 (1997): 16–18. These words come from an address by Dr. Maggay to the World Assembly of the United Bible Societies held in Mississauga, ON, Canada, from 26 September to 3 October 1996.
5   Mac Bradshaw, e-mail to author, 2 December 2003.
6   The term tentmaking refers to earning an income to support oneself while being engaged in Christian ministry. The metaphor is borrowed from the biblical example of Paul the missionary, who worked as a tent-maker while doing evangelistic work in Corinth (Acts 18:3).
7   Maggay, "Time Must Have a Stop," ibid., 63.
8   Maggay, "Flying Solo," *Patmos* 15 (August 2000): 3–4.

9   Maggay, "Crossing the Cultural Divide: Reflections from Down Under," *Patmos* 11 (1996): 14–16, 21.

10 Maggay, *Transforming Society*, Philippine ed. (Quezon City: Institute for Studies in Asian Church and Culture, 1996), 80.

11 Maggay, "Crossing the Cultural Divide," 15.

12 Maggay, "War Against the Roses: On Standing Up to the Powers," *Patmos* 15 (April 2000): 15.

13 Maggay, "Crossing the Cultural Divide," 21.

14 Maggay, "Diversity, Not Homogeneity, is God's Design for the World," *Patmos* 12 (November 1996): 15.

15 Carmen C. Rodriguez [Melba P. Maggay], "Death and Early Sorrow," First Prize, Essay in English category, 2002 Don Carlos Palanca Memorial Award for Literature. In *Ani: 31 Mga Talinghaga ng Puso* [Metaphors of Love] 3 September 2005).

16 Ibid., 5.

17 Ibid., 16.

18 Maggay, "Once upon a Bright Happy Boy," photocopied document, 3. First Prize, Essay in English category, 1999 Don Carlos Palanca Memorial Award for Literature

19 Maggay, "*Mang* Ambo Burns His Last Urn of Ashes," photocopied document, 11.

20 Maggay, "Flor Contemplacion: Requiem for a People," *Patmos* 13 (March 1998): 3–4.

21 Maggay, "Hail Mary, or Why it Might be Good to Sit under a Guava Tree," *Patmos* 1 (1977): 8–9.

22 Melba P. Maggay, interview by author, 21 October 2003, Quezon City, Republic of the Philippines

23 Maggay, "Time Must Have a Stop," 66.

24 Miriam Adeney, interview by author, 16 March 2004, Vancouver, BC, Canada.

Doing A Beautiful Thing

1   Samuel H. Moffett, *A History of Christianity in Asia, Vol. 1, Beginnings to 1500* (San Francisco: HorperCollins Publishers, 1992), 207. Bardaisan, one of the earliest Christian missionaries, wrote about these woman at a time when Christianity was only beginning to spread that far from the center of Edessa, the center of Christianity at that time.

Selected Sources

Acknowledgment
Zwemer, Samuel M. *Raymond Lull, First Missionary to the Muslims.* Internet, written in Bahrain, Arabia, March 1902.

Chapter 1
Prologue
Beaver, R. Pierce. *All Loves Excelling: American Protestant Women in World Mission.* Grand Rapids: Wm. B. Eerdmans Publishing Company, 1968.
————. *American Protestant Women in World Mission: A History of the First Feminist Movement in North America.* Rev. ed. Grand Rapids: Wm. B. Eerdmans Publishing Company, 1980.
Brock, Sebastian P. and Susan A. Harvey, transl. *Holy Women of the Syrian Orient.* Updated ed. Berkeley: University of California Press, 1987.
England, John C. *The Hidden History of Christianity in Asia: The Churches of the East Before 1500.* Delhi: ISPCK and Hong Kong: CCA, 1998.
Moffett, Samuel H. *A History of Christianity in Asia* Vol. I *Beginnings to 1500.* San Francisco: HarperCollins Publishers, 1992.

Chapter 2
Women in Mission
Barr, Pat. *To China: With Love: The Lives and Times of Protestant Missionaries in China, 1860–1900.* London: Hodder & Stoughton, 1975.
Broomhall, A. J. *Hudson Taylor & China's Open Century* Book I, *Barbarians at the Gates.* Sevenoaks: Hodder & Stoughton, and The Overseas Missionary Fellowship, 1981.
Covell, Ralph R. *W. A. P. Martin: Pioneer of Progress in China.* Washington: Christian University Press, 1978.

Donovan, Mary S. "Women as Foreign Missionaries in the Episcopal Church, 1830–1920." *Anglican and Episcopal History* 61 (1961): 16–39.

————. "Women and Mission: Towards a More Inclusive Historiography." *Historical Magazine of the Protestant Episcopal Church* 53 (December 1984): 297–305.

Fagg, John G. *Forty Years in South China: The Life of Rev. John Van Nest Talmage.* New York: Anson D. F. Randolph & Company (Inc.), 1894.

Goodall, Norman. *A History of the London Missionary Society, 1895–1945.* London: Oxford University Press, 1954.

Horne, C. Silvester. *The Story of the L.M.S., 1795–1895.* London: London Missionary Society, 1894.

Hageman, Alice L. "Women and Missions: The Cost of Liberation." In *Sexist Religion and Women in the Church.* Edited by A. Hageman. New York: Association Press, 1974, 167–193.

Heuser, Frederick J., Jr. "Presbyterian Women and the Missionary Call, 1870–1923." *American Presbyterians* 73 (Spring 1995): 23–34.

Hoyt, Frederick B. "When a Field Was Found Too Difficult for a Man, a Woman Should Be Sent: Adele M. Fielde in Asia, 1865–1890." *Historian* 44 (May 1982): 314–334.

Hunter, Jane. *The Gospel of Gentility: American Women Missionaries in Turn-of-the-Century China.* New Haven: Yale University Press, 1984.

Huntley, Martha. "Presbyterian Women's Work and Rights in the Korean Mission." *American Presbyterians* 65 (Spring 1987): 37–47.

————. *To Start a Work: The Foundations of Protestant Mission in Korea (1884–1919).* Seoul: The Presbyterian Church of Korea, 1987.

Kwantes, Anne C., ed. *Chapters in Philippine Church History.* Manila: OMF Literature, Inc., 2001.

————. *Presbyterian Missionaries in the Philippines: Conduits of Social Change (1899–1910).* Manila: New Day Publications, 1989.

Kwok, Pui-lan. "The Image of the White Lady: Gender and Race in Christian Mission." In *The Special Nature of Women?* Eds. A. Carr and E. Fiorenza. London: SCM Press, 1991, 19–27.

Lovett, Richard. *James Gilmour and His Boys.* London: The Religious Tract Society, n.d. [1894].

————, ed. *James Gilmour of Mongolia: His Diaries, Letters and Reports.* New York: Fleming H. Revell Co., n.d. [± 1920].

Paul, John J. "Religion and Medicine in South India: The Scudder Medical Missionaries and the Christian Medical College and Hospital, Vellore." *Fides et Historia* 22 (Fall 1990): 16–41.

Piggin, Stuart and John Roxborogh. *The St. Andrews Seven: The Finest Flowering of Missionary Zeal in Scottish History.* Edinburgh: The Banner of Truth Trust, 1985.

Robert, Dana L. *American Women in Mission: A Social History of Their Thought and Practice. The Modern Mission Era, 1791–1992, an Appraisal.* Series editor Wilbert R. Shenk. Macon, GA: Mercer University Press, 1997.

————. "Evangelist or Homemaker? Mission Strategies of Early Nineteenth-Century Missionary Wives in Burma and Hawaii." *International Bulletin of Missionary Research* 17 (January 1993): 4–6, 8–10.

Romarate, Carla Gay Agus. "The First Baptist *Pastora.*" In *Chapters in Philippine Church History.* Edited by Anne C. Kwantes. Manila: OMF Literature, Inc., 2001, 290–299.

Russell, Thomas. "Can the Story Be Told Without Them? The Role of Women in the Student Volunteer Movement." *Missiology: An International Review* 17 (April 19889): 159–175.

Singh, Maina C. *Gender, Religion, and "Heathen Lands."* New York and London: Garland Publishing, Inc., 2000.

Stuart, Arabella [W.]. *The Lives of the Three Mrs. Judsons.* Comp. & ed. Gary W. Long. First pub. in 1851. Missionary Series. Springfield, MS: Particular Baptist Press, 1999.

Thoburn, James M. *Life of Isabella Thoburn.* Cincinnati, OH: Jennings & Pye, 1903.

Torbet, Robert G. *Venture of Faith: The Story of the American Baptist Foreign Mission Society and the Woman's American Baptist Foreign Mission Society, 1814–1954.* Philadelphia: The Judson Press, 1955.

Tucker, Ruth A. "Female Mission Strategists: A Historical and Contemporary Perspective." *Missiology* 15 (January 1987): 73–89.

————. *From Jerusalem to Irian Jaya: A Biographical History of Christian Missions.* Academie Books. Grand Rapids: Zondervan Publishing House, 1983.

————. "Women in Mission." In *Toward the Twenty-first Century in Christian Mission.* Grand Rapids: Wm. B. Eerdmans, 1993, 284–294.

Wilson, Dorothy C. *Dr. Ida: The Story of Dr. Ida Scudder of Vellore.* New York: McGraw-Hill Book Company, Inc., 1959.

Personal contact:
Madrid, Helen. E-mail letters to author, 1 May 2004, 6 May 2004.

Chapter 3
Mother of Four Rulers—Sorkaktani

Curtin, Jeremiah. *The Mongols.* Boston, MA: Little, Brown & Co., 1908; Cambridge, MA: Da Capo Press, 2003.

De Hartog, Leo. *Genghis Khan: Conqueror of the World.* Paperback ed. New York: Barnes & Noble, Inc. ed. 1989; paperback ed., London: I. B. Taurus & Co., Ltd., 1999.

Gunzel, Stuart and Donald E. Hoke. "The Mongolian People's Republic. In *The Church in Asia.* Edited by Donald E. Hoke. Chicago: Moody Press, 1975, 441–449.

"Khubilai Khan and His Advisors." Internet. Accessed 14 January 2004.

Lamb, Harold. *Genghis Khan: Emperor of All Men.* Bantam Pathfinder edition, New York: Bantam Books, 1963 and New York: Doubleday & Co., Inc., 1963.

———. *The March of the Barbarians.* New York: The Literary Guild of America, 1940.

Lister, R. P. *Genghis Khan.* New York: Dorset Press, 1969.

Mar, Aprem. *Nestorian Missions.* Probe ed. Maryknoll, NY: Orbis Books, 1980.

Missick, Stephen A. "The Assyrian Church in the Mongolian Empire as Observed by World Travellers in the Late 13th and Early 14th Centuries." *Journal of Assyrian Academic Studies* 13 (November 1999): 85–104. Internet. Accessed 15 January 2004.

Moffett, Samuel H. *A History of Christianity in Asia.* Vol. 1, *Beginnings to 1500.* New York: Harper San Francisco: Harper Collins Publishers, 1992, 399–469.

"Mongolian Women." *Women in World History Curriculum @ 2002.* Internet. Accessed 3 March 2003.

Moule, A.C. *Christians in China Before the Year 1550.* London: SPCK, 1930.

Philip, T. V. *East of the Euphrates: Early Christianity in Asia.* Delhi: Christian Sahitya Samithy and Indian Society for Promoting Christian Knowledge, 1998.

Rossabi, Morris. *Khubilai Khan: His Life and Times.* Berkeley: University of California Press, 1988.

———. "Women of Mongol Lands." Lecture. http://www.woodrow.org/teachers/world-.history/teaching/Mongol/women.html. Internet. Accessed 15 January 2004.

Severin, Tim. *In Search of Genghis Khan.* London: Hutchinson, 1991.

"Sorghaghtani Beki, Mother of Great Khans." *Female Heroes of the Regions of the World.* Internet. Accessed 3 March 2003.

"Women." Internet. Accessed 3 March 2003, 15 January 2004.

Young, John M. L. *By Foot to China: Missions of the Church of the East, To 1400.* Tokyo: Radio Press, 1984.

Chapter 4
A Teenaged Pioneer—Harriet Atwood Newell

Eddy, Daniel C. *Heroines of the Missionary Enterprise; or Sketches of Prominent Female Missionaries.* Edited by John Cumming. Third edition. London: Arthur Hall, Virtue, and Co., n.d.

Goodsell, Fred F. *You Shall Be My Witnesses.* Boston: American Board of Commissioners for Foreign Missions, 1959.

James, Sharon. *My Heart is in His Hands—Ann Judson of Burma: A Life, with Selections from Her Memories and Letters.* Durham, England: Evangelical Press, 1998.

Montgomery, Helen B. *Western Women in Eastern Lands: An Outline Study of Fifty Years of Woman's Work in Foreign Missions.* New York: The Macmillan Company, 1910. Reprinted in *Women in American Protestant Religion, 1800–1930.* Carolyn De Swarte Gifford and Donald W. Dayton, eds. A Garland Series. New York, NY: Garland Pub., Inc., 1987.

————. [Newell, Samuel]. *The Life and Writings of Mrs. Harriet Newell.* Revised edition. Philadelphia: Philadelphia American Sunday School Union, 1831.

Pierson, H. W., ed. *American Missionary Memorial, including Biographical and Historical Sketches.* New York: Harper & Brothers, Publishers, 1853.

Robert, Dana L. *American Women in Mission: A Social History of Their Thought and Practice.* The Modern Mission Era, 1792–1991: An Appraisal Series editor Wilbert R. Shenk. Macon, GA: Mercer University Press, 1997.

Stowe, Sarah D. Locke. *History of Mount Holyoke Seminary During its First Half Century (1837–1887).* Springfield, MA: Mount Holyoke Seminary, 1887.

White, Ann. "Counting the Cost of Faith: America's Early Female Missionaries." *Church History* 57 (May 1988): 19–30.

Chapter 5
Letters Home from Japan—Margaret Tate Kinnear Ballagh

Ballagh, Margaret Tate Kinnear. *Glimpses of Old Japan, 1861–1866.* Tokyo: Methodist Publishing House, 1908; Avon, NY: The Abcedarian Press, 1993.

Ballagh, Margaret, *Furuki Nihon no Bekken—Glimpses of Old Japan 1861–1865,* transl. Kawakubo, Tokuo. Yokohama: Yuurindoo, *Heisei* 4 [1992].

Drummond, Richard H. *A History of Christianity in Japan.* Grand Rapids: Wm. B. Eerdmans, 1971.

Chamberlain, Mrs. W. I. *Fifty Years in Foreign Fields, China, Japan, India, Arabia: A History of Five Decades of the Woman's Board of Foreign Missions, Reformed Church in America*. New York: Woman's Board of Foreign Missions, Reformed Church in America, 1925.

Griffis, William E. *Verbeck of Japan*. New York: Fleming H. Revell Co., 1900.

"James H. Ballagh Correspondence." W94–1186.5–James H. Ballagh. History Research Center, The Joint Archives of Holland, Hope College, Holland, MI. Typewritten document.

Jalagin, Seija. "Gendered Images — Western Women on Japanese Women." *Looking at the Other: Historical Study of Images in Theory and Practice*. Internet. Accessed 9 May 2002.

Mizugaki, Kiyoshi, transl. J. A. McAlpine. "One Hundred Years of Evangelism in Japan: A Memorial to the Missionary Labors of Three Generations." W92–1049–Mizugaki. The Joint Archives of Holland, Hope College, Holland, MI. Typewritten doc.

Peeke, H. V. S., *Sketch of the Japan Mission*, rev. and brought down to 1922. New York: Board of Foreign Missions, Reformed Church in America, n.d. [c1922].

Reynolds, Arthur, ed. *Japan in Review*. Tokyo: Japan Evangelical Missionary Association, 1970.

Reformed Church in America Board of Publication. "The Seventy-Eighth Annual Report of the Board of Foreign Missions of the Reformed Church in America and the 53rd Year of Separate Action." *The Acts and Proceedings of the One Hundred and Fourth Regular Session of the General Synod of the Reformed Church in America, June 1910*. New York: Board of Publication of the Reformed Church in America, 1910.

Thomas, Winburn T. *Protestant Beginnings in Japan: The First Three Decades*. Tokyo: Charles E. Tuttle Com., 1959.

Personal contacts:

Moore, James Ballagh, great-grandson of Margaret and James H. Ballagh. Telephone interviews by author, 4 February 2004, 10 February 2005, and several e-mails.

Moore, Lardner, great-grandson of Margaret and James H. Ballagh and elder brother of James B. Moore. Interview by author, Black Mountain, NC, 5 June 2004.

Chapter 6
The Law of Service—Isabella Thoburn

Beaver, R. Pierce. *All Loves Excelling: American Protestant Women in World Mission*. Grand Rapids: Wm. B. Eerdmans, 1968.

Brown, Earl K. "Isabella Thoburn," *Methodist History* 22 (July 1984): 207–220.

Hill, Patricia R. *The World Their Household: The American Women's Foreign Mission Movement and Cultural Transformation, 1870–1920.* Ann Arbor, MI: The University of Michigan Press, 1985.

Montgomery, Helen B. *Western Women in Eastern Lands: An Outline Study of Fifty Years of Woman's Work in Foreign Missions.* New York: The Macmillan Co., 1910. Reprinted in *Women in American Protestant Religion, 1800–1930.* Carolyn De Swarte Gifford and Donald W. Dayton, series editors. A Garland Series. New York: Garland Publishing Inc., 1987.

Oldham, William. "Isabella Thoburn, Christian–Teacher–Missionary, 1840–1901." Photocopied document, 12 pp., n.p., n.d.

Singh, Maina C. "Gender, Mission, and Higher Education in Cross-Cultural Context: Isabella Thoburn in India," *International Bulletin of Missionary Research* 25 (October 2001): 165–69.

Thoburn, James M. *Life of Isabella Thoburn.* Cincinnati: Jennings and Pye; New York: Eaton and Mains, 1903.

Personal contact:
Thoburn, Crawford R, great-grandnephew of Isabella Thoburn. Letters to author, 6 March and 10 March 2004.

Chapter 7
A Woman's Voice In India—Pandita Ramabai Dongre

Adeney, Miriam. "Esther Across Cultures: Indigenous Leadership Roles for Women." *Missiology* 15 (July 1987): 323–337.

Burgess, Stanley M. "Pentecostalism in India: An Overview." *Asian Journal of Pentecostal Studies* 4 (2001): 85–98.

Burton, Antoinette. *At the Heart of the Empire: Indians and the Colonial Education in Late Victorian Britain.* Berkeley: University of California Press, c.1998. Internet. Accessed 18 February 2004.

Deen, Edith. *Great Women of the Christian Faith.* New York: Harper & Brothers Publishers, 1959, 277–287.

Frykenberg, Robert E., ed., *Pandita Ramabai's America: Conditions of Life in the United States.* K. Gomes, translated by P. C. Engblom, transl. ed. Grand Rapids: Wm. B. Eerdmans, 2003.

Hardesty, Nancy A. *Great Women of Faith.* Nashville: Abingdon Press, 1980, 123–128.

Hiebert, Paul. "Mission to Hindu Women: Pandita Ramabai, 1858–1922." In *Ambassadors for Christ* edited by John D. Woodbridge. Chicago: Moody Press, 1994, 166–172.

Kumar, Radha. *The History of Doing: An Illustrated Account of Movements for Women's Rights and Feminism in India, 1800–1900.* London: Verso Books, 1993, 26. Abstract on internet. "Pandita Ramabai (1858–1992): Woman Reformist." *Women's Studies.* Internet. Accessed 18 February 2004.

Lavinia, Byrne, ed. *The Hidden Journey: Missionary Heroines in Many Lands.* London: Society for Promoting Christian Knowledge, 1993.

Macnicol, Nicol. *Pandita Ramabai.* Builders of Modern India series. Calcutta: Association Press, 1926.

Mangalwadi, Vishal. "Women of the Millennium." *The World.* 13 December 1999; www.vishalmangalwadi.com/articles/Ramabai.htm. Internet. Accessed 18 February 2004.

McGee, Gary B. "Baptism of the Holy Ghost and Fire! The Revival Legacy of Minnie F. Abrams of India." *Enrichment.* Summer 1998. Reprint: http://www.agts.edu/faculty/faculty_publications/articles/mcgee_abrams.pdf. Internet. Accessed 18 February 2004.

Montgomery, Helen Barrett. *Western Women in Eastern Lands: An Outline Study of 50 Years of Woman's Work in Foreign Missions.* New York: The Macmillan Company, 1910. Reprinted in *Women in Asian Protestant Religion, 1800–1930.* Carolyn De Swarte Gifford and Donald W. Dayton, series editors. A Garland Series. New York: Garland Publishing, Inc., 1987.

Pandita Ramabai. *A Testimony.* Ninth ed. Kedgaon, India: Ramabai Mukti Mission, 1968.

The Pandita Ramabai Story in Her Own Words. Internet. Accessed 18 February 2004.

Ward, Roland. "The Story of Ramabai." *The Presbyterian Banner,* April 2001. Reprint: Internet. Accessed 18 February 2004.

Wright, Elliott. *Holy Company: Christian Heroes and Heroines.* New York: Macmillan Pub. Co., Inc., 1980.

Personal contact:
Ramabai Mukti Mission. E-mail to author. 22 March 2004.

Chapter 8
Physician to the Korean Queen—Lillias S. Horton Underwood

Brown, Arthur J. "No. 594 — To the Chosen Mission." Letter Arthur J. Brown, Mission Secretary to Presbyterian missionaries in Korea, 7 November 1921.

Egan, Leonora Horton. "Lillie in Korea and Contributing Circumstances," ed. Nancy K. Underwood. Appendix included in a 1977 reprint of Lillias H. Underwood, *Fifteen Years Among the Topknots.* Boston & New

York: American Tract Society, 1904. Seoul: Royal Asiatic Society–Korean Branch, 1977.

Griffis, William E. *A Modern Pioneer in Korea: The Life Story of Henry G. Appenzeller*. New York: Fleming H. Revell Company, 1912.

Huntley, Martha. *To Start A Work: The Foundations of Protestant Mission in Korea (1884–1919)*. Seoul, Korea: Presbyterian Church of Korea, 1987,

Kim, Young-sik. "Americans in Korea in the Late 1800s: A Brief History of the US-Korea Relations Prior to 1945." Http:www.asianresearch.org/articles/1483.html. Internet. Accessed 1 March 2004.

Lumba, Zenaida. "Harris Memorial College: The Spiritual Journey of a Faith Community." *Phronesis: A Journal of Asian Theological Seminary*, 8 (2001): 31–46.

Mathews, Winifred. "Lillias Underwood: She Followed 'A Red-maned Star.'" In *Dauntless Women: Stories of Pioneer Wives*. Biography Index Reprint Series. Freeport, NY: Books for Libraries Press, 1947, 145–164.

Paik, L. George. *The History of Protestant Missions in Korea, 1832–1910*. Pyeng Yang: Union Christian College Press, 1929.

Underwood, Jean Welch. "Horace Grant Underwood and Lillias Horton Underwood." Photocopied document, private, unpublished.

Underwood, Lillias S. H. *With Tommy Tompkins in Korea*. New York: Fleming H. Revell Company, 1905.

Personal contacts:

Harkness, Grace Underwood. Granddaughter of Lillias H. and Horace G. Underwood. E-mail letters to author, 8 March 2004, 12 April 2004. Telephone conversations 30 April 2004, 9 February 2005.

Huntley, Martha. E-mail correspondence and telephone conversations with author, March–April 2004.

Underwood, Jean Welch. Wife of grandson of Lillias H. and Horace G. Underwood. E-mail letters to author, 4 March 2004, 28 April 2004.

Chapter 9
Healing Among the Poor in Manila—Rebecca Parrish

Alejandro, Dionisio D. *From Darkness to Light: A Brief Chronicle of the Beginnings and Spread of Methodism in the Philippines*. Quezon City: The United Methodist Church, Philippines Central Conference, Board of Communications and Publications, 1974.

Deats, Richard L. *The Story of Methodism in the Philippines*. Manila: National Council of Churches in the Philippines, 1964.

Devolder, Mary L. *Rebecca Parrish: A Medical Missionary in Manila*. Cincinnati:

Woman's Division of Christian Service, Board of Missions, The Methodist Church, 1956.

―――――. "The Mary Johnston Hospital: A Remarkable Balance of Charitable Medicine and Evangelistic Outreach." Photocopied document, n.d.

"Dr. Rebecca Parrish – August 1952." Photocopied document, n.d.

Harrington, Mabel E. "Dr. Rebecca Parrish Data." Letter to Rev. John Hinkle, Cebu City, 3 May, 1961.

Hess, Doris. "Dr. Rebecca: Pioneer Extraordinary" *The Methodist Woman* (July–Aug. 1953): 10.

"History is Repeated." *Manila Times.* 26 August 1952.

Lumba, Zenaida. "Harris Memorial College: The Spiritual Journey of a Faith Community." *Phronesis: A Journal of Asian Theological Seminary* 8 (2001): 31–46.

"The Mary Johnston Hospital Story." Internet. Accessed 29 October 2000.

Parrish, Rebecca. *Cabin In Th' Clearin.'* N.p.

―――――. "Damiana Dolorico: A Philippine National Leader," in Leon Wood, "Rebecca Parish [sic]: Who Went to the Philippines," ch. 10 in *The One Who Went and The One She Found.* New York: Woman's Foreign Missionary Society, 1929, 234–46.

―――――. *When I was in Palestine.* N.p.

Wood, Leon. "Rebecca Parrish, Who Went to the Philippines." In *The One Who Went and The One She Found.* [New York]: Woman's Foreign Missionary Society, 1929, 221–248.

Personal contacts:

Fernandez, Ricardo. Interview by author, Manila, 18 February 2001.

Velasquez, Dr. Myrna P. E-mail to author, 28 April 2004, several telephone calls October 2004.

Chapter 10
"She Became the Tiger of the School!" —Tena Holkeboer

"About World Vision." Internet. Accessed 10 January 2004.

Angus, William R. Jr. "RCA Chinese Mission Reports–1941–1946." n.d. History Research Center, The Joint Archives of Holland, Hope College, Holland, MI H00-1381.

―――――. "Customs in Amoy." Typewritten document. n.d. Holkeboer Papers. Board of Foreign Missions, Reformed Church in America. *Tena Holkeboer.* Brochure. Holkeboer Papers.

―――――. *Tena Holkeboer.* April 1948. Brochure. The Joint Archives of Holland, Hope College, Holland, MI W88–0055 "Tena Holkeboer (1895–1965)."

Chamberlain, Mrs. W. I. *Fifty Years in Foreign Fields, China, Japan, India, Arabia: A History of Five Decades of the Woman's Board of Foreign Missions, Reformed Church in America.* New York: Woman's Board of Foreign Missions, Reformed Church in America, 1925.

De Velder, Walter. *Across Three Continents.* Typewritten doc. The Joint Archives of Holland, Hope College, Holland, MI. W88–0033. "De Velder, Walter, (1907–)."

English Department, Hope Christian High School. "School History." *Truth, Life.* Graduation Souvenir, 1957. The Joint Archives of Holland, Hope College, Holland, MI. W88–055. "Holkeboer, Tena–articles–1920–1950."

Holkeboer, T. *God's Bridge, Or the Story of Jin-gi.* Second edition Grand Rapids: Wm. B. Eerdmans, 1945.

———. "Latest News from China." *The Church Herald.* 11 November1949. Joint Archives of Holland. W88–055. "Holkeboer, Tena–articles–1920–1950."

———. Personal papers. This includes letters written to family and friends. 1920–1960. Holkeboer Papers.

———. "Revive Thy Church." *The Church Herald.* 5 February 1943, 7. Holkeboer Papers.

———. "Tena Holkeboer midst of China Air Bombing [sic]." *Holland City News.* 23 September 1937. Holkeboer Papers.

———. *Rooted and Built up in Him: The Story of Our Educational Work in China.* New York: The Foreign Mission Boards RCA. N.d. Holkeboer Papers.

———. "Urging a Decision." *The Church Herald.* 21 May 1942. Holkeboer Papers.

———. "When Revival Fires Swept South Fukien . . ." *The Church Herald.* 18 January 1963. Holkeboer Papers.

———. [Holkeboer, Tena]. "Chinese Visitor Comes to America." *The Church Herald.* 17 October 1946. Joint Archives of Holland. W88–0315. "Chinese Missions."

Lim, Jin-go. *The History of the First Protestant Church in China, After One Hundred Years.* Joint Archives of Holland. W88–055. "Holkeboer, Tena–articles–1920–1950." Typed document.

Nienhuis, Jean. Papers. Joint Archives of Holland. W96–1208 "Nienhuis, Jean (1887–1975)."

Shafer, L. J. "The Chinese Emergency." *Board of Foreign Missions, RCA – A News Bulletin.* 28 October 1937. Joint Archives of Holland. H00–1381."Angus, William. R., Jr., 1901–1984, papers.

Te Winkel, Sarella. "The Amoy Mission, China." *The Sixth Decade of the Woman's Board of Foreign Missions: 1926–1935.* New York: Woman's Board of

Foreign Missions, RCA. N.d. Joint Archives of Holland, Box 3, W 88–303, 20–21.

"The First Letter Written (from China) by the Rev. David Abeel, and sent from Amoy." Hong Kong Baptist University archives, special collection. 1 March 1842.

Van Baak, Edward A. "Dr. Tena Holkeboer." *The Banner*. 10 December 1965, 10.

Woman's Board of Foreign Missions. *1908 – Woman's Work in Our Amoy Mission, China*. New York: New York, 1908. Holkeboer Papers.

Personal contacts:

Alumnae of the Iok Tek (Amoy) Middle Girls' School, one-time students of Dr. T. Holkeboer. Interviews with seven alumnae, who wish to remain anonymous, transl. from Chinese and typed by Dr. Amanda Shao Tan. Manila, October 2000 to March 2001.

Homkes, Chris Holkeboer, younger sister of Dr. T. Holkeboer. Interview by author, Lowell, MI, 21 June 2001.

Joldersma, Genevieve. Letter to author, 2 February 2001.

Mereness, Cecilia A. Holkeboer, daughter of a brother (Oscar) of Dr. T. Holkeboer. Interviews by author, Lowell, MI, 21 June 2001; 19 November 2003.

Rockett, Jean Homkes, daughter of a sister of Dr. Holkeboer, Mrs. Chris Holkeboer Homkes. Interview by author, 19 November 2003.

Shao, Wesley. Former student of Dr. Holkeboer. Interview by author, Manila, 27 October 2000.

Tong, Stephen (Chung Rung). Interview by author, Kowloon, 23 July 2003.

Van Baak, Edward A. Interview by author, Grand Rapids, 10 May 2000.

Vander Ark, Nelle, cousin of Dr. T. Holkeboer. Interview by author, Grand Rapids, 14 May 2000.

Chapter 11
"Do it! Do it! Do it!"—Geertruida Johanna Dreckmeier

Algra, A. *De Geref. Kerk in Ned. Indië: 1877–1961* [sic] *[The Gereformeerde Church in the Dutch East Indies: 1877–1961]*. Franeker, the Netherlands: T. Wever, n.d. [± 1968].

Bunjamin, I. and J. Van Vliet. "Heel de Mens" ["The Whole Human Being"]. *Vandaar*. January 1993, 18.

"Cita2nya Terkabul" ["Her Dream Fulfilled"]. Photocopy of a newspaper article published in Indonesia in 1973.

Dekker, Rienke. "Dokter Geertruida Johanna Dreckmeier (1895–1992): Een Kerk-historisch Onderzoek naar haar Bijdrage aan de Zending, in het Bijzonder aan de Emancipatie van de Vrouw." ["Doctor Geertruida Johanna Dreckmeier (1895–1992): A Church History Research of her Contribution to Missions, Particularly the Emancipation of Women"]. Ph.D. diss., Theologische Universiteit, Kampen, the Netherlands,1998.

Dreckmeier, Geertruida J. Christmas letters of 1988 (*"Lieve mensen"*), 1989 (*"Kerstmis 1989"*) and 1990 (*"Sahaba-sahabat yang baik"*).

————. Dreckmeier, Geertruida J. "De Regionale Conferentie van de YWCA voor Oost-Azië en Australië" ["The Regional Conference of the YWCA for East Asia and Australia"], *De Opwekker* (Jan.–Dec. 1936), 576–581.

————. "Opvallende Toespraak" ["A Striking Speech"]. *Zendingsblad*, May 1971, 113.

————. Photocopy of a congratulatory letter taken from an anniversary album of *Yoga Darma*, 1979.

"Dr. Nn. Dreckmeier 53 Tahun Mengabdi Di Indonesia" ["Dr. Ms. Dreckmeier Served in Indonesia for 53 Years"]. Photocopy of a newspaper article published in Indonesia in 1973.

Dreckmeier, Wilhelmina. *Suwarto en de Toverstokjes [Suwarto and the Magic Wands]*. Oegstgeest, The Netherlands: Raad van de Zending van de Nederlands Hervormde Kerk, 1959.

Gorter, M., S. Holsteijn, M.C. Jongeling, L. Lagerwerf, and A. A. van der Woerdt. "Vrouwen in de Zending: Een Stukje Geschiedenis" ["Women in Missions: A Historical Vignette"]. *Allerwegen* 16 (1985:2): 1–68.

Krijgsveld. W. "Chronologie van Gebeurtenissen in Ambarawa 6" ["Chronology of Events in Ambarawa 6"]. Internet. Accessed 17 October 2003.

Mak, Geert. *De Eeuw van mijn Vader [My Father's Century]*. Amsterdam: Uitgeverij Atlas, 1999.

"Mej. Dr. Dreckmeier Ontving Hoge Onderscheiding" ["Dr. Dreckmeier Receives a High Distinction"]. *Centraal Weekblad*, 6 February 1971.

Merkelijn, Aart. *26 Jaren op het Zendingsveld: Herinneringen van een Missionair Predikant [26 Years on the Mission Field: Memoirs of a Missionary Pastor)*. 's Gravenhage, The Neth.: D. A. Daamen's Uitgeversmaatschappij, N.V., 1941.

Ong Kian Kieu, "Pengenalan Saya Pada Ibu Dr. Dreckmeier" ["My Knowledge of Dr. Dreckmeier"], transl. Ishak Wonohadidjojo. Typed document, written by a former patient, 25 March 2001.

"Programma van de Zesde Uitreiking van de Albert Schweitzerprijs" ["Program of the Sixth Presentation of the Albert Schweitzer Prize"]. *Stichting Albert Schweitzer Prijs.* Amsterdam: "De Blauwbrug," January 1971.

"Riwayat R. S. K. Ngesti Waluyo–Parakan." Anniversary booklet of Ngesti Waluyo hospital in Parakan, Indonesia, 1980, 10–18.

Van der Linden, J. "Herinnering aan Truus Dreckmeier" ["Memories of Truus Dreckmeier"]. *Centraal Weekblad,* 6 November 1992.

Van der Veen-Schenkeveld, Marja. *Stuur Haar Maar: Drie Markante Vrouwen in Gereformeerde Zendingsdienst [Just Send Her: Three Remarkable Women in Gereformeerde Mission Service].* AZ002. Leusden, the Netherlands: Kerkinactie, 1995, 26–45.

Van der Woerdt, A. A. "De Zending van de Gereformeerde Kerken in Nederland en de Vrouw op Midden-Java: Een Historische Studie over de Jaren 1896 tot 1945" ["Missions of the Gereformeerde Churches in the Netherlands and the Woman on Central Java: A Historical Study of the Years 1896 to 1945"]. Unpublished document. Veenendaal, the Netherlands : Kerkinactie, 1985.

Van der Woerdt, Rineke. *Werken Zolang Het Dag Is: Jacqueline Cornélie van Andel-Rutgers (1874–1951), Gereformeerd Zendelinge in Midden-Java [Working As Long As It Is Day: Jacqueline Cornélie van Andel-Rutgers (1874–1951),* Reformed Gereformeerd Missionary in Central Java]. Kampen, the Netherlands: Kampen, 2004.

"Verenigde Vrienden van de *Yayasan* Pa Van Der Steur" ["United Friends of the *Yayasan* Van Der Steur"], Internet. Accessed 1 May 2004.

Personal contacts:

Boer-Ensing, Tine. Letter to author, 15 December 2001.

Brouwer, Edward. E-mail to author, 24 April 2001.

Duim, Feije. E-mail to author, 28 March 2001,14 May 2003.

Hidayat, P. Laksana. Letter to author, 9 May 2002.

Jongeling, M. C. Letters to author, 1 December 2000, 22 March 2003..

Keulemans, A. F. C. Letters to author, 27 January 2002 (two letters), 8 February 2002, 9 February 2002, 2 October, 2002, 30 March 2003.

Kooy-Bakker, Ineke. Letter to author, 7 July 2003,17 July 2003.

Oldhoff, Anneke. Letter to author, 25 March 2003.

Reenders, Hommo. E-mails to author, 24 October 2003 (2 letters), 2 November 2003.

Vander Leuv, Juul. Letters to author, February 2002, April 2002 and September 2003.

Personal visits:
Amstelveen, the Netherlands:
 An intimate friend of Dr. Drekmeier who wishes to remain anonymous, 27 August 2003.
Doorwerth, the Netherlands:
 Oldhoff, Anneke, 29 August, 2003.
 Vander Leuv, Juul, 29 August, 2003.
Magelang, Indonesia:
 Hidajat, P. Laksana, 29 March 2002.
 Mirmamigsih, Urip, 30 March 2002.
 Moeljono, Mr., 29 March 2002.
 Ong Kian Kieu, Mr. and Mrs., 29 March 2002.
 Pandyopranato, Peter, 29 March 2002.
Parakan, Indonesia:
 Sowono, Suyati, 30 March 2002.
 Sutjip, Herry, 30 March 2002.
 Nastitik, Ibu, 30 March 2002.
 Widyanto, Timothy, 30 March 2002.
Utrecht, The Netherlands:
 Duim, Feije, 22 March 2001.

Chapter 12
Mother of Ten, Woman of Prayer—Tong Tan Njien Nio
Tong, Freda Hatfield, *Sons for the Master.* Singapore: Path Seekers, Ltd., 2001.

Personal contacts:
Ang Se Nio. Interview by author, Surabaya, 4 April 2000.
Hartomo, Mrs. Interview by author, Surabaya, 4 April 2000.
Tong, Caleb (Chung Ming). Interview, Manila, 2 December 2000.
Tong, Freda Hatfield, daughter-in-law of Tong Njien Nio. Numerous e-mail letters during the period 2000–2004.
Tong Solomon (Chung An). Interviews by author, Surabaya, 3 April 2000, 4 April 2000.
Tong Stephen (Chung Rung). Interview by author, Kowloon, 23 July 2003.

Chapter 13
"I Am a Fifth-Generation Japanese Christian"—Minato Akiko
Buss, Siegfried. "In the Shadow of the Rising Sun." *Christianity Today.* 8 April 1991, 30, 32.
Kantzer, K. S. "Christian Scientist Dr. H. Minato." Photocopied page dated March 1978.

Minato, Akiko. "A Challenge from the Asian Mission Congress '90." *Japan Update*. 1990, 2.

———. "An Equal-opportunity Church?" *Christianity Today*. 8 April, 1991, 30, 32.

———. "A Two-Way Spiritual Bridge Across the Pacific." Photocopied document. Note on document "Message given at Trinity College, 1989 or 1990."

———. "Expectations Concerning the Laity in Contemporary Japan," *The Japan Review* 64(1998): 66–73.

———. "The Biblical Role of Women: 'The Women's Era that Has Now Begun in Japan!'" *Japan Harvest* 52 (Summer 2000): 3, 22.

———. "The Biblical Role of Women in Japanese Society." Photocopied document, n.d.

———. "The Japanese Church's Most Critical Issue." *Christianity Today*. 8 April 1991, 30.

———. "Women's Jiritsu and Christian Feminism. *The Japan Christian Review* 59 (1993): 7–17.

Ogoshi, Aiko. "A Reexamination of Shinran's Views of Women," *The Japan Christian Review* 59 (1993): 19–26.

Seagrave, Sterling and Peggy Seagrave. *The Yamato Dynasty: The Secret History of Japan's Imperial Family*. London: Bantam Press, 1999; Corgi Books, 2000.

Wisley, Sandi. "Interview with Professor Akiko Minato." *Leadership* (Tokyo Christian Theological Seminary publication) (Spring–Summer 1993): 3.

———. "Spotlight on Akiko." *Japan Harvest* 43 (Spring 1994): 8–9.

"Tokyo Woman's Christian University." Internet. Accessed 24 October 2003.

Personal contacts:

Buss, Siegfried. Retired TEAM missionary. E-mail to author, 24 October 2003.

Minato, Akiko. Personal interview by author, Tokyo Woman's Christian University, 8 April 2003. E-mail 22 January 2004, letter 3 March 2004.

Wright, JoAnn. Baptist General Conference missionary. E-mails to author, 6 November, 10 November, 2003.

Chapter 14
A Missionary to Her Own People—Lucy del Carmen Apostol

Apostol, Lucy del Carmen. "The Unshackled." In *A Century of Bible Christians in the Philippines*, edited by Anne C. Kwantes. Manila: OMF Literature, Inc., 1998, 199–208.

Apostol, Lucy del Carmen and Vince Apostol. Letters to friends, 1986–1995. Board of Christian Reformed World Missions. CRWM file, "Apostol, Vince and Lucy." Grand Rapids, MI.

————. Reports, 1964–1983. Board of Christian Reformed World Missions. CRWM file, "Apostol, Vince and Lucy." Grand Rapids, MI.

Apostol, Lucy del Carmen and Allen V. del Carmen. "Against All Odds." In *A Century of Bible Christians in the Philippines*, edited by Anne C. Kwantes. Manila: OMF Literature, Inc., 1998, 110–118.

Personal contacts:

Advincula, Lori Apostol, daughter of Lucy Apostol. Several e-mails during the period 2000–2002.

Apostol Lucy del Carmen. Interviews by author, Iloilo, 6 November 2000, 15 February 2001.

Apostol Lucy del Carmen and Vince Apostol. "A History of the Christian Reformed Church in Panay." Oral presentation at a Christian Reformed World Missions meeting. Bacolod, early 1992.

————. "Words of Wisdom." Oral presentation at a farewell speech during the last mission business meeting before their retirement. Christian Reformed World Missions meeting. Manila, 13 February 1996.

Blankers, Clarice. E-mails to author, 10 November 2000, 4 February 2001, 7 February 2001.

De la Peña, Nita. Letter to author, 4 December 2000.

De Kam, Ivan. Written comments to author, 17 October 2002.

De Kam, Joy. Interview by author, Grand Rapids, 14 October 2002.

De Vries, Judy and Henry. Two e-mail messages to author, 21 January 2001.

Hogan, Patty. Interview by author, Manila, 15 March 2001.

Chapter 15
Thinker, Writer, Christian Activist—Melba Padilla Maggay

Maggay, Melba Padilla "Breaking Up Tears Apart Family, Society." *Patmos* vol.13 no. 2 (March 1998): 3–4.

————. "Create Community." *Patmos* vol. 15 no. 2 (August 2000): 5.

————. "Crossing the Cultural Divide: Reflections from Down Under." *Patmos* vol. 11 no. 1 & 2 (July 1995): 14–16, 21.

————. "Diversity, not Homogeneity, is God's Design for the World." *Patmos* vol. 12 no. 2 (November 1996): 14–15.

————. "Flor Contemplacion: Requiem for a People." *Patmos* vol. 11 no. 1 (April 1995): 6–8, 20–21.

————. "Flying Solo." *Patmos* vol. 15 no. 2 (August 2000): 3–4.

_____. "Hail Mary, or Why it Might be Good to Sit Under a Guava Tree." *Patmos* vol. I, no.I, (1977): 8–II.

_____. "In Remembrance of Grandmothers Past." *Patmos*, vol. 14 no. 13 (July 1999): 4–6.

_____. *"Mang* Ambo Burns His Last Urn of Ashes." *Solidarity Journal*, no. 147–48, 1995– 1996: 112–17.

_____. "Mothering Mother." *Patmos* vol. 14 no. 3 (February 1999): 18–20.

_____. "Once Upon a Bright Happy Boy." First Prize, Essay in English Category, 1999 Don Carlos Palanca Memorial Award for Literature.

_____. "Our Text in Context: Shaping a Life-giving Word for Today." *Patmos* 13 no.I (November 1997): 16–18.

_____. "Raising a New Generation for the 21st Century." *Patmos* 17 no.I (1997): 4–7, 32.

_____. "Time Must Have a Stop." In *An Asian Palette: Personal Journeys of Christian Writers.* ed. Bernice Cheng. Singapore: Armour Publishing Pte. Ltd., 1998.

_____. *Transforming Society.* Philippine ed. Quezon City: Institute for Studies Asian Church and Culture, 1996.

_____. "War Against the Roses: On Standing Up to the Powers." *Patmos* 15 no.I(April 2000): 14–15.

Rodriguez, Carmen C. [Maggay, Melba P.] "Death and Early Sorrow." First Prize, Essay in English Category, 2002 Don Carlos Palanca Memorial Award for Literature. *Ani 31: Mga Talinghaga ng Puso [Metaphors of Love]* (September 3, 2005)

Tala, Luningning S. [Maggay, Melba P.] "Mother of Stories." Second Prize, Essay in English Category, 1997 Don Carlos Palanca Memorial Award for Literature.

Personal contacts:

Adeney, Miriam. Interview by author, 16 March 2004, Vancouver, British Columbia.

Bradshaw, Mac. E-mails to author, 2 December 2003, 8 December 2003.

Dyrness, William. Telephone interview by author, 12 January 2004.

Maggay, Melba Padilla. Interview by author, Quezon City, Philippines; 14 April 2003.

Index

About the Autho

Born of missionary parents in pre-World War II Indonesia, the author was raised in the Netherlands and Canada. She has always been fascinated by history, especially that of Christian missions in Asia.

Anne C. Kwantes (Ph.D. in Philippines Studies; M.A. in Asian Studies, University of the Philippines; A.B. in Asian Studies, International College, Sophia University, Tokyo) taught missions courses and the history of the Christian Church and Missions for some twenty years, and was on the faculty of the Asian Theological Seminary in Quezon City, Philippines (1994–2003). She has authored numerous articles and books which include *Presbyterian Missionaries in the Philippines: Agents of Social Change (1899–1909)* and edited *A Century of Bible Christians in the Philippines* and *Chapters in Philippine Church History*.

She and her husband have recently retired in Victoria, British Columbia, Canada.